EX LIBRIS

I pray that this book will bring Inspiration and Blessing into your Life.

With my prayers and Best Wishes

Pete R [signature]

Pat Robertson will forever be known as one of the most influential Christian leaders of our time. His groundbreaking leadership has touched every facet of our culture and will live on through the lives he has connected to Christ around the world. In *I Have Walked With the Living God*, Pat recalls his incredible journey with humor, warmth, and the godly wisdom that can only come from a lifetime of lessons learned at the foot of his Savior. I'm blessed to know him and inspired to serve God with the same unrelenting dedication and conviction.

—STEVE GREEN
PRESIDENT, HOBBY LOBBY STORES
FOUNDER AND CHAIRMAN, MUSEUM OF THE BIBLE

I have enjoyed watching Pat Robertson climb his glorious ladder upward. *I Have Walked With the Living God* is a chance for everyone who reads it to acknowledge that God lives in the heart of every human being, if we only believe.

—GEORGE FOREMAN
FORMER PROFESSIONAL BOXER

Pat Robertson's new book, *I Have Walked With the Living God*, is honest to the core, bold as a lion, and a guidebook for success. This is the one we've all been waiting for!

—KENNETH COPELAND
HOST, *BELIEVER'S VOICE OF VICTORY*

Pat Robertson's latest book, *I Have Walked With the Living God*, is a story of hope, inspiration, and faith. Pat's life story and visionary, Spirit-led leadership have been used to bless millions around the globe. This book will have a life-shaping impact on the reader.

—JAY SEKULOW
CHIEF COUNSEL, AMERICAN CENTER FOR
LAW AND JUSTICE
COUNSEL TO THE FORTY-FIFTH PRESIDENT OF
THE UNITED STATES

I HAVE WALKED

With the

LIVING GOD

PAT ROBERTSON

CHARISMA
HOUSE

Library of Congress Cataloging-in-Publication Data:
An application to register this book for cataloging has been submitted to the
Library of Congress.
International Standard Book Number: 978-1-62999-873-2
E-book ISBN: 978-1-62999-874-9

20 21 22 23 24 — 7 6 5 4 3
Printed in the United States of America

I will walk among you and be your God, and you will be my people.

—LEVITICUS 26:12, NIV

CONTENTS

ACKNOWLEDGMENTS

As I congratulate people, I want to thank my dear wife, Dede, who has, for sixty-five years, always been a hope and an inspiration.

My son Gordon has played a key role in insisting that I explain in detail how my personal devotional life works so that readers may enter into the experience.

My previous books have been written in longhand on yellow legal pads and then transcribed. On this one, I am following the example of Winston Churchill, who dictated all of his manuscripts, and I must commend my faithful assistant, G. G. Conklin, for taking down my words on her laptop and organizing the appropriate chapters.

I also want to salute my dear friend Edie Wasserberg, who has brought together all of the elements to make this book available and appealing to the readers.

I also commend my friend Joe Dillabough for his work on the physical appearance of the book, and I especially commend my attorney, Lou Isakoff, for going through the appropriate negotiations to be sure that the publisher and author were in harmony.

My thanks also go to the Content Development staff at Charisma House who edited the words and phrases and checked the book's accuracy.

PREFACE

M Y NAME IS Pat Robertson. I am now ninety years old. During my lifetime I have been privileged to found a major international broadcasting company called The Christian Broadcasting Network Inc., otherwise known as CBN, which has been responsible for the salvation of hundreds of millions of people across the globe.

Our Lord led me to start a humanitarian organization called Operation Blessing, which has brought food, clothing, shelter, and medical assistance to at least three hundred million people around the world.

Our Lord also led me to start a graduate and undergraduate university that was first called CBN University and is now called Regent University. This splendid school now has over eleven thousand students[1] studying multiple disciplines ranging from nursing to computer analytics to cybersecurity, as well as other important courses that should be available in a major liberal arts institution.

In my lifetime I've seen prayer and Bible reading taken from the schools and seen cherished evidences of our Christian faith removed from the public square. As I prayed about what to do, the Lord led me to start the American Center for Law and Justice (ACLJ), which has a distinguished record of trying and winning cases before the US Supreme Court and US District Courts and Circuit Courts.[2] This organization is one of the leading appellate advocacy groups in America.

During my lifetime our Lord led me to start the Family Channel, which grew to an amazing eighty million paying subscribers.[3] Later taken public on the New York Stock Exchange as International Family Entertainment (IFE), the company was acquired by a joint venture between Rupert Murdoch's News Corp and Saban Entertainment for the sum of $1.9 billion.[4]

Because of my involvement in the political life of this country, I ran for the Republican nomination for president of the United States in the 1988 election. Although I did not win that election, I placed third,[5] and from that came a grassroots movement called the Christian Coalition, which played a significant role in national and state elections throughout the 1990s and especially in the 2000 presidential election.

Over the years, I've had wonderful cohosts on *The 700 Club*, such as Ben Kinchlow and Sheila Walsh. *The 700 Club* welcomed the lovely former Miss America Terry Meeuwsen in 1993. Terry has been such an able prayer partner and cohost over these many years and a great blessing to the CBN ministry.

As I look back, there has been an ongoing life of excitement as the love of God for the world and His people has poured through these effective organizations and me. In *I Have Walked With the Living God*, I want to tell you about some of the wonderful things that have happened to me. I hope the experiences and stories I share will build your faith. I hope what has happened in my life will lead you to a deeper understanding of God and inspire you as you set forth on a course to serve Him.

On these pages I will share many of the things that God has spoken to me and the miracles that He has accomplished. At one time He said to me, "Do not fear the future, for I am the future." When you step out into the future, you step out into the hands of a loving God, whom you can trust not only for tomorrow but for the next day and forever. He is all-powerful and all-knowing, and I can testify that the God I serve and know is very present with each of us. If we listen to His voice, He will say, "This is the way, walk ye in it."[6]

I pray that the events I am about to describe will prove to be a blessing to you and will bring forth glory to almighty God.

—Pat Robertson
Virginia Beach, Virginia

1

From Commune to Broadcaster

S ELL YOUR POSSESSIONS and give to the poor." Little did I know in 1959 that this verse of Scripture from Luke 12:33 (NIV) would call me into Christian broadcasting. Perhaps God in His wisdom knew I couldn't handle the full picture all at once. It would take me some time to understand where He was leading me. Time is something with which the Lord has blessed me. I turned ninety in the spring of 2020, grateful that I still have my mental faculties but keenly aware that the sands of time have nearly run out of the top half of the hourglass.

A man my age is allowed a certain amount of introspection as well as a recollection of past events. This seems to be as good a time as any to get started. *I Have Walked With the Living God* will likely be my final memoir of the incredible life that God has allowed me to experience over the last nine decades.

During my lifetime I have walked with God along a supernatural path. It has been my privilege to behold extraordinary miracles. I have spoken to large crowds of people. I have seen unusual healings. I have encountered demonic possession. I have listened to God's direction. I have been led by the hand of God in supernatural ways, and without question what I have seen proves the existence of the God of the Bible. He is real and powerful and available to those who trust Him.

You probably know me as the founder of the Christian Broadcasting Network, more commonly known as CBN. Our faith-affirming programming is seen in 96 percent of US homes and broadcast internationally in 159 countries. Quite often when I'm in public, people ask me, "How did you get started?"

It's a story that only God could orchestrate using the tools of mass communication at a time when modern television was in its infancy. I know because I was there, but at the same time, as I look back, I'm well aware that I was swept along by events and needed to rely upon the Lord every day of this incredible journey.

Many people are not aware that I grew up the son of a US senator, graduated from Yale Law School, served in the Marine Corps as a second lieutenant, and had plans to make it big in the business world until the Lord got ahold of my life in my midtwenties.

After attending the Biblical Seminary on East 59th Street in midtown Manhattan in the mid-1950s, I got my start in Christian ministry as a youth pastor at Bayside Community Church on Long Island. As I walked more each day with the Lord, the Holy Spirit began directing my path more and more. I was learning the clear truth of these words of the prophet Isaiah: "Whether you turn to the right or to the left, your ears will hear a voice behind you, saying, 'This is the way; walk in it.'"[1]

I had married a nursing student named Dede Elmer several years earlier, in 1954, and we were raising two children, Timothy and Elizabeth. As a young husband and father, I took my role as provider seriously. I began an earnest quest to know God's plan for my future and received several attractive offers to serve in large churches along the eastern seaboard. Each offer represented a good opportunity for my family and me; however, as I looked more deeply, I discovered doctrinal differences that in my mind did not square with clear biblical teaching. A comfortable income with a pleasant parsonage and a friendly congregation would have provided a nice life, but I felt in my heart that God had something else for me.

At that time, Dede took our two children to her childhood home in Columbus, Ohio, for a visit with her parents. I was left alone praying in our apartment in New York. A strong feeling came over me that I needed to be free of any encumbrances to follow the leading of the Holy Spirit. As I prayed, I felt led to the twelfth chapter of Luke's Gospel and the thirty-third verse, which reads, "Sell your possessions and give to the poor" (NIV).

I wrote a long letter to Dede and described to her how God had spoken to me out of Luke 12:33. She immediately wrote back, "Dear, do whatever the Lord leads you to do."

With that in mind, I put an ad in the local newspaper advertising that our early American furniture was for sale. Of course at the time, we owned no antiques, but we had attractive factory-made sofas, chairs, and more. Right after the ad appeared, a number of people visited me and bought all of our possessions except the baby beds and our eating utensils. I took the proceeds of the sale (some six hundred dollars), canceled our apartment lease, transferred the telephone, and moved in with Dick Simmons, an ordained Presbyterian minister, in a parsonage owned by the Classon Avenue Presbyterian Church in the Bedford-Stuyvesant area of Brooklyn, New York.

This prompts me to recall what the founder of another "superstation," Ted Turner of Atlanta-based CNN, once said: "I was cable before cable was cool."[2] With what Dick Simmons had set up in his parsonage, I can honestly say I lived in a hippie commune before communes were cool.

Dick's parsonage was an old brownstone in a neighborhood where crime and muggings were relatively commonplace. Residents included a former pimp who had been delivered from demon possession, a Jamaican who was slightly demented, and the protégé of a well-known Broadway singer who was afflicted with a serious congenital disorder.

Shortly after I moved in, Dede called me at the parsonage number and said, "Why are you taking calls in Brooklyn?"

I said, "I've sold our furniture and have moved into Dick Simmons' parsonage at the Classon Avenue Presbyterian Church."

"You what?!" she exclaimed.

"I told you that God was speaking to me out of Luke 12, and you said go ahead."

"I guess I should have read your letter more closely."

"From now on you should. It's too late to turn back now."

Dede had signed on for better or for worse. This part was now the *worse*. Dede and I and our two children shared one and a half rooms in the parsonage. We strolled to the Fulton Street Market in downtown

Manhattan and purchased leftover vegetables at bargain prices after the vendors had sold a majority of their produce.

I remember buying a case of rutabagas for one dollar, which we had as a staple day after day until I hoped I would never see another ruta-baga in my life. We stored our stock of vegetables in a pantry behind the dining room, where we kept large traps to catch the rats that came to feed. Many dinners were interrupted by the snap of rat traps exploding to catch our unwanted visitors.

One day Dick Simmons grandly announced that we would begin a Daniel Fast.

"What is a Daniel Fast?" Dede asked.

"We won't eat meat or dessert," Dick replied.

Dede spoke up angrily. "We haven't been eating meat or dessert for some time, so what's the big deal?"

A small group of us living in the parsonage gathered to worship the Lord. In our worship service we prayed to be led by the Holy Spirit. As we waited on the Lord, we would feel led to read a psalm and sing a song out of the Presbyterian hymnal. We were delighted to find many times that the psalms we had received by revelation were already set to music in the hymnals to which the Lord had led us. This was a great training ground for walking with the Lord.

Obviously if we felt led to sing a particular song and we were wrong, there was no great consequence. Later in life God's leading would have enormous consequences when we entered into major ministry.

2

PACKING OUR BAGS

To a rational person, our youthful exuberance must have appeared fanatical. I was ready for whatever God had for us next, but before I could fulfill God's destiny for my life, my wife needed to enter into God's perfect will for hers.

I came up with the idea that we could buy a former house of prostitution located next door to the parsonage and start a ministry in Bedford-Stuyvesant. Dede reluctantly gave her consent. Then she agreed to be baptized by our good friend Harald Bredesen, a Lutheran minister passionate about introducing people to what was known as the baptism of the Holy Spirit. On a beautiful day in October 1959 she was baptized in Long Island Sound. After she came out of the chilly water, a heavenly glow surrounded her. Our friend Pastor Paul Morris from the Jamaica Avenue Presbyterian Church in Queens, New York, was caught up in the spirit of the moment and declared to me, "You have spoken to handfuls of people. Soon you will be speaking to millions." I filed that away in my memory.

I knew it was time to get serious about God's plan for the rest of my life. I set a time for an extended fast, and took a sleeping bag and seven cans of fruit juice and walked over to the old Classon Avenue Presbyterian Church in Brooklyn to seek an answer from the Lord.

At that time God confirmed to me Paul Morris' prophetic word that in the future I would be speaking to millions of people. Then, as I prayed further, God's Spirit led me to a beautiful verse of the Bible: Jeremiah 16:2.

When I opened my Bible, I read, "You shall not take a wife, nor shall you have sons or daughters in this place." I took that to mean no more hippie commune, no more mission to the poor of the New York slums. I firmly believed that God had a new life and a new future out there for us—somewhere. I jumped up from the church pew and ran up the street to the parsonage. I called out to Dede, "Pack your bags! We are getting out of here!"

I rented a five-by-seven-foot U-Haul trailer, hooked it up to our old DeSoto sedan, loaded some pots and pans and baby beds, thanked Dick Simmons and his wife for their hospitality, and headed south toward Lexington, Virginia, and my family home. I figured that it was an excellent place to start.

As we boarded the Little Creek-Cape Charles Ferry and crossed the Chesapeake Bay to Virginia, I felt somewhat like Moses crossing the Red Sea into the Promised Land. I was welcomed by my mother to our family home in Lexington. She told me that I had an invitation for the following Sunday to preach at the small church that she attended, called Grace Covenant Presbyterian Church.

My message was well received. At the end of the service two businessmen in the church approached me unexpectedly. After introducing themselves, one of them said, "We would like to sponsor you to preach for fifteen minutes a day on our local radio station, WREL."

Suddenly, here before me was an open door to fulfill the Lord's direction: "Go to your home and tell of the great things the Lord has done for you."

On the second day of the broadcast I drove from my home toward the station on the north side of town. Halfway there I stopped at the local post office, where I encountered a high school classmate named George Lauderdale. George's father was the pastor of the Associate Reformed Presbyterian Church of Lexington. His son, George, had followed him into the ministry.

George told me an amazing story. He was living in Norfolk, Virginia, on the coast and said he had had a vision of a man from Lexington saying to him, "Your mission here is not complete. You must return to Lexington."

On the strength of that vision, George got into his car and drove more than 225 miles to Lexington, a five-hour journey in those days. I encountered him as he stopped at the post office—a totally random occurrence. I invited him to ride with me to the radio station. On the drive he told me that there was a television station in Portsmouth, Virginia, that had gone off the air and that I should claim it for the Lord.

To me this seemed like a ridiculous suggestion. I didn't even own a television *set*, so buying a television *station* didn't make any sense. Besides, I knew absolutely nothing about television broadcasting. But could this possibly be God's future for me?

That night, I walked down from my mother's house to the tiny football field where I had played as a high school sophomore. Under the stars that night, I said, "God, if this television station is of You, how much will it cost?"

The Holy Spirit answered, "Thirty-seven thousand dollars."

Here was the situation: the Federal Communications Commission had allocated Channel 3 and Channel 10 to the Norfolk-Portsmouth ADI, or area of dominant influence. Then it added Channel 13. When this happened, the operators of UHF stations 15 and 27 signed off the air and made an application for the Channel 13 license.[1] What was available in Portsmouth was a broken-down studio with one black-and-white television camera, a thousand-watt UHF television transmitter, and a three-hundred-foot self-supporting television antenna with a low-powered antenna on top.

When I entered the studio of this run-down facility, I witnessed a scene of total chaos. The studio floor was covered with paper, and someone had urinated on a section. The plate glass between the studio and the control room had been shattered. Someone had ripped the lens from the film projector in the control room. One side of the building was broken off and looked like a large wedge of cake. The trees outside were festooned with film that had been vandalized from the control room.

What was left of the facility belonged to someone we in the South call a "good old country boy" named Tim Brite, who had been born in the rural area of southwest Virginia. Tim owned a used car lot named Starlight Motors. He had been using the television station as a vehicle to sell secondhand cars from his dusty lot. I wrote to Tim and said, "I understand that you have a TV facility for sale in Portsmouth, Virginia. How much do you want for it?"

His reply was succinct: "I want $25,000 for the equipment alone or $50,000 for the real estate plus the equipment." The figure that the Lord had put in my mind was right in the middle, which I presumed was the actual asking price.

My next step was to enlist prayer, so I printed ten thousand prayer cards asking people to pray for Christian television in the Norfolk-Portsmouth, Virginia, area known as Tidewater. My next step was to draft articles of incorporation for a nonstock, nonprofit corporation called the Christian Broadcasting Network Inc. The cost for this was thirty-five dollars, which I mailed, along with an application, to the Corporation Commission in Richmond, Virginia. Within a few days I received my official corporate documents. I now had an option, a corporation, and almost no money.

It turned out that RCA, one of the major electronic companies at the time, had a first lien on all of the equipment in the station, and it was quite possible that the City of Portsmouth might begin proceedings against the abandoned facility and seize it.

Tim finally agreed to come to Portsmouth to meet with me, and I drew up a deed giving the equipment and real estate of the television station to the Christian Broadcasting Network. All that was left was to agree on a price.

When we met, I explained to Tim my desire to begin Christian broadcasting in Tidewater and pointed out to him the potential liability he faced if he continued to hold on to the abandoned facility. During our lunch together I suggested that he might be able to get a huge tax break if he donated the facility to a charitable institution such as the Christian Broadcasting Network. I showed him the deed of gift and then drove him to his car.

While he was sitting there thinking about the liability he faced, he said, "Pat, do I have to sign this thing?"

"Yes, Tim, you do," I replied. He signed, and to this day I remember with gratitude the "good old country boy" who donated our first television station and the land beneath it to the Christian Broadcasting Network. A Christian friend of George Lauderdale's heard of my venture and sent me my first contribution—three dollar bills tucked into an envelope. Since I was the president and treasurer of the company, I thought the safe place for our treasure was a drawer in a bedroom bureau. I put the three dollar bills in the drawer and after a while opened it to see if they had multiplied. Regrettably there were still only three dollar bills in the drawer. So I decided I needed a bank account and drove around the city of Portsmouth looking for the most stable financial institution I could find.

Clutching my corporate treasure, I marched into the bank and inquired where I should go to open a bank account. I was directed to a young lady who said, "Do you wish to open a corporate or a personal account?"

"A corporate account."

"What is the name of your corporation?"

"The Christian Broadcasting Network Inc."

"Who are your directors?"

At that time my board consisted of Robert Walker, founder of *Christian Life* magazine; my old high school chum George Lauderdale; Lutheran pastor Harald Bredesen; my wife, Dede; and me.

After receiving the necessary data, the bank clerk said, "I know you will want some checks. We have two colors: gold and green."

I thought gold sounded more stable than green and chose that color for my checks. By then I figured I was home free, but she looked at me knowingly and said, "In matters of this nature, it's appropriate to make an initial deposit. How much will yours be?"

I shyly reached into my pocket and pulled out three dollar bills. "My initial deposit will be three dollars," I said. When I quickly reminded her that Jesus had multiplied the loaves and the fishes, she acknowledged that she was aware of the story. Then she told me that my checks would cost six dollars. So I must confess that the first business transaction of the Christian Broadcasting Network left me three dollars in the hole.

Shortly after that I was approached by a nursing home operator whom I will call Mr. Dangler. He told me that he was willing to underwrite my initial expenses of getting the station on the air. In return he wanted the use of a boat slip behind the TV station on a body of water known as Scott Creek. With this assurance I began making a few financial commitments. Then suddenly Mr. Dangler came to me and said he was revoking his commitment.

I had been operating on the assumption that the Spirit of God would lead His children in the right way. Now I felt that my concept of the guidance of the Holy Spirit was wrong and God had misled me. That was the first and only time in my Christian life that I questioned the goodness of God. Fortunately, He forgave me for this moment of doubt. Nevertheless, I resolved that I could not continue a venture that involved borrowing money that I was unable to repay. So I told the Lord and myself that unless a miracle happened by the next Wednesday, I was going to close down my fledgling corporation and seek another line of work.

On the preceding Sunday my mother had been deep in prayer and was given a vision by God. She saw her son on his knees with his hand outstretched to heaven and then saw a large packet of banknotes fall from heaven into his outstretched hand. My mother didn't tell me about her vision, for fear that I would consider her fanatical. Nevertheless, here's what happened: On Tuesday night—the eve of my self-imposed shutdown—Paul Morris showed up unexpectedly at my house and said, "The Lord has sent me down to you, and there is something I must do."

He then pulled out a checkbook, wrote out a check, and handed it to me. I quickly looked at the number: eighty dollars. I thought that was a nice gift, but it wouldn't come close to meeting my financial needs. Then, as I looked at the check more closely, I noticed the amount was not $80 but $8,000, which was more than enough to meet the outstanding obligations and move us along.

Once more I felt the watchful care of a supernatural God and was grateful that the Christian Broadcasting Network was still alive.

3

On the Air

ON MARCH 22, 1960, I celebrated my thirtieth birthday. I had realized from reading the Bible that the age of thirty marked the beginning of many significant Old Testament ministries, starting with the Levites, who could not begin their service until age thirty. I felt my thirtieth was the true beginning of a very special service.

I set about restoring the equipment to prepare to go on air, and I hired a couple of guys to do the work. I was well aware of RCA's prior lien on the equipment. The electronics company warned me in no uncertain terms I was not to turn on the transmitter until I had paid them the full amount of the lien, which was $15,000. Of course, other than RCA's permission, I also needed a license from the Federal Communications Commission to operate a television station.

I visited a lawyer in Norfolk to get advice about how to proceed with the FCC. The lawyer gave me a wise glance and, in a sonorous voice, said knowingly, "They won't even let you in the door of the FCC unless you've got five million dollars."

I didn't believe in naysayers, so I traveled to Washington and went to the FCC building myself. I inquired about the location of the office that gave out broadcast licenses. I was given directions to the office of a Mr. Levy. I walked down the marble-lined hall, knocked on the appropriate door, went in, and announced myself.

"Mr. Levy, I'm Pat Robertson. I have founded a small broadcast company in Portsmouth, Virginia, and I would like to know how to obtain a license."

Mr. Levy reached into a drawer, pulled out a couple of pieces of paper, and handed them to me. "Fill these forms out with the necessary exhibits, and send them back to me," he said.

I did that, and after a couple of weeks I called Mr. Levy to ask how my application was going.

"We've read your application, and it doesn't look like you have enough money to do it. I guess that you'll get it somewhere, so we'll grant you the license," he said. His reply delighted me.

Shortly thereafter the official certificate arrived granting the Christian Broadcasting Network the privilege of operating on Channel 27 in the Norfolk-Portsmouth metropolitan area. I had initially tried to get the call letters WTFC, which stood for Television for Christ. They were taken, so I changed my application to WYAH, which I had chosen after the Hebrew name for God, which is Yahweh, the *Hiphil* tense of the Hebrew word "to be," which can be translated "he who causes to be."[1] That call sign was granted.

In the fall of that year, I was hoping for an influx of substantial funds to help carry the network forward. I was invited to attend a regional meeting of the Full Gospel Business Men's Fellowship International (FGBMFI) in Washington, DC. This large organization with chapters all over the world had drawn its membership from well-to-do businessmen brought together in their belief in the power of the Holy Spirit. I was hoping that among these men I would find several donors. My heart was burdened with the responsibility I was carrying.

In one of the large public meetings the men raised their hands and worshipped God. I joined in the worship, and as I did so, God spoke to me in a clear voice: "This is My work. I'll carry the burden." No longer was there any thought of selling the business and getting out of television broadcasting. I left Washington a different person. A heavy load was lifted.

When I got home, I was approached by a local printer, who said, "I would be willing to print material for you." Someone else gave a gift of newsprint. I published a flashy tabloid with the banner headline "GOD'S DECISION NO SALE!" Now I had a way to get the word out, and I was on my way. The burden was on His shoulders, not mine.

Although my principal interest was television, I also learned that FM licenses were being granted for the asking. In those days AM (which stands for amplitude modulation) was the preferred medium for radio. Radio was in almost every home, and the major broadcasters had been granted what were called fifty-thousand-watt clear channels that, because of the characteristics of AM, were able to be heard a thousand miles away at night. A pioneer was KDKA in Pittsburgh, owned by the Westinghouse Broadcasting Company.[2]

Other equally well-known stations were WSB in Boston, WOR in New York, and similar powerhouses in Atlanta and Chicago. During the Great Depression, President Franklin Delano Roosevelt captivated America with his radio-delivered "Fireside Chats."[3] Jack Benny and Fred Allen dominated radio comedy during the 1940s.[4] Procter & Gamble felt that radio dramas would help sell soap, so they sponsored shows such as *The Guiding Light* before television became popular in the 1950s. Because of their sponsorship, they became known as soap operas.[5] As a youngster, I avidly listened to radio shows such as *The Shadow* and *I Love a Mystery*.

AM radio yielded tremendous reach into the nation's heartland but was lacking in fidelity, so the FCC opened up bandwidth for what was called frequency modulation, or FM.

FM had vastly superior fidelity and was not affected by stormy weather, but it could only be heard within the coverage area provided by the height of its tower and the strength of its signal.

I met an engineer named Dexter Phibbs, who told me he could put together an FM radio station out of his garage on Sparrow Road in Chesapeake, Virginia. He had been given an antique federal FM transmitter and had a homemade FM antenna on a seventy-foot creosote pole outside of his garage. I acquired the run-down facility from Dexter and applied to the FCC to broadcast on FM at 104.5. The FCC granted me a license with the call letters WXRI—XRI being the first three letters of the Greek name of Christ.[6] For better or for worse, we were able to cover our broadcast area from this run-down facility.

I was then visited by Stewart Brinsfield, a pastor from Maryland interested in acquiring a couple of broadcast facilities. I told him that I would sell him our radio facility for $5,000. Before he left town, he wrote me a check for the full amount for the radio station. A short time later he decided he did not want to get into the radio business but told me I could keep the money to use toward my television venture.[7] Now that was a big surprise!

I now had $5,000, but I was $10,000 short. Where would the other money come from?

In my devotional time my eye came across a prophetic word: "Even those from afar shall come and build the temple of the Lord."[8] I kept that in mind.

Not too much later I received a letter with another check for $5,000 from someone with Furr's cafeterias in Texas. The $5,000 check included an explanatory letter that said, "I've heard about your Christian broadcasting endeavor, so here is a contribution to help you."

I remembered God's prophetic word and was deeply touched. West Texas is located "afar" from Portsmouth, Virginia. The word had been that "those from afar shall come and build the temple of the Lord." With that $5,000 contribution, His Word was dramatically confirmed.

As I was working to put our TV station on the air, I was invited to join a men's Bible study and breakfast group that met Saturday mornings at the hair salon Taylor Burgess, located on the second floor of an office complex at Wards Corner in Norfolk. Among the members was a man named Jim Coates, a vice president of the Norfolk Shipbuilding & Drydock Corporation, owned by his wife's wealthy family.

One day Jim was doing yard work on the family property when a passerby stopped and said, "How much do you charge for yard work?"

Jim wiped the sweat off of his brow and said with a smile, "My hourly rates are very reasonable, but I have one extra benefit—I get to sleep with the lady of the house." At that, the visitor rolled up his car window and sped off in disgust.

I had set October 1, 1961, as the day of our first television broadcast on Channel 27, which, as I mentioned, I had named WYAH. As I prayed that Sunday morning, the word of the Lord came to me: "The salvation of the Lord is at hand." I left for the station and on the way passed Jim Coates, who was driving in the opposite direction. I invited him to come down to the station at noon to participate in our inaugural television broadcast. When Jim joined us at 11:45 a.m., I told him that we were $5,000 short of having the money necessary to turn on the transmitter. I remember he put his head in his hands and then looked up and said, "I'll give you the last $5,000."[9]

I then went back to the control room and told Harvey, our part-time chief engineer, that I had received the money necessary to get us on the air at noon.

Harvey's reply dumbfounded me. "I didn't think you could get the money, so I didn't get the equipment ready to go," he said.

The Lord had taken away my colorful Marine Corps expletives, but I let Harvey know in no uncertain terms that I wanted that rig turned on that day or else. Harvey turned a few screws and joined a few connections, and we actually had the transmitter operating at about one o'clock Sunday afternoon.

Though we were late on that first day of October in 1961, the first television station ever licensed to broadcast 50 percent or more religious content went on air.[10]

Imagine what our few viewers saw. Our backdrop was a gray curtain subject to dry rot. We had two pieces of cardboard taped together to form a cross. We had a poorly constructed pulpit for a speaker to stand behind. We had one black-and-white camera. There was no adequate monitor in the studio, and we had to run down to a convenience store a block away to see if we were even on the air.

When the Bible says, "Do not despise these small beginnings,"[11] I can certainly voice that with a hearty amen!

Little did I know where this first day on the air would take this embryonic TV station.

But I couldn't wait to find out.

4

Early Days

MY FATHER WAS A. Willis Robertson, who was quite the athlete growing up at the turn of the twentieth century in Virginia. While attending the University of Richmond, he played four years of varsity football without a substitute. In track he held the state record for the hammer throw. He was an accomplished tennis player, and his great love of hunting and fishing resulted in him being named Sportsman of the Year by *Field & Stream* magazine.

My father trained as a lawyer and opened a law practice in Buena Vista, Virginia, which had modeled itself after the City of Philadelphia. This small town of several thousand, set in the Blue Ridge Mountains, never reached that height.

Just a few miles from Buena Vista was a town called Lexington, which was the home of two universities, the Virginia Military Institute and Washington and Lee. My father opened a law practice in Lexington and soon after that was elected Commonwealth attorney for Rockbridge County.

After that he won a seat to the Virginia State Senate. His seatmate at the time was a young man from Berryville, Virginia, named Harry Byrd, a descendant of the distinguished Byrd family prominent in colonial America.

My father was named chairman of the Virginia Commission of Game and Inland Fisheries,[1] and his State Senate seatmate, Harry Byrd, was elected governor of Virginia.[2] While in Richmond, Byrd recognized that the political power in Virginia was held by court clerks and other officials, who appointed their followers to various key political posts throughout the state.[3]

Byrd, a political genius, gained allegiance from almost all of the court clerks throughout the state, and they in turn formed what was called the Byrd Machine.[4] In those days the nomination of the Democratic Party was tantamount to victory for a political candidate. As a result, an endorsement by the Byrd Machine assured victory for Byrd's selected candidates.

The 7th Congressional District comprised a valley of Virginia that ran from Lexington through Staunton and Harrisonburg on to Winchester. In those days the political parties were allowed to select their candidates for public office by party caucus. In 1932 the 7th District Democratic Party held its congressional caucus in Winchester, Virginia. As the delegates assembled, Harry Byrd slipped in unannounced to a back room.

Then he called his trusted aides to see him. He quietly passed this word to them: "Our choice for the Democratic nomination for the 7th Congressional District will be Willis Robertson." Byrd's key lieutenants then cornered caucus delegates and instructed them on whom they were to vote for. Shortly after that the press announced that the Democratic nominee for Congress in the 7th congressional district was A. Willis Robertson, chairman of the state's Commission of Game and Inland Fisheries. From there the election was a certainty, and in 1932 my father was elected to the US Congress.[5]

A dedicated public servant who gave himself unstintingly to his service, my father was scrupulously honest and held in high esteem by all of his colleagues while serving as a congressman from 1933 to 1946 and as a US senator from 1946 to 1966, a span of thirty-four years in Washington.[6] He was so well loved by his Senate colleagues that at his funeral in 1971, over forty sitting senators traveled from Washington to Lexington, Virginia, to be in attendance.

Besides a great love for the outdoors, along with hunting and fishing, my father loved working with field dogs and taking long walks in the country. The most tender side of him that I have ever seen is the letter that he wrote to my mother when she accepted his proposal of marriage, a letter that I still hold dear.

My mother, Gladys Churchill Willis, was a renowned beauty who was led to faith in Jesus by Dr. William Lumpkin, the pastor of the small Manley Memorial Baptist Church in Lexington, Virginia. As the years passed, she withdrew from the demands of the social life of Washington, DC, and spent countless hours in prayer to the Lord. Without a doubt her beautiful spirit played a significant role in shaping who I would become.

Two years before my father went off to our nation's capital, on March 22, 1930, I was born the youngest of two sons. My father, who was forty-two at the time I was born, named me Marion Gordon after his college roommate and distant cousin, Marion Gordon Willis.

When I was a baby, my older brother, Willis Robertson Jr., whom everyone called Tad, was five and a half and often looked after his little brother. He liked to pat my cheeks and say, "Pat, pat, pat." Everyone around thought it was adorable, and the name Pat stuck. From that moment on I was not Marion Gordon but Pat Robertson. As much as I honor St. Patrick and all of my good friends from Ireland, my nickname has nothing to do with St. Patrick or Ireland.

I laughingly say that when I was two years old, in 1932, I first learned the words *mama*, then *daddy*, and then *constituent*—a word I heard a lot. I was always being told, "Do this," or, "Do not do that," followed by, "What would the constituents think?" That attitude instilled in me what the French would call *noblesse oblige*—nobility obligation—because I felt I had a responsibility to behave myself in the public eye. I have carried that responsibility throughout my life. Those early days proved to be excellent training.

In 1932 the government of the United States was much smaller than the monstrous bureaucracy it has become in the twenty-first century. The US Congress was much closer to the Founders' concept of a body that comprised farmers, businessmen, lawyers, and doctors who for a short time left their personal responsibilities behind and assembled in Washington to pass laws that affected the lives of people just like themselves.

In the days of the Depression a congressman's salary was $8,500 a year,[7] which was adequate to maintain a comfortable middle-class lifestyle but was hardly the road to riches. So in keeping with this custom of his fellow congressmen, my father packed his wife and children into the family Plymouth, and we drove from our home in Lexington to Washington, DC, in January, and then we returned home to Lexington in early June.

I remember in one of those years they rented a home in Foxhall Village in Washington, DC. This was a Tudor-style grouping of homes and businesses built around a small shopping center. Across the road from the shopping center was the Rose Lees Hardy School, where I was enrolled as a student in what I believe was either the fifth or sixth grade.

During the following year my father rented a home about a mile away from Foxhall Village on Dexter Street; however, I was still enrolled as an elementary school student in the Rose Lees Hardy School. In order to get home from school in the afternoon, I had to walk about a mile along a small stream that separated the neighborhoods.

As a little boy out on his own, whether from fear or spiritual longing, I began to spend time talking to God during those walks. This was my first real experience of spiritual communion with my heavenly Father. Perhaps what was happening reflected my spiritual origin.

My great-aunt Julia Holman lived with us for a time. When I was a baby, she would hold me in her arms and pray God's blessing over me. She hoped that I would be another George W. Truett, who at the time was pastor of the First Baptist Church in Dallas. Her father, Russell Holman, was a pastor in Birmingham, Alabama, who recruited and equipped the First Baptist missionaries to the state of Texas.

I am convinced that God remembers the prayers of His godly saints to affect generations yet unborn. Years later I can still remember the cry of my youthful heart to know God, to know His presence, and to have Him in my life.

5

HARDER THAN A ROAD GANG

AFTER A FEW moves to Washington, DC, from Lexington, my parents decided it was too much trouble to keep moving the family. They determined that we would remain in Lexington instead of renting a house in Washington. Therefore, I attended sixth grade at a decrepit Lexington elementary school.

It soon became apparent that my grades in sixth grade were sufficiently high for me to be one of the subjects of a new experiment that the local school system was putting in place. Under their plan, some of the more promising students were allowed to skip seventh grade and go directly to eighth grade. Because my grades were good, I was allowed to start eighth grade a year ahead of schedule.

In our school system, though, eighth grade had become a dumping ground for those students who didn't have the academic qualifications or aptitude to go on to high school. I found myself sitting in a classroom with some very old, big boys from the mountains, and I was a fresh-faced youngster in their midst. The school made no attempt to shield the students from bullying or even physical violence, so bare-knuckled fistfights and bloody noses settled many of our disputes.

Fortunately for me, some of the bigger boys in eighth grade decided to take me under their wing and give me their protection. So as packs of boys planned aggressive action against me, these big fellows from the mountains became my protectors. I'm unscathed today because of them.

Something else stood out. Those boys and girls who would come down from the mountains were the victims of severe poverty. My grades generally put me second or third in my class standing; the person who was first in my class was a girl who, for purposes of this book, I'll call Ellen Davis.

Ellen was brilliant, but she was desperately poor. She didn't have adequate clothes, her nutrition was poor, and everything about her, except her brilliant mind, showed deficiency.

I realized at that time—and I carry this memory even now—that girls and boys like this who have such ability should always be given an opportunity to excel. Unfortunately their economic situation was so poor that boys and girls of great ability were often denied the advantages they might have had if they came from more affluent surroundings. Nevertheless, going to school day to day with these gifted people gave me a vivid understanding of poverty, an understanding of the abilities of people, and a profound sense of gratitude for what God had made available to me personally.

When I graduated from eighth grade and went on to high school, my parents decided that I would benefit from military training. They enrolled me in the McDonogh School outside of Baltimore, Maryland, which meant I would be boarding. The McDonogh School was located in the country but was not far away from Baltimore Street, the infamous address of seedy bars, burlesque theaters, and other nefarious activity. Later in life, as I recall in a subsequent chapter, the spiritual roots of Baltimore Street burst vividly in my consciousness.

At McDonogh the cadets wore uniforms and went through military-style exercises. I remember standing at attention in the freezing cold in the early morning hours while the flag was being raised on the campus flagpole and the company bugler played an appropriate martial tune. After the flag raising, a couple of drummers beat their drums, and the young cadets marched to the McDonogh dining hall, where we were often fed a mysterious mixture of pork called scrapple. I could barely eat the stuff, which is why I still recall that my time at McDonogh was marked by inadequate nutrition and constant hunger.

Fortunately for me, my parents relented after one year and let me go home to Lexington, where I entered Lexington High School as a sophomore. LHS had a small football team, and I played right tackle on the second team. It would be nice to claim that, at this stage of my life, I was devoted to becoming a better football player and developing my intellect, but I have to admit that my main pursuit was youthful romance during my high school years.

I developed a puppy-love crush on a young lady called B. T. She lived with her uncle Bill, a dentist whose home was on a hill opposite that of my parents' home, so it was easy for romance to blossom. In her senior year B. T. was named the most beautiful girl at Lexington High School, and she and her young boyfriend—that would be me—were named Lexington High School's Biggest Case in the yearbook. While having a gorgeous girlfriend in high school showed that I might have something going for me, it was not necessarily something spiritual.

During my young life my family members were prominent members of the Manly Memorial Baptist Church in Lexington. My father was a trustee, a deacon, and a Sunday school teacher. Sometime in my early teen years I went forward at an invitation to receive Jesus Christ as Savior, as most of my peers did at one time or another. I shook the hand of the pastor and officially joined the church. Following that I submitted to water baptism. In all candor I must confess that this did not represent a spiritual transformation at the time, but it did show that in my early days I was not immune to the spiritual call of God on my life.

That summer after my sophomore year of high school, my father decided I would profit from rigorous farm work, so I was sent to a farm in Rapidan, Virginia, owned by Robert Tinsley and his wife, Elsie, of the prominent Garnett Family.[1] Looking back, I am amused to see our current debate about raising the minimum wage for young workers to fifteen dollars an hour. I was paid the princely sum of fifteen dollars—not for an hour, but for an *entire month* of physical labor, which, I might add, would start at five or six in the morning and many days did not conclude until nine o'clock at night.

One of my tasks was driving a team of mules pulling a crosscut mower. I became an expert at loading hay wagons, and during the digging season I marched down row after row picking up potatoes, after which I transferred the same spuds from buckets to hundred-pound sacks.

In an amusing incident I recall the time I drove my team up near the fence at the end of the property and looked across the road. A truck was taking on a number of workers from a road gang. I asked a person who was with me what was going on since it was only four o'clock in the afternoon.

"These men are now finished with their work for the day," he replied, "and they are going back to their barracks, where they will have dinner and spend the night."

Somehow I thought that would be a wonderful deal if I could get on the road gang and get out of the tremendous work I had to do on the farm. Nonetheless, the farm is where I learned the value of hard work…and I mean it was *hard work*. If you have ever stood on a mound of straw, trying to control the output of a threshing machine blower on a hot, sweaty July day while getting blasted with itchy dust, you will never forget it.

Here's something else that I learned that has stayed with me: During the past several decades there has been an ongoing struggle to reconcile the races. We have seen the spectacle of a little African American girl needing armed guards to gain access to an all-white school.[2] We have seen angry police dogs and fire hoses turned on innocent African American people.[3] We have heard the inspiring words of Dr. Martin Luther King Jr., who dreamed of a time when people would be judged by the quality of their character rather than the color of their skin.[4]

Whatever struggles might have been going on in other parts of the country, I can testify that on the Tinsley farm there was no thought of who was black or white. We worked side by side. We sweat and labored together. When we took a drink of water from a spring, there was no sign saying "Whites Only."

We had one rusty tin cup, and each of us drank from it. The segregation in the South was certainly not my experience on the farm. I think of one special African American gentleman. He lived in a little house along the dirt road up from the farm. As a youngster I would go to him just to listen to his wisdom. He had no formal education, but God had given him both great dignity and great common sense. There is no way I could ever demean that dear friend because of the color of his skin.

I cherish each building block that shaped my personal life. My experience on the Tinsley farm was one of them. Learning the reward of hard work is something I have carried with me all my life.

6

GOLDEN GLOVES HEAVYWEIGHT

ONE OF MY classmates at Lexington High School, Jimmy Adair, was extremely handsome and had an upper body like a young Adonis. During our sophomore year he inherited a brand-new automobile from his father. In those days Virginia permitted a young teenager to drive a car, which opened the door to a lot of freedom for a couple of randy high school boys.

Lexington's state-supported military college, Virginia Military Institute (VMI), was the alma mater of none other than "Old Blood and Guts" himself, Gen. George S. Patton.[1] VMI had austere barracks modeled after those at West Point. The VMI cadets were subject to scrupulous discipline, including restrictive nighttime check-ins.

These rules proved a major opportunity for Jim Adair and me. The VMI cadets would invite their prom dates to come to Lexington. For us, their twelve o'clock curfew meant that the night was just beginning. As soon as the cadets were safely in the barracks, a few of us high school students would arrange a late-night rendezvous with their dates. I still marvel at the indulgence of my dear mother, who allowed her wayward son to stay out until two or three in the morning. However, my parents' indulgence eventually came to an end when my father and mother opted to send me to another military school.

McCallie School in Chattanooga, Tennessee, was founded by two Presbyterian men, Park and Spencer McCallie. The McCallie brothers, deeply spiritual men, instilled a spiritual ethos that was extremely beneficial to those who attended the McCallie School.

McCallie was famous for its athletics. Around the chapel walls were banners proclaiming the noted championship teams in football, track, baseball, wrestling, and tennis. Each student was required to participate in a sport during three seasons of the year—fall, winter, and spring. I played football in the fall and participated in the shot put in the spring but chose boxing for my winter sport. As part of the McCallie team I fought in the novice heavyweight division in the Chattanooga City Tournament and also the Chattanooga Golden Gloves. A couple of the matches stand out in my mind.

In the Chattanooga Golden Gloves tournament my opponent in the semifinals was a student from a local high school. For some reason I still cannot understand, the young man had built up a fear of facing me in the ring. Instead of a rigorous training schedule, he allayed his fear by filling up on junk food.

After a few minutes of desultory sparring early in the match, I threw a right-handed jab at his face. When he covered up, I struck him with a full shoulder punch with my left hand straight into his midsection. The junk food inside of his stomach didn't seem to like that blow, and it appeared that he was getting ready to throw up.

The referee approached me with a stern look on his face. I was just a kid and didn't know if I had done something wrong until he reached for my right hand and lifted it high into the air, giving me a technical knockout. As proof of this victory, I was handed a small silver glove as the runner-up champion in the novice heavyweight division of the Chattanooga Golden Gloves.

Perhaps my most notable fight was against a wild man from the town of Ooltewah, Tennessee. I remember sitting in the dressing room with my gloves on, waiting to be called. At the time, a tall, rawboned young man opened the door and came in.

"I fought your opponent yesterday afternoon and was knocked out and just woke up," he said. "I've come to tell you how you should deal with him."

I thought, "If a guy as tough as this was knocked out for hours, what chance do I have against him?"

It was too late to call off the fight, so I courageously stepped into the ring. When the bell rang, the Ooltewah Terror charged across the ring and unleashed a flurry of blows that knocked me through the ropes and out of the ring. I wasn't really hurt, so I bravely climbed back in.

At that time a number of my McCallie classmates said to each other, "We can't stand to see a McCallie boy beaten that way, so we're going to leave." They walked out and left me facing the Terror by myself. I had two things in my favor: the Ooltewah Terror had never fought a left-hander before, and he always telegraphed his punches. Each time he started to swing at me, he made guttural noises like an animal, and I could easily step out of his way. Then I'd hit him with my left hand, prompting him to shake his head and then again make strange sounds.

I really think that I won that fight, but because he knocked me through the ropes in the opening round, the judges insisted that I would have to deliver a knockout to counter the earlier debacle. So the Ooltewah Terror won the match and claimed the Chattanooga Golden Gloves championship.

After these two examples of my amusing ring prowess, I did not enter any further Golden Gloves engagements. A few years later, though, I had some modest success as a college novice heavyweight wrestler.

McCallie School was committed to the Westminster Confession of Faith, and its motto was "Man's chief end is to glorify God, and to enjoy him for ever."[2] Scholastically and physically my time at McCallie played a key role in my formative years.

God, in His graciousness, shapes us so that we will grow and learn of Him. At that point in my life He had a lot of shaping to do of me.

7

THE FROZEN HILLS OF NORTH KOREA

I GRADUATED FROM McCALLIE School just after my sixteenth birthday and was scheduled to attend the University of Virginia in Charlottesville. Remember, I had skipped a grade.

Just before my college classes began, I was shocked to hear the news that happened at the Theta Delta Chi fraternity house. When a fistfight broke out between two students, one of them fell against the base of a stately column in front of the fraternity house. He struck his head and tragically died.

I decided that I was too young to get killed at the University of Virginia, where students bragged that they lost their amateur status as drinkers. At the last minute I turned to my hometown college of Washington and Lee and was accepted into the freshman class. My major was history, and the college experience turned out to be absolutely delightful.

Washington and Lee had a storied history. George Washington made a $50,000 gift—a sum equivalent to nearly one million dollars today—to its predecessor, Liberty Hall Academy. The name Washington Academy was then given to the school, and fifteen years later it was renamed Washington College.[1]

After the end of the Civil War, Southern general Robert E. Lee became the president of Washington College, and later the name was changed to Washington and Lee.[2] The school was set in the middle of the beautiful mountains of the Shenandoah Valley in an atmosphere that could be described as most genteel.

When I attended the all-male institution, there was a custom that students and professors would greet one another in passing. Washington and Lee also prided itself on its honor code. Students could leave their books or money lying unattended on the campus with the knowledge that nobody would dream of stealing anything. There was a code of honor about cheating, about lying, about theft, and about all the things that would be considered ungentlemanly for the students. There was also a dress code that obligated students to wear coats and ties wherever they went on the campus.[3]

I dove right into my classwork, and in the first semester I was placed on the dean's list. Those on Washington and Lee's dean list were relieved from the burden of having to attend class unless they chose to do so. Often I decided not to go because I found it more profitable to study on my own and learn from the textbooks as opposed to taking notes at the lectures.

In my freshman year fraternity life loomed large. We freshmen were "rushed" (as the saying went) by fraternities in the hopes that the most desirable of us would join the fellowship of these exclusive clubs. I pledged the Sigma Alpha Epsilon fraternity and was received as a member.

Shortly after that my exhaustion from Rush Week led to a case of mononucleosis, characterized by high fever, swollen glands, and general physical malaise. It took me several months to recover, but recover I did. I then launched into a hectic round of parties, weekend outings, and "familiarization" trips to the adjoining girls' schools of Sweet Briar, Randolph-Macon, and Hollins.

I was living at home at the time and must congratulate my dear mother, who insisted that I burn the midnight oil to prepare for exams. The Lord, in His goodness, gave me the ability to read textbooks and spot exam questions. It was uncanny how the underlining in my textbooks would show up later on the exams. I found out that without too much trouble I could achieve a report card that contained more A's than B's.

After a couple of years I was inducted into an honorary society, Phi Beta Kappa, made up of members with high academic achievement. When I graduated, my degree would be accompanied by three Latin words: *magna cum laude*, which is an academic honorific title meaning "with great distinction."[4]

Before the end of my sophomore year, in 1948, I was alarmed to learn that the president of the United States had instituted a draft for college-age people such as myself. Rather than be drafted into the army, I decided to enlist in the Platoon Leaders Class of the Marine Corps. I went to the Marine Corps School at Quantico for two summers. The first summer, I was ranked as a corporal, and the second, I was ranked as a sergeant. I went through all of the necessary drills needed to train me to be an infantry platoon leader. A marine officer attended my graduation and awarded me a commission as a second lieutenant in the US Marine Corps. My father, in his first term as a US senator, beamed when his son became a newly minted lieutenant in the USMC.

Because I had done relatively well in my studies, my parents rewarded me with a trip to Europe, along with tuition for a course at the University of London titled The Arts in Britain Today. I was able to rent a room located on Tottenham Court Road a few blocks away from the British Museum.

Our coursework was extraordinary. We were privileged to hear T. S. Eliot read his poetry. We attended a performance of the Royal Opera Company in which the great ballerina Margot Fonteyn danced to Tchaikovsky's *Swan Lake*. In our classes we received lectures from the drama critic of *The Times* (London). At other times we were given tours of the museums and the London art gallery. I couldn't have imagined a better graduation present.

During my time in England I took the opportunity to travel frequently across the channel to Paris, where I enjoyed the *haute cuisine* and sights and sounds of the City of Light. One lovely summer day I was sitting at a Parisian sidewalk café reading a French newspaper. I noticed the headline "La guerre dans Corée." Even though I had taken French classes in school, I must admit that I didn't know what the English word for Corée is. All I knew was that a certain land was engaged in war.

As I read on, I learned that a group of Fusiliers Marins had been called to duty. That was a French term I did know: Fusiliers Marins were navy soldiers, which, of course, was their designation for US Marines. I realized that the commission I had gained at graduation was being called upon very quickly, and I later learned that I would be sent to an unknown land called Korea—Corée in French.

Around 1950 the Russians installed an expatriate lieutenant colonel named Kim Il-sung as the head of North Korea. He could barely speak Korean, but the Russian propaganda machine went into overdrive to shout his praises. As a result, the North Korean people began to idolize him. In fact, he became like a god to them.[5]

Under Russian influence the North Koreans invaded South Korea and overran its defenses in a lightning strike. Soon all that was left of South Korea was a small enclave around the city of Pusan, which is now known as Busan. Korea had been made a UN Protectorate, and the UN considered the aggression by North Korea as an attack against the UN itself. Because of disagreements on policy the Russian representative on the Security Council had boycotted the meetings. While that boycott was in place, President Truman directed the US representative to put forward a resolution committing the UN to what was later called a Police Action against North Korea.[6]

Simultaneously with this action, General MacArthur left Toyko and flew to Pusan to gain firsthand knowledge of the situation on the ground. He determined that the plight of South Korea needed American forces and first one regiment; then several divisions of American troops were sent to reinforce the Pusan perimeter. When other armaments were added, the North Koreans were unable to overrun that last small part of the Korean Peninsula. They struggled to survive, but with the addition of armaments airlifted in, the perimeter around Pusan held firm and the North Koreans were prevented from taking over the entire Korean Peninsula.

Then MacArthur conceived a brilliant plan. He brought in navy squadrons to bombard the Port of Inchon on the West Coast of Korea and then began to unload several divisions of American troops. MacArthur had managed a pincer movement, which effectively annihilated the North Korean forces that had invaded the South. MacArthur did not stop there. He determined to invade North Korea and win a dramatic victory. He divided his forces into two parts—one was designated the Eighth Army under Four-Star General Walton H. Walker; the other forces were designated the Tenth Corps, to which was added the First Marine Division. Both of these forces moved deep into North Korea with little or no opposition.

However, the Chinese had sent clear signals that they were alarmed by the presence of major US forces on the Korean Peninsula, and the Russians had made clear that they were prepared to defend their proxy, Kim Il-sung. US Army patrols captured a few combatants who were clearly Chinese nationals. Intelligence estimates were received by army intelligence indicating the presence in North Korea of sizable numbers of Chinese troops. Reports that I have read indicate that MacArthur, who had so roundly defeated the North Koreans, chose to ignore the intelligence reports pointing to massive Chinese involvement. As his forces pushed deeper into North Korea, massive Chinese armies blowing trumpets and firing weapons descended upon the Eighth Army, which apparently was unprepared to deal with this severe onslaught and began a rapid pullout back to the 38th parallel. Regrettably the First Marine Division, which I later joined as assistant adjutant, was left stranded at a place called the Chosin Reservoir. The marines found themselves surrounded. At that time their principal enemy was not just the North Koreans but also the bitter cold that swept down from Manchuria. The marines were dressed in summer fatigues with lightweight leather shoes, cotton socks, no overcoats and no warm headgear. Many of these brave Americans lost their lives in temperatures so cold that even the firing pins of their rifles could not fire rounds.[7]

The commanding general of the First Marine Division ordered an attack to clear the way for a withdrawal to the sea. As they trudged out in the freezing temperatures, the marines took vicious fire from North Koreans hidden in the hills. The brave marines fought their way to the safety of the seacoast, but many lost their lives in this time of tragedy. The battle in the Chosin Reservoir went down in the history of the US

Marine Corps, along with its heroism in places such as Iwo Jima and Guadalcanal.

The defeat of US forces in Korea may well go down in history as one of the worst tragedies ever suffered by our armies. Nevertheless, General MacArthur's desire was to use American air power and ground forces to liberate all of North Korea. To do so, he conceived a plan to move beyond the Yalu River into Manchuria.

To the civilian leadership in Washington this plan looked like an attempt to double down on disaster. In the long run Truman fired MacArthur. MacArthur's two successor generals brought the conflict to a stalemate at a demilitarized zone on the 38th parallel, which left Kim Il-sung and his descendants in charge of North Korea. The United States' aid and support helped create a remarkably vibrant and successful democratic nation in South Korea.

As I write this, I am conscious that North Korea, under the family of Kim Il-sung, had become perhaps the most oppressive dictatorship in the world with a starving, oppressed population that now, under the grandson Kim Jong-un, possesses an arsenal of nuclear weapons and the launch vehicles that may one day threaten the western coast of the United States with thermonuclear destruction.

So we ask ourselves, Were Douglas MacArthur and the militants correct, or were Harry Truman and the peace party correct? What had really happened? Had there been no coordination between the Eighth Army and the Tenth Corps? Were the marines not told that their left flank was now totally exposed?

I had always believed that MacArthur's strategy of moving deep into North Korea and sealing the northern border of that country would have been a historical win for our nation. In truth our forces had suffered one of the worst military defeats in our history, and the marines were left to suffer.

The political leadership of America did not wish a major Asiatic conflict with China, nor did they wish a major conflict with Russia, which now had nuclear weapons in its arsenal.

They lacked the courage to stand up to the Chinese and demanded that Truman force MacArthur to back down. There was a subsequent example of insubordination by MacArthur against Truman. The Joint Chiefs determined that MacArthur should be relieved of command. It was then that the most distinguished general in American history was forced to resign as commander in chief of the Allied Forces in the Far East.

Had MacArthur's advice been followed, America would have a peaceable Korean Peninsula modeled after our strong ally, South Korea. To my way of thinking, a unified Korea would have proved a welcome addition to the family of nations. But that apparently will not be the case. I leave it to history to sort out whose actions were correct.

Now to get to my part of the Korean conflict, I returned to the States in October 1950 and had orders waiting for me to report to duty at Camp Pendleton in California. I spent a couple of weeks at my home in Lexington and then arranged for transportation on military aircraft to San Diego, where a ship was waiting to take me into the Korean conflict. I'll never forget the feeling I experienced sitting in the wardroom of the troop ship as a local San Diego radio station played the song "Enjoy Yourself (It's Later Than You Think)." I thought I'd better enjoy what I could because before long I was going to be joining the First Marine Division in Korea.

I arrived in Kobe, Japan, and received orders to report to Camp Otsu near Kyoto, where my initial assignment was to train troops wounded in the Korean War and to bring them back into physical shape to reenter the Korean conflict.

After I had been in Japan for a few months, I was given orders to fly to the headquarters of the First Marine Division in a place called Chondo-ri, which is north of the 38th parallel in what we now know as North Korea. As I sat in the processing tent, the officer in charge noted that I had proficiency in communication skills and was planning to study law.

"Well," he said, "we need an assistant adjutant with communication skills for the division, so we'll send you south to Masan." I spent several months in Masan and was then ordered up to the Forward Command

Post of the First Marine Division, which was locked in combat against the Chinese and North Korean enemies near a place that has been popularized in literature as Heartbreak Ridge and the Punchbowl.[8]

We were living in tents at First Division headquarters, and I must say it was bitter cold. When icy winds would sweep down from Manchuria, the temperature would fall to minus 20 degrees, and we were sleeping in canvas tents. It was so cold that it would be necessary to break our shoes loose from the frozen ground when we got up each day.

The frigid weather was so intense that the Marine Corps awarded three battle stars to members of the First Division who endured the extreme cold. I remember a Christmas in that frozen environment. I had been partaking rather liberally of what we called "Class VI Ordnance," and in a drunken haze I stood outside on a hill in North Korea and cried out to the Lord, "God, why? Why is this happening? Please show me what is going on. Give me an understanding and let me know what life is all about as I'm facing what we have in this place."

After the bone-chilling winter was crowded out by a pleasant summer, the Defense Department ruled that the time of my overseas service had come to an end and I was entitled to return to the United States. The troops who were being rotated out along with me were loaded into trucks that made their way through the darkness from the center of Korea out to the port city of Hamhŭng. There we went aboard loading craft that took us out to oceangoing troop ships, where we climbed rope ladders thrown over the sides of the ships. As I swung my legs over the side of the ship and onto the deck, someone said to me, "Lieutenant, you have just been named the mess officer. You have twenty-two hundred troops to feed. It's time for their lunch."

I was dumbfounded. My military occupation specialty was combat infantry. I certainly had never gone to Marine Corps cooking school, so I asked somebody on the deck what I was supposed to do next. He looked at me and said, "Find yourself a good gunnery sergeant and tell him to get the food ready."

The standing joke in the armed forces is that noncommissioned officers are more knowledgeable than their superior officers. This was certainly the case on our troop ship because the sergeant I chose did a masterful job of organizing the galley to feed a shipload of hungry marines from Korea to California.

My active-duty service in the Marine Corps was officially over in July 1952, and I was grateful to have served my country while remaining in one piece. Now it was time to do what I really wanted to do: follow in my father's footsteps and become a lawyer.

8

ON TO LAW SCHOOL

Y FATHER HAD a close friend, Raymond Guest, who was
a member of the Palm Beach elite and counted among *his*
close friends a number of the leaders of Yale University. Because of Mr.
Guest's associations Yale treated me like a legacy and guaranteed my
admission to Yale Law School, provided I could pass the Law School
Admission Test (LSAT).

Fortunately for me the LSAT was a test of word association and
reasoning as opposed to stored knowledge. I've always been good with
language and had no difficulty not only passing the LSAT but scoring
in the top 6 percent of those who took it. When I gained admission to
Yale Law School in the fall of 1952, I was twenty-two years old.

I soon realized that I was running on a fast track. I found out that
88 percent of my class members were members of Phi Beta Kappa or
the equivalent at their respective colleges. My class members included
the valedictorians at Notre Dame, City College of New York, and
Williams College. After two years in the military my academic proficiency was quite rusty; nevertheless, I wholeheartedly undertook the
enormous amount of reading required of every law school student.

Yale University was an amazing place. A number of the ornate buildings were erected during the Depression, when the cost of construction was quite low.[1] For example, the Payne Whitney Gymnasium was
outfitted for the sons of the rich and famous. The so-called Cathedral
of Sweat had two Olympic-style swimming pools, a workout room, a
dry steam room, a wet steam room, and even an area with a mechanical horse so that people could practice their polo strokes indoors. In
short the facilities were magnificent.

The Yale Law School itself was quite beautiful, with Gothic architecture, complete with gargoyles. My first dorm room wasn't all that

spectacular. But later, when I was able to move to a better room, I had oak paneling, leaded windows, a wood-burning fireplace, and beautiful amenities. In short the sons and daughters of the rich were not supposed to camp out when they went to school, and I was happy to be included in that opulent setting.

In its past Yale had been noted for its spiritual revival. A clergyman named Timothy Dwight was the leader of a great revival at the turn of the nineteenth century,[2] and other chaplains and teachers were known for their spiritual piety. I must say when I got to Yale, there wasn't much evidence of that piety—a reality reflected in *God and Man at Yale*, the brilliant book by William F. Buckley Jr., which he wrote while he was still a student there.

Choral singing was a prominent student activity at Yale. The most famous Yale singing group, which sang a cappella, was called the Whiffenpoofs.[3] Their best-known song was "The Whiffenpoof Song," which wasn't a lusty drinking song or a stirring challenge for victory on the gridiron. Instead, "The Whiffenpoof Song" mentions God's mercy and eternal damnation.

Does "The Whiffenpoof Song" represent a parody of the warning given by pious parents to their sons to change their dissolute ways or face God's punishment? Or is the song a genuine cry from one seeking forgiveness by God? I will let you be the judge. Here are some of the lyrics:[4]

> We're poor little lambs who have lost our way
> Baa, baa, baa
> We're little black sheep who have gone astray
> Baa, baa, baa
>
> Gentleman songsters off on a spree
> Doomed from here to eternity
> Lord have mercy on such as we
> Baa, baa, baa

The Yale law professors were advocates of the concept of judicial supremacy. In the three years I was a student, I never studied the US

Constitution as such. We were taught from casebooks. The first case in our Constitutional Law class was called *Marbury v. Madison*. In that case Chief Justice John Marshall had written that the Supreme Court had the power to overrule an act of Congress.[5] The issue before the Court had to do with the appointment of a collector of customs in a port city. The case did not touch the lives of ordinary American people in any way at the time, and the seed of judicial supremacy was virtually unnoticed. Nevertheless, the seed, once planted, began to grow and grow until the weakest of the three branches of government—as the Framers intended—became the most powerful.

Here is how that concept has ripened in our day: The liberal elites realize that they cannot impose their views on the majority of the American people. The electorate is generally conservative. However, by skillful judicial reasoning and a strategy of bringing forward winnable cases, the ACLU, many of the Harvard law faculty, and others with a similar mindset seek to influence the nine-member Supreme Court and, therefore, change the moral structure of the United States. That is the teaching that is represented by the Harvard Law School and is certainly carried out in large measure at Yale Law School as well.

Back when I was at Yale, though, things were different. I can remember studying under very brilliant professors. Professor Boris Bittker taught me from his textbook on US tax law. Professor Fred Rodell was also a noted writer about US taxation. Professor Corbin's book on contracts made him a leading authority in the field, and who could forget Professor Moore, a native of Montana whose multi-volume books titled *Moore's Federal Practice* became the acknowledged authority in that field.[6] One of my tort professors, Fleming James, had represented the New Haven Railroad before the courts. And Professor Fowler Harper had written extensively on other aspects of the state laws governing tort litigation. In short I was privileged to study law under men who were the leading experts in the nation.

In today's world the Yale Law faculty has shown a more radical bent. For example, the outstanding Supreme Court Justice Samuel Alito is himself a Yale Law graduate. Yet the Yale Law faculty vehemently opposed his nomination to the Supreme Court by President George W. Bush.

In 2006 I returned to Yale Law School for a fiftieth-anniversary reunion and was invited to participate in a forum to discuss "Yale University and ROTC." Yale University had gone on record as withdrawing support for the Army ROTC program because of the Defense Department policy dealing with homosexuality in the military called "Don't Ask, Don't Tell."

I argued during the debate that if Yale University was the recipient of hundreds of millions of government dollars for various programs, it was hardly in a position to exercise any righteous indignation over a Defense Department policy. The Defense Department sued Yale to have the ROTC program reinstated, and Yale countered with a claim of educational independence. Yale lost. The *Wall Street Journal* headlined its editorial "Army 9, Yale 0."

I will say this about the Juris Doctor (JD) that I earned at Yale: I learned a great deal, including how to form corporations and partnerships. I learned about classes of stock and the rights of shareholders, bondholders, and corporate officers. I learned about tax law, estate law, and the laws that govern our nation. I was given the technical ability to draft the founding documents for a number of institutions and ministries that have facilitated multiple blessings to hundreds of millions of people around the world.

Liberal bias notwithstanding, I'd say that my time at Yale Law School was quite valuable.

9

I Meet JFK and Jackie

THE SUMMER FOLLOWING my first year of law school, I was hired as a staff member of the US Senate Appropriations Committee headed by Senator Styles Bridges from New Hampshire. The small team with whom I worked were all ex-FBI agents who regaled me with stories about J. Edgar Hoover's FBI. The secretary of this working group was Angie Novello, who later became the personal secretary of Robert Kennedy, the brother of President John F. Kennedy.

As is the case today, the largesse of the federal government can make or break important scientific initiatives. The National Institutes of Health is responsible for significant medical discoveries. A prominent advocate for increased funding for the National Institutes of Health was a New York philanthropist, Mary Lasker.[1]

There's no doubt that Mary Lasker was an extraordinary woman. In her college days she studied extensively in France as an art student. She was the friend of struggling Impressionist painters who later became famous. With a keen eye for what could become valuable works of art, Mary Lasker quietly accumulated a major collection of Impressionist paintings.

Mary had married a renowned advertising executive, Albert Lasker. They owned a lovely home on Beekman Place in Manhattan. After her husband's death Mary Lasker devoted her energies to influencing key members of Congress to support her passion of raising funds for the National Institutes of Health. She then bought a home in the Georgetown area of Washington, DC, and hired Florence Mahoney as a representative. Florence was given the task of cultivating and entertaining key members of the Appropriations Committees of the US House of Representatives and the US Senate.

Mary Lasker had a fantastic flair for decorating. In her homes in

New York and Washington the background was always white. The walls were white, the furniture was white, the lampshades were white, and the rugs were white. Then against the white walls she hung magnificent museum-quality Impressionist paintings. And throughout the houses were gorgeous displays of brilliantly colored flowers. Upon visiting Mary one evening, my father remarked that he was afraid to sit down on the white furniture for fear that he might soil it.

Florence Mahoney had gotten to know my father, a vital member of the important Senate Appropriations Committee. She was kind to his Yale Law School son as well. She invited me one evening to attend a dinner with her friends at the Shoreham Hotel in Washington. We were blessed with a lovely summer evening that allowed the guests to eat together on the outdoor terrace.

Across from me was a young senator from Massachusetts named Jack Kennedy. Sitting next to him was a roving photographer for the *Washington Times-Herald* named Jacqueline Bouvier. Someone asked me at the time whether it looked like their relationship was serious. My reply showed a complete lack of understanding when I said, "She looks like a starstruck young actress. I don't think it will go anywhere." I felt foolish when later on, this young photographer became Mrs. Jack Kennedy, a worldwide celebrity, and the mother of two famous children.

Invitations to Sunday lunches at Mary's Manhattan apartment were highly desirable. I was honored to be included in the guest list that included prominent New York businesspeople, members of the performing arts, and various important public officials.

In 1956 while living on Staten Island, I organized a "Stevenson for President" campaign in support of the former governor of Illinois Adlai Stevenson, the nominee of the Democratic Party against General Dwight Eisenhower. I was pleased that Mary and her guests were interested in my views about Stevenson. As I recall, my opinion was that Governor Stevenson should stop making amusing quips and get serious on the campaign stump, or he would be defeated.

Little did I realize at the time how right the American electorate was when it gave General Eisenhower an overwhelming victory over Stevenson. As charming and literate as Stevenson was, he lacked the determination and steely resolve crucial for the leader of this nation.

This was my first foray into national politics, and I learned a lot.

10

THE SOULISH MAN MUST DIE

WHILE I WAS in law school, I had momentary urges to be a little more righteous whenever the cards were dealt for some really serious games of poker. I determined that I would tithe my winnings, but since I lost so much at the table, I decided to double the amount of my losses and give that amount to the church.

I was attending a Congregational Church in downtown New Haven and began a regimen of rather substantial giving. I suspect that I may have become one of the largest regular donors of the congregation, so I was not totally surprised when the pastor called on me at Yale Law School, perhaps to thank me for my generous gifts. I didn't tell him the source of the money he was receiving.

I would spend my evenings playing poker, sometimes until three or four o'clock in the morning, and then I would go over to the magnificent Whitney Gym and straight to the steam room, where I would sweat out some of the imperfections of the night. It wasn't a very healthy environment and was hardly a spiritual exercise.

While all of that was true, I was becoming more and more obsessed with the concept of going into business, starting companies, playing the market, making a lot of money, and doing whatever it took to pursue worldly goals. I also was becoming more and more arrogant, which is easy to do when you're in an environment like Yale Law School, where everyone experiences a false sense of superiority. The fact that I had gotten to know some prominent people in New York and Washington also contributed to my sense of arrogance. My life was not a pretty picture.

When I read the Bible now, I see that God resists the proud but gives grace to the humble. Back then I sensed that sooner or later something was going to happen that wasn't going to be pleasant. The

Bible says that Moses was trained in all of the wisdom in Egypt when he grew up,[1] but he had to be humbled on the backside of the desert.

In my situation I had learned the way business works. I had learned the way government works. I had seen the good, the bad, and the indifference. I had been on the inside of political intrigue and machinations. The more a person is exposed to these influences, the more hardened or callous he or she will become. That happened to me. It wasn't a pretty thing, and I was hardly a candidate for God's work.

In 1 Corinthians 2:14 the apostle Paul says, "The natural man receiveth not the things of the Spirit of God: for...they are spiritually discerned" (KJV). The apostle Paul also said, "I am crucified with Christ: nevertheless I live....And the life which I now live...I live by the faith of the Son of God, who...gave himself for me."[2]

If anyone tells you that crucifixion is fun, don't believe him. But for the new man to be born, the old man must die. If they attempt to live side by side, there will be constant warfare. There will only be peace and power if the spiritual man becomes dominant and he is led by the Holy Spirit of God.

In other words, there is no way that God Almighty will ultimately use somebody whose life is filled with pride and whose goal is material gain.

For God to begin His work in me, something had to happen.

11

A BIRTHDAY I'LL NEVER FORGET

LOCATED ONLY BLOCKS from the Yale Law School, the Yale School of Nursing, especially its Master of Nursing program, was considered one of the best in America. Some of the young women in the nursing school thought it would be fun to meet some of the law school students, so they organized a mixer and sent out invitations.

One of the nursing students I met that night was a lovely girl from Columbus, Ohio, named Dede Elmer. She was a graduate of Ohio State University, a runner-up in the Miss Ohio State Contest, and named the beauty queen of the Kentucky Military Institute. After working a short time in the juvenile justice system in the Ohio courts, Dede had decided to pursue a career in nursing.

During the mixer a rather obnoxious law student was attempting to monopolize Dede's time. She tried to escape his attentions by busying herself at the refreshment table.

Unfortunately, in her haste she got too close to the candles on the table, and her hair caught on fire. I noticed the problem, rushed over to her, and put the fire out. In recounting the incident later, she sweetly told friends, "He put the fire out in my hair but started a fire in my heart."

They say the best way to a man's heart is through his stomach. The reverse is true as well. Since the dormitory food at the Yale School of Nursing was less than desirable, I used to invite the girls to enjoy dinners of wood-cooked tenderloin steak and wine. I had a wood-burning fireplace in my quarters at the Yale Law School, perfect for these social events.

My birthday was on the 22nd of March, and Dede thought she would surprise me with a birthday cake as long as I provided the steaks and the wine. We enjoyed a delightful birthday dinner in my quarters, just the two of us, during which we finished a bottle of red wine. It wasn't long before we found our way to the bedroom in my suite, where we consummated our relationship.

Only God Himself knew at that time that the merging of the life force of Marion Gordon Robertson of Lexington, Virginia, and Adelia Florence Elmer of Columbus, Ohio, would bring forth four extraordinary children, fourteen remarkable grandchildren, and fifteen exceptional great-grandchildren, all of whom have a fine intellect, are physically healthy, and have a love for God. God knows things beyond our understanding, and only He knew how a night of romance would completely change my life.

Several months later, as I was sitting in my dorm room, there was a long-distance call on the downstairs telephone. When I answered, I heard the voice of a gruff lawyer hired by Dede's father, who informed me that Dede was pregnant with my child, and he wanted me to own up to the responsibility of being a father. I couldn't believe it. I was the young, hotshot future attorney, budding entrepreneur, society playboy, and Marine Corps officer. The well-thought-out plans that I had for myself had suddenly vanished.

Dede's father was a vice president of the Hanna Paint Manufacturing Company in Columbus, Ohio. For him there was no choice but that his daughter would be married to me. It didn't seem that I had any choice but to comply with her father's wishes. The State of Maryland had, within its jurisdiction, localities that permitted marriage without any waiting period or particular formalities. Dede and I drove from New Haven to Elkton, Maryland, where we found a justice of the peace who sold us a wedding license and performed a simple civil ceremony.

For my bride and me there was no formal wedding—no lovely wedding dress, no beautifully clad bridesmaids, no rehearsal dinner, no laudatory statement in the society pages—nor was there any romantic honeymoon at an exotic location. Instead, there was a night in a nondescript motel in Cape May, New Jersey. With that momentous day, everything that I had been hoping for came crashing down. I now faced a different life and a different world. Later on I would see God's magnificent hand in it all, but at the time, all I felt was despair.

I went to work for W. R. Grace, a huge chemical conglomerate, in New York City, and Dede took a train home to Columbus, where her parents looked after her when she gave birth to the first of our children, whom we named Timothy Brian Robertson.

W. R. Grace had in its far-flung portfolio a cement manufacturing operation in Bolivia. This plant provided 100 percent of the cement for the entire country. I went to La Paz, Bolivia, and then traveled to what is called the Altiplano, where Grace's huge kilns were turning out the raw materials for the cement. It was clear that having 100 percent of any nation's product was a good thing. The plant was operating profitably, and I reported that we should keep it and possibly enlarge it.

I returned to New York from Bolivia and asked Dede to meet me in New York. I had booked a suite in a residential hotel in downtown Manhattan. The two of us met together at that place, which proved to be one of the most memorable weekends of our lives. Our previous wedding had been perfunctory; this weekend was the real thing. I committed my love to her for the rest of my life. I determined that we would build a family with our young son. We recited our marriage vows and pledged to each other our lifelong love.

Amazingly, despite our difficulty, we began life together as few couples are able to do. There was no deception, no dishonesty, no hidden secrets, no games.

That weekend of true love has held us together in sickness and in health, for richer and for poorer, during the nearly sixty-five years of our marriage and will provide a bond for the rest of our lives.

12

THE LITTLE CLOUD THAT
SEEMED LATE

WHILE DEDE COMPLETED her master's course at the Yale School of Nursing, her parents watched Timothy in Columbus, and I continued to work in downtown Manhattan. When her schooling was over, she arranged to bring our young son from Columbus and join me in New York.

After a quick overview of rental prices in the New York area, it was clear that finding a place on Staten Island would be much more favorable than anyplace in the metropolitan area. I zeroed in on a gate-keeper's cottage located on Todt Hill Road overlooking the New York Harbor. The dwelling we leased had been part of a wealthy estate that was subsequently acquired by the Catholic Church to use as a novitiate for their young nuns. From our hilltop on Staten Island we could look down at the ocean and see the massive ocean liners as they turned out of the New York channel to head toward Europe.

I had the privilege of decorating our rental property along a rather avant-garde style. I had the walls painted orange, covered the furniture with black slipcovers, and hung a huge print of a seated Modigliani nude on the wall behind the sofa. In that little house we had a nice-sized living room, a small kitchen, and a loft bedroom.

As an executive trainee I was making about $6,000 a year, which was more than enough to cover our bills. Each day, Dede would drive me down the hill to the train that would take me to the ferry, which sailed across New York Harbor to Lower Manhattan, where I could either walk to work or take a subway to midtown.

The work as a W. R. Grace trainee was exhausting. Each of us looked like a cartoon cutout with a Brooks Brothers suit and striped rep tie, sitting at a small desk complete with a desktop calculator. We were assigned to add up columns of figures that would support Wall Street's valuation of W. R. Grace stock.

For some reason the pressure on each of us seemed intense, and within a short time I started developing what was called an executive ulcer. I knew if I stayed at Grace, I would eventually be promoted to a good-paying corporate job, but I wanted more. I wanted freedom and independence and the ability to chart my own destiny.

I got together with two friends from law school. Together we discovered an invention that we believed we could manufacture and sell. The invention was a flexible electrostatic speaker with a remarkable range in the upper level of high fidelity. The inventor was a timid man named Curry, and we formed the Curry Sound Corporation.

His electrostatic speaker consisted of a sheet of polyethylene surrounded by two sheets of aluminum, all encased in a rubber shell. The aluminum sheets were then activated with high-voltage electricity, and the high-frequency sound was superimposed upon them. The idea of a high-frequency, electrostatic, flexible tweeter should have had quite an appeal to people who enjoyed high-fidelity music. There was only one problem with this device. Although it had very little current, it was charged with about two thousand volts of electricity, and if a person got on the wrong side of it, he would get the daylights shocked out of him. We demonstrated this device to the officials of Trans World Airlines, but when they realized the problem of our voltage, they politely declined to carry forward with any further discussions.

It was clear at the time that God had something much more significant for me. Inside of me was a yearning for something better. I remember the words of St. Augustine, who had written, "Our heart is restless until it finds its rest in thee."[1] I thought the answer would be to leave the business world and enter the ministry. I shared what I was contemplating with my dear mother, who was a born-again Christian with an intimate knowledge of the Lord. When I asked for her advice, she challenged me, if I really knew Jesus, and recommended that I contact a friend named Cornelius Vanderbreggen.

Cornelius, who served with the marines during World War II, had written a book titled *A Leatherneck Looks at Life*. When I contacted him, he was staying temporarily in Philadelphia and was associated with a traveling group called the Reaper's Fellowship. He suggested that we meet at a stately hotel in an upscale part of Philadelphia.

The waiters in the hotel were elegantly dressed in white ties and tails. After we had been seated, Cornelius pulled out a big black Bible and placed it on the table. I was embarrassed by such a show of religiosity and was sure that we would be escorted out of that elegant dining room for being "religious fanatics." My fear was realized when one of the waiters marched across the room toward us. I thought, "This is it… out we go!"

Instead, the waiter said, "Gentlemen, the man at the table across the room is interested in what you are talking about."

At that moment, Cornelius added to my shame by pulling a little booklet from his pocket and handing it to the waiter. "This will tell him what we are talking about." The waiter thanked him and took the little tract to the other guest.

Then Cornelius smiled at me. "Now, Pat, tell me what's on your mind," he began.

I told him that I had been in big business and felt that I should serve God by going into the ministry. I probably mumbled something about wanting to do something good for humanity.

When I had finished, Cornelius looked at me and said, "Pat, any Muhammadan could have told me what you just did. Isn't there something more?"

For the first time in my life I blurted out, "Yes, there is. I believe that Jesus Christ died for the sins of the world and for my sins too."

As I said that, a voice spoke to my heart the words that I had read from the Book of Romans: "If you confess with your mouth the Lord Jesus, and believe in your heart that God has raised Him from the dead, you will be saved."[2] At that moment, in a fancy hotel dining room in Philadelphia, I knew in my heart that Jesus Christ was my Savior. The Bible says, "If anyone is in Christ, he is a new creation; old things have passed away; behold, all things have become new."[3] That simple confession in early April 1956 transformed my life. Jesus came into my heart, and I became a new man.

I traveled back to New York to our cottage on Todt Hill Road on Staten Island. I went into the kitchen, opened a cabinet door, took out an expensive bottle of Ballantine's Scotch, and poured it down the drain.

Dede watched in horror. "What are you doing? Don't you know that is good stuff?"

"I don't need to drink anymore."

People have asked me subsequently if I had any trouble stopping drinking. The answer was clear to me: "I have become a child of God. I am now free in Christ."

Since Cornelius had played such a pivotal role in my conversion experience, I looked to him for ongoing advice and counseling. He in turn advised me to attend a camp at the Lake of Bays in Canada, north of Toronto, called Campus in the Woods. At this point Dede supported my decision to seek the Lord but was reluctant to give up her husband for a month's absence. When I arrived, I found a beautiful setting. The people were all dedicated Christians, and for me the retreat proved to be an important transition from the business world of New York to a world of the Spirit.

We lived in rustic cabins, bathed in the freezing cold waters of a Canadian lake, took our meals in a communal setting, and attended spiritually uplifting sermons and lectures. It was in the wilds of Canada that I began to feel the presence of the third person of the Trinity, the Holy Spirit. It's hard to define the feeling, but it was clear to me that He was introducing Himself to me.

As I was getting settled in, my friend Cornelius and his team left in the middle of the night. He said that the Lord had directed them that it was time to go. This left me stranded, but I now realize the wisdom of it. God had plans to take me beyond areas where Cornelius had gone.

After Cornelius left, I wanted the chance to lead people to the Lord. We were at a small island in the lake with few people around, but back onshore was a resort where a large number of young college students worked as summer employees.

I thought it would be nice to schedule a worship service for them and sent out the necessary invitations to bring us together. As I planned the event, I decided it was essential to have it rain over their hotel so they would not be engaged in outdoor sports and would want to attend our service.

On the day of the event, however, the morning dawned clear and bright. The sun was shining, and there wasn't a cloud in the sky. Before I took an open boat across the lake, I got on my knees by my bunk and cried to the Lord, "Please send the rain!"

Then a miraculous thing happened. I heard the sound of rushing wind in the air outside. As I walked to the dock, I looked behind me and spotted a tiny cloud scuttling through the sky. "Too little, too late," I thought. But that cloud went ahead of the team and me, and while we crossed the lake on an open boat without any rain, the little cloud moved over the resort and poured down rain.

When I got to the meeting, the room was filled with eager young people who were more than happy to hear the Word of God. That day God in His goodness showed me that He controls the weather, and He will use the weather at the command of His saints when it serves His purposes.

What happened that day in Canada was an incredibly faith-affirming experience.

13

A New Dimension of Spiritual Reality

As a newborn child in the kingdom of God, I had an intense hunger to know more about Him. For lack of thorough knowledge, I developed a technique of receiving God's guidance. I would pray intensely to learn His will, and then I would take a Bible in my hand, open it prayerfully, and put my finger on a verse. I now know that our Lord has better ways of communicating than that, yet I believe our Lord will move heaven and earth before He allows one of His sincere children to be misled.

It was the first of August when I returned to New York, and Dede was two weeks away from giving birth to our second child. She was glad to have me back at home, and I temporarily put aside all thoughts of jobs and careers. We were going to be parents again, and we took that time to focus on our family.

Our daughter Elizabeth was born on August 14, 1956, and after Dede returned home from the hospital, I prayed with her about God's plans for our lives. We sought the Lord together for how and where He wanted me to prepare for ministry.

I decided that if I were to be a properly credentialed minister, I had to receive theological training. The school that seemed to have the most promise was Gordon Conwell in Boston. This was a lovely school with a splendid curriculum located in a country setting. Before I enrolled, I asked the Lord if this was His perfect will for me. The Lord's direction, however, led me to a different course. The word He gave me was clear: "Say there are not yet four months until harvest. Lift up your eyes, for the fields are already ripe for harvest."

I was in New York City, one of the largest places on earth and teeming with people who needed to know the Lord. This was the place God had for me—not Boston. Friends advised me that a magazine called *Faith at Work* had been started by Rev. Sam Shoemaker, the pastor of Calvary Episcopal Church in downtown Manhattan. I worked as a volunteer at *Faith at Work* for a short time, made some good friends, and gained valuable insights into the spiritual life of New York City.

When I suggested that I wanted to attend seminary, my newfound friends recommended that I inquire about Biblical Seminary, located on East 59th Street. Biblical Seminary was a strong evangelical school that had been founded by Rev. Wilbur White for the purpose of teaching seminary students courses based on the English Bible.

Dede and I had been fortunate enough to locate a rent-controlled space at Boulevard Gardens Apartments, located just off Northern Boulevard in Queens. The rent for two bedrooms, a living room, a kitchenette, and a single bath was the amazing sum of fifty-six dollars a month, a perfect fit for a young family with a seminarian's budget. I learned of an opening at the Bayside Methodist Church in Bayside, Long Island, and was hired as its youth minister at a modest stipend.

While I was at Biblical Seminary, I wanted to reach out to the people of New York, so my next post was with a fledgling group called Christian Soldiers, which maintained a telephone ministry in a one-room office in midtown Manhattan. I stood on the sidewalk outside Grand Central Station and handed out slips of paper inviting people to call in. It would be the height of folly to think that the passing throngs eagerly received this type of ministry on the sidewalks of New York.

Two remarkable things happened at about the same time. I was invited to the Presidential Prayer Breakfast in Washington, DC, and while there I met Bob Walker, the publisher of *Christian Life* magazine. Bob wanted to know if I was familiar with the work of the Holy Spirit, and I told him, "Not as much as I would like, so I am interested."

Soon thereafter, through Christian Soldiers, I met Harald Bredesen, a Lutheran minister and one of the most unique people I had ever met. He was absolutely fearless in witnessing for the Lord. At the same time, he was a total eccentric. Those who knew him well can bring forth hundreds of so-called "Harald stories."

Harald gave himself over wholeheartedly to the service of the Lord, yet at the same time, he had to have an assistant with him to make sure he didn't get lost in some foreign country. One tour group in the Middle East had lost sight of him so many times that they sang a song, "Where's Harald?"

Yet in all that, Harald and I would spend an entire day just crying out to God for more of His presence. He was serving the First Reformed Church of Mount Vernon, New York. He rode a bicycle to my apartment in Queens to tell me more about the baptism of the Holy Spirit.

We developed a warm friendship, and with him I would pray all day long on a Saturday. On other occasions, I'd meet him in Mount Vernon, walk the halls of his old Gothic church, and cry out for more of God. I doubt if I've ever had more intense hunger for spiritual things in all of my life. It wasn't just in Mount Vernon. I went to other churches and attended other prayer meetings, asking for God to fill me with His Holy Spirit.

Then one evening my toddler son, Tim, contracted a severe illness. His temperature was running sky-high, his eyes rolled back in his head, and he was having convulsions. Dede, a registered nurse, put cold towels on him, but to no avail.

Tim was lying on the couch in the living room of our apartment, and I was on my knees next to him. "God, please heal him! Please heal him!" I cried out. But then I realized that God loved my boy thousands of times more than I ever would, so I stopped begging and lifted him into the hands of a loving God.

As I did so, a miracle happened. The fever broke, and Tim got up and went to the bathroom. He came back and lay down, and by morning he was completely healed. I was so grateful that I began to praise God. Then something from the depth of my being was given a voice, and I started to speak in a language that sounded like some African dialect. My spirit was in touch with the living God, and I knew that I was entering into a new dimension of spiritual reality.

Dede was sitting in a nearby chair. Her first thought was, "How long has this been going on, and why didn't he tell me?" In her wonderful Midwest wisdom she said, "I told you that you didn't have to go to all of those churches to receive the Holy Spirit. You could receive the blessing sitting in your living room." And that is what happened. I had now walked into the Book of Acts and was no longer a spectator but an active participant in the works of a miracle-making God.

This opened a whole new chapter for me of seeking God's guidance. Up to this time, I would open the Bible and ask God to lead me to find a verse of Scripture that would answer the particular need of the moment. Now I was being led by the Holy Spirit, and as I prayed, the Holy Spirit would speak to me a specific verse of the Bible. When I opened the Bible to that verse, there would be the miraculous answer. As the Bible says, "As many as are led by the Spirit of God, these are sons of God."[1] It was wonderful for Dede and me to know we had sources of guidance beyond what we could experience through our senses. And this was just the beginning.

I entered more deeply into the manifestation of what are called the charismata (or gifts of the Holy Spirit). The Bible says, "Let the peace of God rule in your hearts."[2] When a person is baptized in the Holy Spirit, the peace of God is a true indicator of what course should be taken. When waiting upon God in prayer, the Spirit would speak to my spirit to show me the action that I should take.

John Wesley once wrote, we sought "the oracles of God."[3] I knew exactly what he was talking about as I began to ask God for clear direction from His Word. Later on, when my dear wife, Dede, was baptized in the Holy Spirit, we could pray together and ask God to speak to us specific verses from the Bible. Then we could open our Bibles independently and see what God had told us.

14

James Dies, and Satan Takes Aim at Gordon

I N THE SPRING of 1957 four of us students at seminary decided that we would take a weekend to go on a prayer retreat where we could fast, pray, and seek more of God. A friend owned property in New Preston, Connecticut, a small town that bordered the New York state line. We drove up to this rural property on a Friday and put our sleeping bags down in a rustic and empty log house. Since it was a weekend of fasting, we had no need for cooking utensils. We prayed together and shared a simple Communion.

In the group was Eugene Peterson, who would later translate the New Testament into what he called *The Message*. Another was a former classmate named Dick White, who would later earn a PhD from Ohio State University and become a tenured professor at Clemson University. The last member of our group was Dick Simmons, who, as you know from the opening chapters of this book, would come to play a significant role in my life.

When we woke up the first morning, I left the group and took a walk around the property. I was amazed to find a placard that read "The Birthplace of Evangelist Charles Finney."

I had heard about him. Finney's lectures on *Revivals of Religion* was a classic that I had eagerly devoured in my seminary days. Born in 1792 on the spot where I was standing, Charles Finney, as a young man, had been transformed by the power of the Holy Spirit. He brought spiritual revival all over upstate New York.

One example of the extraordinary presence of God in his life stood out in my mind. Finney was asked to speak at a New York factory that employed a number of young women. As his audience looked at this gangly preacher, they began to laugh at his appearance. Finney's eyes began to blaze, and he stared at them without saying a word. Suddenly the power of God came upon them, and they broke down and began to weep and call on God for repentance. That weekend, I knew it was no coincidence that I had felt led to pray at the birthplace of this great man, and I hoped to receive an impartation of his spiritual anointing in my personal life.

As I look back on the significant moments of my life, I realize that God Himself was orchestrating a narrative that would shape my thinking. I had certainly not been brought to this place in upstate New York by accident. To me it seemed like an accident, but God had a purpose in directing me to a man whose teachings in life would prove so foundational.

When I returned to New York, I learned that Dede, who had been pregnant with our third child, had miscarried during my absence. God had previously shown me through a word of Scripture that He quickened to my heart that our third child would not survive. Of course, I didn't share that thought with Dede. We had chosen the name James if God gave us a boy, but the Lord did not allow our third-born to live.

Our second child, Elizabeth, had been born in the summer of 1956 when we had lived on Staten Island. Elizabeth was an extraordinary child, full of fire and beauty and a head of lovely red hair. During her toddler years Dede made them matching mother-daughter outfits out of dark green cloth with rose accents. As this gorgeous young mother and her beautiful daughter walked down Madison Avenue together, the heads of cynical New Yorkers turned in amazement.

Following Dede's miscarriage, she was able to conceive again, and Gordon Perry Robertson was born on June 4, 1958.

I want to take a moment to tell you about Gordon's amazing story. As I've mentioned, I attended college at Washington and Lee as an undergraduate and then went to Yale Law School for a law degree. Gordon reversed that process by taking his undergraduate degree from Yale and then a law degree from Washington and Lee. Upon graduation from law school, he easily passed the bar exam to be certified as a lawyer in Virginia and was hired by one of the most prestigious law firms in the city of Norfolk, Virginia, where in a short time he made partner in the firm in charge of the real estate section.

Although Gordon was dedicated to running away from ministry, the serious call of God was on his life. John Gimenez, the pastor of Rock Church in Virginia Beach, recognized that call and arranged for Gordon to travel with him on a mission trip to Rajahmundry, India. Early in the morning Gordon watched devout Hindus bathing in the Godavari River. He further witnessed scenes of idol worship. When he asked God for wisdom, Jesus Christ literally appeared to him. From that moment in 1994 my third son, Gordon, was a transformed human being. He devoured the writings of the great men of faith, and in the process he developed a ministry of miracles, which is the wonder of all who see it.

I then sent him to the Philippines to learn about CBN's ministry there. While Gordon was in Bacolod City, he had a dream about sending Filipinos to be missionaries, so he moved his family to Manila to start the Asian Center for Missions.

Then the enemy struck. As Gordon was traveling along the border of Myanmar and Thailand with a group of Filipino missionaries, he was bitten by a mosquito. Such a bite is common, and the resulting malaria is both common and treatable. But it quickly became apparent that something worse had happened to Gordon, so he was taken to a hospital in the Philippines for treatment.

An infectious-disease specialist told us she thought perhaps Gordon was suffering from dengue fever. A close friend of hers was an expert in tropical diseases on the same hospital floor where Gordon was being treated. This doctor analyzed Gordon's condition and determined that Gordon did not have dengue fever but a rare form of malaria from which only 20 percent of victims survive. Advanced antibiotics were of no value in treating this exotic form of malaria, so Gordon was given quinine, one of the oldest treatments for malaria. By this time Gordon's liver was shutting down. His eyes were yellow, his skin was yellow, and he was unable to get out of bed.

Our staff at CBN began to pray, and God spoke to Gordon's pastor in the Philippines, Joey Bonifacio, and told him to go pray for Gordon. Miraculously Gordon began to recover. Through the power of God Gordon survived because God had an important role for him to play.

Gordon had become an experienced broadcaster, a ministry leader, and a man who walked in the miraculous power of God. He also was conversant with the more modern means of communication that were increasingly eclipsing standard broadcasting. As a result, in late 2007 I was able to enthusiastically recommend Gordon as my successor as the CEO of The Christian Broadcasting Network, of which I remain the chairman of the board.

Gordon married Katharyn Banks in 1989, right after her graduation from the College of William & Mary with a degree in economics. Gordon and Katharyn have three children: Evelyn, Patrick, and Lauren Adelia. Katharyn's father had been a high school coach, and he took his young grandson, Patrick, under his wing. Patrick Robertson was named the captain of his high school's football, wrestling, and track teams. Patrick holds the school record in discus at Norfolk Academy and in the hammer at Washington and Lee University.[1]

I am chilled now as I think back on how the enemy desired to cut Gordon's life short. But praise our almighty God; His power and purpose always prevail.

15

A New Thing ... "Go and Tell!"

M<small>Y BIRTHDAY, ON</small> March 22, seems to herald significant events in my life. One such incident took place in 1959 as I was working as an assistant to Harald Bredesen at the First Reformed Church of Mount Vernon. The church has a storied past, but it had fallen on hard times by the time Harald got there. Things immediately turned for the better on Harald's first Sunday in the pulpit when the collection plate offering doubled. The joke was that the collection went from three to six dollars.

The church was guided by a board of elders who had little or no knowledge of the things of God. On one occasion they accused Harald Bredesen of speaking in tongues. "Paul spoke in tongues," Harald replied, to which one of the elders said, "Who is Paul?" Nevertheless, the pastor was always concerned about the feeling of the consistory, or governing body of the church, which at the time was controlled by a brother and sister named Wedlake.

Behind the old Gothic church building was a sparsely furnished event hall where a few of my friends gathered to celebrate my twenty-ninth birthday on the 22nd of March. After the potluck supper was over, I left the social hall and entered the church.

That night the church was lit by a small cross that hung over the pulpit area. Shortly after I arrived, Harald Bredesen began walking up and down the floor of the church and suddenly burst forth in a heavenly language. He started spinning around and clapping his hands as he brought forth this unique message in English, saying, "Why are you afraid of those who themselves are servants of Satan? I am doing a new thing on the face of the earth. Go and tell! Go and tell!"

When he finished, Harald pulled me aside. "I believe that we should share what God is doing with Mrs. Norman Vincent Peale."

Ruth Stafford Peale's husband, Norman Vincent Peale, was the famous pastor of Marble Collegiate Church in downtown Manhattan and author of a runaway best seller titled *The Power of Positive Thinking*.[1] Ruth was the publisher of a popular monthly magazine called *Guideposts*, which she cofounded with her husband. Marble Collegiate Church was a member of the Reformed Church in America,[2] which included the First Reformed Church in Mount Vernon. Therefore, there was a denominational connection between Marble Collegiate and First Reformed. I have to admit that I looked askance at Harald when he mentioned meeting with Ruth Peale. "Sure, Harald. I'll believe it when I see it," I said with more than a touch of skepticism.

We said our goodbyes. Then I went home and was sitting in our little kitchenette the following morning, sipping my coffee and reading the *New York Times*, when the telephone rang. Harald was on the line with a breathless question: "What are you doing tonight?"

I knew answering a question like that from Harald was dangerous, so I replied, "Harald, what do you have in mind?"

"We're having dinner tonight with Mrs. Norman Vincent Peale," he announced.

"You've got to be kidding."

"When I spoke to her this morning and said I wanted to share something with her about the things of God, she replied, 'I'm leaving on a trip, but I will make time. Can you come tonight to our apartment for dinner?'"

After eating together in her lovely Fifth Avenue apartment, we adjourned to a sitting room to have coffee. After we were seated, Harald asked Mrs. Peale if we could pray together. As we did so, God gave one of us—Harald had brought a colleague—a message in tongues and the other the interpretation of that message. Mrs. Peale was visibly moved but excused herself because she had to pack for her trip to attend a meeting of the *Guideposts* board of directors and editors.

When the editors assembled to talk about future editorial ideas, Mrs. Peale told them, "I've just had three young ministers in my apartment, and they prayed in tongues and had an interpretation. Can you find out more about this phenomenon?"

One of the editors was a gifted writer named John Sherrill, who received this challenge and began to investigate the Pentecostal experience. His subsequent book, *They Speak With Other Tongues*, became a classic.

One of John's friends was a wealthy insurance executive named W. Clement Stone of Chicago. All of us knew a skinny preacher from Pennsylvania named Dave Wilkerson who had come to New York to minister to teenage gangs. His ministry was called Teen Challenge. John Sherrill asked Clement Stone to make a substantial donation to Teen Challenge. As he did so, Sherrill was intrigued by what Teen Challenge was doing. There was clearly enough material for another book. This one would feature Dave Wilkerson and would be called *The Cross and the Switchblade*, which would not only become a best-selling book but also be made into a motion picture.

Young Catholic students at Duquesne University in Pittsburgh began reading these two books, which caused an intense spiritual hunger to boil within them. As they continued to pray, God baptized them with the Holy Spirit, and from this prayer meeting this phenomenon became known as the Catholic Charismatic Revival.

It all started with a message to Harald Bredesen on the night of my birthday at a little church in Mount Vernon when the Lord said, "I am doing a new thing on the face of the earth. Go and tell! Go and tell!"

Little could we have dreamed of the extent of that outpouring of God's prophetic word. What began on October 1, 1961, when WYAH-TV, a UHF station, went on air with barely enough power to transmit beyond the city limits of Portsmouth, Virginia, has grown into a worldwide broadcasting network reaching the farthest corners of the globe.

16

INTRODUCING MR. PINGO
AND JIM AND TAMMY

W<small>E'VE REACHED THE</small> point in my life that I covered in the opening chapters of this book. If you recall, God spoke to me, I sold all we had, and my small family and I moved into a Brooklyn Brownstone with Dick Simmons before we eventually followed God's leading to move back to Lexington. I then bought a television station, obtained a license for WYAH, paid off the lien on the equipment, and on October 1, 1961, I had seen the transmitter turned on.

If you know anything about television, then you know that I was only skimming the surface of what needed to be done. In today's world a television station operates at least eighteen hours a day and must be fed programming hour after hour, day by day, week by week, month by month. In short I had to create programs for my new television station to put on the air.

An extraordinary young man named Neil Eskelin contacted me. Neil and his father, Ernie, were itinerant evangelists for the Assemblies of God. He was brimming with creativity but to the best of my knowledge had not received any seminary training, possibly not even Bible school training. Still, Neil knew how to touch the hearts of audiences. He became our first program director for the princely salary of one hundred dollars a week.

Our first live show featured Neil and a little toy bear named Mr. Pingo. Neil would talk to Mr. Pingo, and Mr. Pingo would reply with a series of squeaks made possible by a small device located in his underside.

Neil took Mr. Pingo on several adventures. In one that I recall, he put the toy bear into a fishbowl filled with goldfish. For sound effects our audio man blew through a straw into a glass of water, making the sound of bubbles.

Around that time, the United States had sent astronauts into space. Mr. Pingo was quick to follow. We set off a loud explosion in the studio to mimic a launch, but the explosion filled our small studio with a cloud of smoke. The choir members for the following program had to struggle to find their voices amid the fumes.

We only had one camera in those days, so to obtain multiple shots, our director would dip to black and then swing the camera to a mirror, which could provide us a side shot of the person involved.

We couldn't afford to buy commercial programs, but we found several companies that made interesting travelogues as vehicles for their commercial products. These films were free. One particular program, *Of Lands and Seas*, actually allowed us to gain a respectable audience when we aired it.

On one occasion our travel film showed people drinking cocktails, one of which I recognized as a Manhattan—a cocktail made with whiskey, vermouth, and bitters. I yelled at Neil to get that liquor scene off the air. He assured me that they were drinking fruit juice, but I wasn't sure. Because of his strict upbringing, he'd probably never seen a Manhattan before.

Our transmitter had two sides: one was for video, and the other was for audio. One night a tiny little mouse crept into the audio transmitter and was fried dead. I opened the door of the cabinet, looked in, and saw the little fellow staring out at me. Using a pair of gloves, I was able to get him out, but the audio part of our station was off the air until we could make permanent repairs.

The next program in our lineup was with Rev. John Stallings, a minister who had grown up with deaf parents and was an expert in sign language. His program was called *The Deaf Hear*. We continued the broadcast in sign language but only for the deaf because we had no sound coming from our transmitter.

In those days hardly anybody was able to receive UHF television. And when I told people that I was working at Channel 27, they seemed to show great delight in replying, "I can't get that on my TV." Later on Congress passed a law mandating that all television sets sold in America would be able to receive UHF television. But that would come much later for us.

After a couple of years I scraped together enough money to upgrade the facility of our radio station, WXRI, and the audience grew. The station was still located in an old facility on Sparrow Road in Chesapeake, but the quality of our broadcasting had improved dramatically. We began airing some popular radio ministers with national audiences. I also did a fifteen-minute program called *The Deep Things of God*.

Our daily morning broadcast block scored significant audience ratings throughout our area. We played beautiful Christian music that touched the hearts of many. We had one program called *Revival Prayer*, with an introduction as follows: "Every day at noon the staff of WXRI bows to pray for revival in Tidewater and for the rest of the world." After these prayers had been going on for six years, an amazing thing happened in the seventh year that I'll tell you about shortly.

A couple of years after we started television broadcasting, Neil Eskelin moved on, and in 1965 I hired a young couple with a ministry to young people. They came as a team—Jim and Tammy Faye Bakker. Jim billed himself as a former rock 'n' roll disc jockey, and Tammy (the former Tammy Faye LaValley from a small town in Minnesota) was a children's entertainer and singer. I put them on at five o'clock in the afternoon. *The Jim and Tammy Show* became an enormous success. Neighborhood children flocked to be in the audience, and before long Jim and Tammy were local celebrities.

From 1961 to 1963 I had tried to follow the example of the godly clergyman in England George Müller, who had cared for thousands of orphans by only making an appeal in prayer to the Lord. As I prayed about my commitment, the Lord made it clear to me, "I did not call you to be George Müller. I called you to preach the gospel." That released me to begin asking people for financial help to underwrite our broadcast needs.

At that time our projected budget for the entire operation—radio and television—was $7,000 a month. I determined that if 700 people in our community would give just ten dollars a month each, we would meet our budgetary goal. So I went on air with what I called *The 700 Club Telethon* and asked if 700 people would come forth to help keep us on the air. My appeal was halfway successful: we recruited about 350 people, not 700.

In 1964 I determined that the rickety installation of WXRI had to be changed, and the station should move to our headquarters in Portsmouth. We laid out plans to construct a suitable radio building built out of cinder blocks at right angles to our existing building. I can still recall the Thanksgiving morning when I was perched up in the air, nailing roof joists for the new building. With some professional help, we completed an addition that housed a new transmitter, a control room, an on-air studio, and a couple of offices. I was able to get RCA to finance our equipment package for a reasonable price, and shortly thereafter we began broadcasting at fifty thousand watts, which made us the most powerful FM station in the area. We ran our transmission line out of the newly constructed wing to a new antenna that we mounted on our television tower. At the same time, I was able to secure a more open frequency at 105.3 FM, meaning that we essentially abandoned 104.5.

As we continued operating, though, we built up a deficit of $40,000. I went to see my benefactor/philanthropist, Fred Beazley, and told him my problem. I asked if he would endorse a note at the bank so that I could borrow the money.

He didn't see things my way. "In my career I have never endorsed anybody's note, and I don't think I can start now. I think you should sweat it out," he said.

Who, you might ask, is Fred Beazley? That in itself is another story.

17

THE DESIRE OF MY HEART

W HEN I ARRIVED in Tidewater, my principal calling was starting a television ministry. However, like the apostle Paul, I had to sew some tents to keep a roof over our heads and food on the table.

As I mentioned earlier, my mother had been led to faith in Jesus Christ by the pastor of our Baptist church in Lexington, Dr. William Lumpkin. Since that time, Dr. Lumpkin had received a call to become the pastor of the historic Freemason Street Baptist Church in downtown Norfolk. I contacted Dr. Lumpkin to learn if his church needed a youth minister. Indeed it did, and I was delighted to be hired on the staff of that stately downtown church. I worked diligently with the youth of Freemason Street Baptist Church, but my heart was committed to the television ministry that God had set forth for me. Still, the steady paycheck helped the family finances a great deal.

The chairman of the board of trustees of the Freemason Street Baptist Church, Toy Savage, who was a namesake partner of the prestigious law firm of Wilcox Savage, asked to see me. When we got together, Toy said, "How do you like your work?"

"I think I'm doing a good job with the young people of the church, and I'm at it at least forty hours a week," I replied with a smile.

"That's nice, but I want to know what you think about when you shave in the morning." So I told him honestly that my main concern was starting a television ministry, not working at Freemason Street Baptist. "If that's the case," he said, "I will have to ask for your resignation."

I was stunned. And although I didn't realize it at the time, Toy Savage had done me a great favor. I was good in my work with young people, but a youth minister in a small church is torn. If he leads his young charges into a deep spiritual walk, he will often find that he quickly comes up against the material, secular goals of their parents. This conflict can be exhausting.

I remember when I served as youth minister of the Bayside Community Church in Long Island, New York, while I was a student at Biblical Seminary. I encountered severe problems. I asked the Lord for help, and He led me to a simple verse in the Old Testament that said, "If you have run with the footmen, and they have wearied you, then how can you contend with horses?"[1] God knew that I did not have enough strength to deal with the problems of the youth at the church *and* their parents while at the same time putting together a major television ministry.

Of course, I still needed a job and some income. I had heard that a large church down the street from the television station was looking for an interim pastor. I contacted the chairman of the deacons of Parkview Baptist Church in Portsmouth and offered my services. He was delighted to provide me with a position and said, "Here's what we are looking for: we need someone who will preach at the Sunday morning and evening services, lead the Wednesday night prayer meeting, marry the wed, and bury the dead. If you do that, we can pay you $6,000 a year."

That money was a good deal more than I was paid at Freemason Street Baptist, and the job required less work. I had a wonderful time at Parkview Baptist Church. I loved the people, and they loved me. Unfortunately they had no intention of supporting a television station, even if the station was just a few blocks from the church.

After several months serving as pastor at Parkview Baptist, I had a call to visit one of its most prominent members. His name was Fred Beazley.

Fred had made a fortune in the coal and ice business. He then turned his attention to philanthropy and had purchased from the federal government a major tract of government housing. At one time his low-income housing projects were home to twenty-five thousand people.

Then Fred, in his wisdom, noticed a huge government facility near Portsmouth on the Nansemond River. This facility was called Marford, which stood for Marine Forward Depot. Marford had a dock to handle deep-draft vessels. A rail spur ran through it. Next to the spur were cavernous warehouses that held large quantities of military equipment.

Back on the property dozens of separate bunkers were used to hold explosive ordnance such as artillery shells. The commanding officer was given quarters in a pre–Civil War mansion on the edge of the property. To this day I don't know what the Defense Department had planned for Marford, but it was clear that one or more marine divisions could be equipped and launched overseas from this place, or in case of an invasion similar divisions could mobilize for homeland defense.

Under the law that still exists today, surplus government equipment and facilities could be given to state-sponsored charities, such as the Beazley Foundation. The chairman of the Beazley Foundation was Virginia Supreme Court Justice Lawrence I'Anson, who contacted Senator Harry Byrd to see if he could use his influence with the Defense Department to permit the transfer of the post–World War II Marford to the Beazley Foundation for use as a four-year liberal arts college. Senator Byrd was successful in that quest, and Marford was transferred to the Beazley Foundation. That's when Fred Beazley set about transforming the facility into what he named Frederick College.

When I met Mr. Beazley, he welcomed me into a spartan office at one of his housing projects. "I've heard about your broadcast ministry, and I want to help you," he said. "I want to put you in a position where you won't have to be looking for contributions to keep yourself going. How much do you think you will need?"

I told him I thought I could get by very nicely on $6,000 a year.

Mr. Beazley thought for a moment. "I have a house that I own in the Parkview section of Portsmouth. You and your family can stay there if you wish," he said. I was floored. That was just the beginning of my relationship with this incredible human being.

Dede and I and our three children moved into a modest house

in Parkview, but this was hardly an ideal environment for us. The upstairs rooms were small. On the first floor there was no subflooring, so during the cold winter, freezing air would blow through the cracks in the floor. We would huddle together in the kitchen and turn on the stove to try to keep warm.

A neighbor was carrying on a love affair while her husband was serving in the military overseas. A rebellious teenager would stand under a stoplight across the street and scream vile profanities. I said to my dear wife, "I know this is bad, but whatever you do, don't complain. Don't complain! If you do, we'll never get out of here. So let's thank God now for His goodness." And thank God we did.

Dede did a marvelous job teaching the young people at the church and then resumed her nursing career at a local hospital. About a year of this was all I could take, however, and I determined that I wanted to build a house of my own. So I went back to see Mr. Beazley and said, "Mr. Beazley, I think it's time for our family to move."

He nodded. "I know few young ministers who would put up with what you have. What did you have in mind?"

"What would you think of my building a house?"

With a twinkle in his eye, he said, "If God told you to build a house, He's wrong." Then he quickly added, "Why would you build a house when I have a lovely home on the grounds of Frederick College? I don't want to hurt you with kindness, but go out there and see if you'd like to live in it."

I drove from Portsmouth out to the grounds of Frederick College and found the house Mr. Beazley had told me about. Frankly what I saw was the fulfillment of a dream: a stately, pre–Civil War dwelling with columns in the front and a spacious lawn with a massive magnolia tree and several maples. The mansion, actually, backed up to a body of water called Streeter Creek, which flowed into the Nansemond River and ultimately out to the Chesapeake Bay. The immaculate property came with a complete horse barn with a tack room and loft for holding hay and feed and was adjoined by a thousand acres of farmland. I hadn't mentioned it to anybody, but the deep desire of my heart had been to own a farm in the country where I could live with my family and keep horses.

There was a time when rural land sold for a few dollars an acre. But the influence of government money into northern Virginia and the influence of high-paid actors from Hollywood in the West had run the price of rural land into the stratosphere. There was no way that I could afford to buy a farm anywhere. Yet here was a fulfillment of my dream given to me—for free.

The residence on the property was splendid, but the Marine Corps, in order to make the place seem more utilitarian, had stripped out the lovely crown molding and chair rails in the public rooms. One of the Parkview Baptist Church members was a skilled carpenter. I bought the appropriate length of crown molding and chair rail, and then he and I went out to my future home to restore these gracious accents. Of course, I wasted no time in telling Mr. Beazley that I had visited the property and was more than delighted to accept his offer. We quickly moved our furniture and happily settled in. Life was idyllic.

There was an extra benefit. We now lived on the campus of Frederick College, and Dede was quickly hired as an assistant professor of nursing at that school. From a first cousin I acquired a couple of fine riding horses. My children—including a fourth child, our daughter Ann, who was born on April 24, 1963—had a place to build a tree house and a big yard to play in.

I was truly enjoying the fulfillment of the word in Psalms that says, "Delight yourself also in the LORD, and He shall give you the desires of your heart."[2]

And another desire of my heart was that *The 700 Club* would find a place in people's homes as well.

18

THE LIGHT OF GOD BREAKS THROUGH

OUR THIRD ANNUAL *700 Club* telethon was held in November 1965, which also happened to be the beginning of the seventh year that I had come from New York to Tidewater. During this time *Revival Prayer* had been broadcast every noon requesting prayer for revival in Tidewater. Then something amazing happened.

We started the telethon and asked for people to join the 700 Club. The telethon was broadcast not only on television but on radio as well. I asked for seven hundred people to pledge to give ten dollars a month. The pledges were coming in, but I also asked for prayer requests—and those flooded in too.

As we started praying, the power of God descended as in the days of the Bible. One woman called in and said, "I'm walking softly in my house because the power of God is coming through your radio." Homemakers who had no experience with the miraculous were answering our phones and recording extraordinary miracles.

As the broadcast continued, the miracles intensified. Jim Bakker emotionally began to cry out, "We owe $40,000, and if we don't get it, we'll go bankrupt. We need your help." The volume of giving intensified. One man called and said, "I woke up in the middle of the night, and I can't sleep until I make a pledge."

Hour after hour we prayed for the needs of the people. The telephones rang incessantly as callers reported miracle after miracle. No human program director could have come up with programming more exciting.

On either Wednesday or Thursday of that week, a reporter for our local paper called and said, "What have you got going on over there? Is this the second coming of Christ?"

"This isn't the second coming," I replied, "but it is a heaven-sent revival for Tidewater."

Up until this time our area had been under the strong influence of Edgar Cayce, a self-professed clairvoyant, and what was known as the Association of Research and Enlightenment, which maintained a large center in Virginia Beach. As a result, a dark cloud had been hovering over our area for decades. One pastor actually declared, "It's impossible to pray through in Tidewater."

A spirit of poverty gripped local ministries such as ours. During the week of our telethon that spirit was permanently broken. The light of God was shining on us. We could pray for miracles of healing, and God answered our prayers. We could expect miracles, and God would perform them. We could sense the blessing of God in our homes and families.

Even in financial terms the spirit of poverty had been broken. Not only did we match our telethon goal, but we exceeded it. A bright future lay before us.

What we experienced was so wonderful that I hated to stop; however, I was scheduled to fly to London as a member of the Full Gospel Business Men's Fellowship. I was looking forward to returning to London and couldn't wait to see what God had in store.

19

HIPPIE HAIRCUTS NEAR BUCKINGHAM PALACE

OUR CROWD OF Full Gospel Business Men arrived at London's Heathrow Airport, then made our way to the London Hilton hotel, an elegant facility located just up from Buckingham Palace in the exclusive Mayfair district of London.

The decision was made that we would spend our first day down in the Soho district to find drug addicts and lead them to the Lord. What ensued was absolutely ludicrous. We found a profusion of heroin addicts and then witnessed to them before bringing them back to the Hilton. These Christian businessmen thought that evidence of conversion would indicate the presence of a haircut, so they brought in a barber and stationed him on one of the upper floors of the Hilton, where he proceeded to cut hippie-length hair.

I will never forget the sight of one particular young man. He had long red hair and was wearing a tuxedo jacket with a T-shirt and blue jeans. Over the lower legs of the blue jeans, he had fur-lined puttees, or leg wraps. On his head was a black bowler hat. He had been totally strung out on heroin, and I remember him telling me that his parents had thrown him out of the house and he was homeless. After his haircut he said he couldn't wait to tell his mum that he had been converted to Christ.

As this strange assortment of drug addicts filled the lobby of the hotel, the concierge decided I must be one of the sane ones. "Mr. Robertson, you've got to get these people out of here. They are ruining our image!" she declared.

I told her I would see what I could do, but I couldn't give her much hope of stopping the procession of spiritually delivered derelicts.

The next night, we were scheduled to attend a church, and the venue selected was the famed Westminster Chapel headed by Rev. Martyn Lloyd-Jones. I joined an evangelist from Oklahoma named Oral Roberts in the lobby. As we stepped outside, he said, "I'd like to walk. Would you come along with me?"

It was November. It was England. It was pouring down rain outside. I had an overcoat but not a hat. But I felt reluctant to tell America's leading healing evangelist that I might catch a cold. So we set out from the Hilton and walked as fast as we could in the pouring rain. We passed the guard at Buckingham Palace and then arrived at the church. The service was stifling hot, and we were falling asleep. After sitting for fifteen minutes, Oral said, "Let's get out of here," and I said, "I'm with you."

We put our wet overcoats back on, went back out in the pouring rain, and then practically jogged past the guard at Buckingham Palace on our way back to the Hilton. We later shared a light supper and told a few stories about what God had been doing in our lives, and I was then finally able to get out of my wet clothes and take a warm shower. I count it as a miracle that neither Oral nor I contracted any serious respiratory illness on account of that crazy night in the cold London rain.

During our time in London, Oral preached at a fabulous healing service in the Royal Albert Hall. Again, many English businessmen and legislators were profoundly touched by the encounters with our group of Spirit-filled Americans.

Along with our team in London was a singing group of former drug users called the Addicts. They were members of a Puerto Rican church in the Bronx, and their leader was John Gimenez. I'll have more to say about him later.

In the fall of 1966 it was time for another *700 Club* telethon. Was it possible to believe that God would visit us in the same fashion as He did the year before? I could hardly imagine such a thing was possible, but to my amazement when we opened the phones for prayer, a similar visitation of God's Spirit touched our audience. I remember hearing about a mother's prayer for her son who had a disfiguring birthmark on his face. After praying over the air, something like a giant hand moved across his face and took away the birthmark. People in our area would call relatives out of state and let them listen to our prayers, at which time they were healed. Once again, it became heaven on earth.

It was clear that we could not continue in a fundraising telethon mode forever. Our solution in early 1967 was to close our broadcast day at 10 o'clock at night with a program of prayer and praise that we called *The 700 Club*. Our telephones would be open for prayer requests. If we were experiencing a spiritual visitation, it would be possible to stay on the air until after midnight. If nothing was happening, we would sign off the air at an early hour.

But a lot was happening.

20

PRAY FOR THE WORLD

IN 1967 IT was clear that our modest studio and office facility was inadequate to meet our growing demands. A local architect offered what financial types like to call "an elegant solution." We would build an addition on top of our existing facility and attach a large metal prefab structure that could hold two studios and a set of offices on top of the main building.

We broke ground on the renovation of the WYAH facility on June 5, 1967. As we were undertaking a brief groundbreaking ceremony with the mayor of Portsmouth, my friend Paul Morris hurried up to me and said, "Have you heard the news?"

"What are you talking about?" I asked.

"War has just broken out in the Middle East," he replied.

This was the beginning of the Six-Day War, during which Israel captured the Old City of Jerusalem and an area of Israel known as the West Bank.[1] This war became the sudden fulfillment of the prophetic word of Jesus Christ in which He said, "Jerusalem will be trampled by Gentiles until the times of the Gentiles are fulfilled."[2]

This was a momentous day in biblical prophecy. The fact that we had begun to build our new addition on that very day told me that the destiny of the Christian Broadcasting Network was forever linked to the nation of Israel. But there would be more…much, much more.

Not too long after that I took my first trip to Israel. I was on a British European Airways jet from London to Tel Aviv on a moonlit night. As we were flying along the coast of Turkey, the Lord spoke to me so clearly that it still resonates in my spirit today. He said to me, "You've made mistakes in Virginia. You've made mistakes in New York. You are entering Israel, the land of the Bible. You don't make any mistakes here."

79

When we touched down at Lod Airport, I realized that I was entering into a land of prophecy, and our Lord would watch over His prophetic word to guarantee the integrity of what had been set down in His holy Word.

Meanwhile, back home our general contractor made short work of the construction project at hand, and when I returned to Virginia, he brought me the good news that our new offices and television studios were ready to be put in service. He also gave me a bill that totaled $200,000. Our new second-floor office complex included seven individual offices surrounding an open area suitable for secretarial desks. I carried most of my books upstairs to my new office while our construction workers moved the accompanying furniture.

At noon we stopped for prayer, and I remember kneeling beside a desk in the open area outside one of the small executive offices. My desperate need at the time was for the $200,000 needed to pay the general contractor. As I beseeched the Lord, God spoke to me and said, "Don't pray for $200,000; I want you to pray for the world."

As I shifted my prayer focus, I had a vision of Jesus holding a small globe in His hands. He then reached out and placed that globe in my heart. I was transformed. Up to that time, my focus had been on broadcasting in an urban area of Virginia.

From that moment on, my vision for CBN was not just for Virginia, or even America, but for the world. And our first international venture would take us into the heart of Latin America; a whirlwind began— including a radio station in Bogotá, Colombia, with an outreach all over Latin America.

21

Moments of Joy at Nuevo Continente Sociedad Anónima

N OT TOO LONG after, I received a call from a minister named Sixto López, a brother-in-law of Carlton Spencer, who in turn was the president of Elim Bible Institute and College, a small Christian school in upstate New York.

Sixto and Carlton had married a pair of sisters, and Sixto was active in ministry in the nation of Colombia. Sixto told me that an AM station in Bogotá had become available for sale and that I should look into buying it.

The Bogotá station was broadcasting at 1490 on the AM radio dial, and its strong signal covered the entire area of Bogotá. Efraín Páez Espitia owned the station and was asking $50,000 in US dollars, a relatively moderate price.

I flew with Sixto to Bogotá and met with Senor Espitia. The station had a relatively good audience and featured a Latin version of rock 'n' roll.

I wasn't a native Spanish speaker by a long shot; nevertheless, it was easy to find parallels between American and Spanish corporate terms, such as words for shareholders, corporate directors, and officers. I founded a corporation called Nuevo Continente Sociedad Anónima. I found five Colombian nominee shareholders. They were given voting control of the corporation, but they endorsed their shares to me in blank. If these nominee directors decided to misuse the assets of the corporation, all that was necessary for me to remove them was to put new names in the blank spaces in their shareholdings. With that protection I began the ministry in the only country in the world other than Spain that had a concordat, or treaty, with the Vatican.

In Colombia's rural areas at that time, the Catholic population's hatred of evangelical Protestants was intense. In the United States we took as normal our freedom to lead people to faith in Christ or to pray for their spiritual or physical needs over the air. I was warned that doing such a thing in Colombia could lead to a violent reaction.

Our flagship program in the States was called *The 700 Club*. In Spanish that translates to "El Club Siente Cento." Sixto López felt such a title would not resonate in the Hispanic spirit. He suggested something much more melodious: *Momentos de Gozo y Alabanza*, which means "moments of joy and praise." We went with that name.

I decided that I hadn't come into Colombia to be timid, so the first night on the air, I opened the mic and began praying for people. Sixto translated my fervent prayers into Spanish. Instead of anger, a fountain of faith erupted all over Bogotá. People by the thousands were being touched by God and healed. Instead of rage, one Catholic priest called in and said, "You are men of faith and valor. I commend you."

Throughout Colombia opportunities opened up to obtain choice broadcast frequencies. Despite tempting opportunities throughout the country, I did not feel led to purchase any other stations besides Nuevo Continente. This was before the rise of the Medellín Cartel and the vicious drug wars that have since plagued Colombia.

I traveled freely and unafraid all over that beautiful land and was grateful that the Lord opened incredible doors for us in Colombia.

For me, doing broadcast ministry in a foreign country was as natural as riding a horse.

22

My Encounter With the
Original Horse Whisperer

Between missionary endeavors and my broadcast duties, I began to indulge in my favorite pastime, which is horseback riding. As a teenager, when I had worked at the Tinsley Farm in Rapidan, Virginia, I loved galloping over country roads on the single horse they had on the property.

Now it was the '60s, and my first cousin, Frank Peters, had a beautiful farm outside of Charlottesville, Virginia. Frank heard that I was looking for a couple of horses and offered to give me a gentle show jumper named Tuffy and a large gray pony named Colonel, who had once belonged to Bobby Kennedy. I spent countless hours on the weekends riding that wonderful horse, Tuffy, all over the property and up and down the banks of the Nansemond River.

A horse's age can be compared with that of a human when it is multiplied by a number depending on the age of the horse. Tuffy was at least twenty-five years old, which meant he was about seventy-five in human years.[1] My father warned me that it was dangerous to try to jump a horse of that age.

I had read in our local paper about a lady named Margret Gafford, who was breeding and selling horses of the Trakehner breed. These horses had a storied past. They were bred as cavalry horses in the Trakehnen area of Prussia. When Hitler invaded Russia in World War II, he did so not only with tanks and half-tracks but also with mounted troops. After his decisive defeat during the Russian winter, the Trakehner horses were put on the roads back to Germany with little or no food. During the "Long March" most of the horses died on the way. The survivors were considered by the German breeders as superior stock to be used to build back the classic breed.

I drove sixty miles to Petersburg and visited Margret Gafford at her farm. Margret was a skilled dressage rider whose son had won first place in the National Junior Dressage Competition while riding Margret's big Thoroughbred, Why Jump.

This victory was unusual because Margret herself never achieved a national championship for one simple reason: she worked her horses too long and too hard. Horses, like people, need a time of rest, but Margret's horses never got that, and consequently in major competitions they lacked a little spark of brilliance that the judges looked for in the top horses.

One of Margret's horses that appealed to me was a yearling stallion named Aristocrat. I bought him from Margret and took him to my barn, where he grew to be a gorgeous 16.2-hand three-year-old.

Aristocrat and I became fast friends, but I had no intention of trying to break in a three-year-old stallion. Instead, I turned to a good friend from Pennsylvania named Johnny Berguson, who'd trained his Arabian horse, Sheik, to do amazing things. Johnny could ride Sheik without a bridle. He liked to think the horse's thoughts. He treated his horse like a member of the family, and the horse responded.

Johnny came to Portsmouth, picked up Aristocrat, and took him to his farm in Pennsylvania. When he brought Aristocrat back to me nine months later, I discovered to my delight that my young stallion had been trained to kneel, bow, come when called, back up on command, and be a perfect riding companion.

Shortly thereafter I had as my guest a trainer named Monty Roberts, who later became famous as the original "horse whisperer." Monty had watched horses in the wild and realized they utilized a nonverbal language that he called "Equus."

In his early days his father, a horse trainer, had severely abused him because Monty refused to use the brutal horse-breaking methods in vogue at the time: sharp spurs, cruel bits, painful hobbles, and strong whips. The audiences in many of Monty's lectures included married women who had had abusive husbands. Somehow these women could identify with the abused and suffering horses that Monty endeavored to set free.

Monty recognized that horses were herd creatures that hated to be separated from the herd. He believed that every horse learns instinctively to follow the herd leader, and he learned that horses use their ears to signal their moods at any given time.

He then developed a technique of horse training that was vastly superior to anything then in use. In our television demonstration for the *700 Club* audience, we took a young horse that had never been ridden and turned him over to Monty, and within thirty minutes Monty had trained the horse to accept a bit and bridle, a saddle, and a rider without any bucking or sign of rebellion.

Up to that time, I had been a farm rider. I enjoyed the sport, but I wasn't terribly good at it. One of my neighbors was Sue Ashe, who was proficient in every conceivable type of equestrian activity, including flat racing and steeplechasing. Sue had become a certified judge in an equestrian sport known as dressage, a French word for training that involves a degree of riding skill daring as far back as the Greek philosopher and riding master Xenophon. Sue offered to come by and give me some lessons, and I eagerly accepted.

The riding ring adjoining my house was ideal for Aristocrat. Unfortunately workers had covered the ring with too deep a layer of sand. As Aristocrat was working on that surface, he twisted a foot and pulled a suspensory ligament in his front leg.

If you watched the motion picture *Seabiscuit*, you might remember that Seabiscuit also pulled a suspensory ligament,[2] but fortunately his owner was able to get him rehabbed in time to race in the Santa Anita Handicap, which he won.[3] My vet said that he saw no hope for Aristocrat and that I should let him retire at Margret Gafford's farm.

On the day that he was supposed to go, Aristocrat somehow knew that he was leaving. That amazing animal performed every single trick he had learned, as if to say, "Boss, please don't send me away." Unfortunately I knew that his health required it.

Horses engaged in dressage are given classifications according to their level of skill. Young horses are classified as Training Level. From there, according to their abilities, they can go to First Level, Second Level, Third Level, Fourth Level, and then a category called Prix St. George, followed by Intermediate, and finally Grand Prix.[4]

Years later I discovered a big Portuguese-bred Lusitano horse that had been trained to the fourth level. I asked Sue Ashe to take a look at this horse and give me a report. He was located in California, was quite an accomplished dressage horse, and vetted sound except for what is called a seedy toe. His name was Ufano, which in Portuguese means "proud."[5] And proud he was! He was 17.3 hands high and became the best horse I ever owned.

I arranged to buy him at a reduced price and had him shipped to Virginia. As part of my training in Equus, I knew that horses blew in each other's noses to become acquainted. So as Ufano came off of the truck, I blew in his nose to let him know he was among friends. A mare will also nibble on the withers of her baby. I knew this was a friendly technique, so with my fingers I massaged Ufano's withers. I was also aware that when a horse is completely relaxed, it will hang its head and let out a sigh. So when I began riding Ufano, I relaxed my body and gave a big sigh. Then before any work began, I let Ufano walk around freely in the ring to let him know that this was going to be a fun experience. Nobody was going to ask him to do anything he didn't want to do.

I required a three-step stool in order to get on him because he was so big. But that horse was extraordinary. He could perform a piaffe, which is a trot standing in place. He could perform the passage, which is a piaffe where the horse moves forward in an elegant gait. He could perform a half-pass at a canter. He could do a pirouette, which is a canter in a tight circle. With the right signal he would do a hand gallop running at full speed across the ring, and with a slight touch he would stop. He would do beautiful transitions. He could do flying changes of lead, but for the Grand Prix a horse must perform a one-tempi change of lead, which looks as if the horse is dancing. Ufano could maybe do a four-tempi, but not a one-tempi.

Riding a high-level dressage horse was exhilarating. The rider can direct a horse just by the movement of his seat bones. After the horse is brought back into what is called collection, the only pressure required on the reins would be a slight squeeze of the hand. I learned that well-trained horses can somehow read pictures in the minds of their riders. I could think in pictures; Ufano would respond.

From my experience with horses I learned what the Bible means when it describes Moses as the meekest man on earth.[6] Moses was a man of great power, and yet he was totally under the control of his God. These huge animals I was riding can weigh as much as fourteen hundred pounds, and yet with all that strength they totally yielded to my slightest command.

I also learned that horses have a remarkable memory. After I finished riding each day, I would give Ufano a little treat. Whenever our exercise session ended, he would turn his head, and I would hand him something that he gratefully received.

Tragically this beautiful animal was bitten by a tiny tick carrying Lyme disease. Veterinarian treatments were unsuccessful, and I was forced to give my incredible friend away to a lady in Suffolk who had a small horse farm.

I have a piece of advice for any of you who happen to be fledgling riders: Horses expect to be led by a herd leader. They want firm direction. If a rider gives conflicting signals, a horse can become angry and dangerous. He needs to trust his rider and to rely on his rider's judgment. If you don't know what you are doing, I suggest you get a mechanical horse, not a live one.

For those of you who may wonder why a book on my life and the miracle power of God includes a rather lengthy chapter about horses, I would refer you to the Book of Revelation chapter 19: "I saw heaven standing open and there before me was a white horse, whose rider is called Faithful and True.... The armies of heaven were following him, riding on white horses and dressed in fine linen, white and clean."[7]

Now that is something this inveterate horse rider is looking forward to seeing one day.

23

Miracles in Atlanta, Houston, and Dallas

In 1968 I focused my attention on improving the quality of our television and radio programs. I knew that people loved Christmas carols at Christmastime, so right after Thanksgiving we broadcast our first-ever "Festival of Christmas Music." Stores that wanted to build their Christmas business began playing our station, and our audience grew dramatically. At the same time, I dipped my toe in the commercial television program arena and bought rerun episodes of a charming situation comedy called *Leave It to Beaver*.

We operated on a limited schedule on television and slowly began to fill our broadcast hours with programs of interest to the audience. In retrospect I must admit that what we were doing was anything but high-quality television.

At the time, I acquired some early-model color cameras and modified our television transmission equipment so that we could begin broadcasting in color. At the same time, I learned that the FCC had allocated UHF Channel 46 in Atlanta. I applied to the FCC for that channel, which was granted to us. We now had our second television station. Since most of our programs were live, our team had to travel to Atlanta to produce live television broadcasts, which stretched us thin.

Once again, I experienced deep love and affection for God's people. And once again, as we prayed on the air, members of the audience received miraculous answers—and miracles became the norm. But we really couldn't be live everywhere when we needed to be. The question became, How can we produce programs at one place that can be sent to another?

In those days videotape was not as common as it is today. Nevertheless,

I was able to acquire a pair of Ampex two-inch videotape recorders. Then programs produced in Portsmouth could be sent to Atlanta, and programs produced in Atlanta could be sent to Portsmouth. Before long we developed a daily block of four hours that could be sent by express to any station equipped with a videotape player.

Not long after this I read that Ted Turner, who owned a billboard company in Atlanta, had obtained a license for Channel 36 in Charlotte, North Carolina. His station was losing money, and he laughingly said, "I think my company should be called Marginal Media."

Even though his venture was totally commercial, Ted had gone on air to ask for donations from his viewers to sustain the cost of operating his station, so I called Ted with an offer.

"Ted, I understand you sign on at four o'clock in the afternoon in Charlotte. We will take your unused time from noon to four for our programs. We will then hold a telethon to help pay the bills." Ted liked my idea, so we opened up in Charlotte, and he became a CBN affiliate.

We recruited volunteer phone counselors, built our set in the studio, and went on air. Any words that I could think of to describe our love with Charlotte would be an understatement. The people there were warm, welcoming, and aglow with the Holy Spirit of God.

One day as the counselors were praying before we went on air, God gave us this prophecy: "There are many wells across my land, and I will pour living water out of all of them." I was enormously encouraged and realized that there were dozens of struggling UHF stations all across America that would welcome the same arrangement that I had made in Charlotte.

My trusted lieutenant and dear friend at that time was a Canadian named Stan Ditchfield, who'd been a regional marketing manager for *Reader's Digest* as well as a bomber navigator for the RAF during World War II. If anyone else is to share the credit for starting the Christian Broadcasting Network across America, Stan has to be the one. He traveled far and wide—Buffalo, New York; New York;

Detroit; Chicago; Houston; Fresno, California; and many other cities throughout America.

In those days the interconnection of television stations was stymied by the prohibitive rates of long-distance telephone service. For each point in the network there was an added set of mileage charges so that the monthly costs of interconnection could quickly run into the millions of dollars. Our only means of interconnection was through the shipment of videotape, coupled with live telethons. The telethons would begin on Fridays at noon and run to midnight, followed by noon on Saturday to midnight, and then from noon on Sunday to two in the morning. In one year I set a record of twenty-three telethons and became so exhausted that on several occasions I forgot what city I was in. The show business term is "paying your dues." I certainly paid mine.

Our affiliate in Houston was Channel 26. Before I went there, the Lord spoke to me these words: "Your affiliate in Houston will be blessed of God, so much so that you will see with your eyes and will not believe it, yet it will come to pass."

We placed our set in the Channel 26 studio with fifty telephones to take calls. We went on air at four o'clock in the afternoon Houston time. The show scheduled for that time was called *Monster Man*. When the camera light turned red, I said, "I want to tell you about someone more powerful than Monster Man. I want to tell you about Jesus Christ."

And then I gave an invitation for people in the audience to receive Jesus as Savior. Then we showed on the screen the telephone number for them to call.

An explosion of calls followed. Every telephone in the studio lit up and rang incessantly hour after hour after hour. I walked up and down the row of phones, encouraging people to call in and then saying to myself, "I don't believe it. This can't be happening." But it was happening. Literally thousands of people throughout Houston were finding the Lord. Every time I prayed, more and more miracles of healing and deliverance were taking place.

Once again, God's word to me had been fulfilled literally. I have experienced many spiritual highlights, but this weekend has to rank among the most significant of them.

When we signed off early Monday morning, we caught a few hours of sleep and then flew to Dallas, where I had been told there was a television station that we might be able to acquire.

No fiction writer could have spelled out what happened next.

A Pentecostal pastor had decided that he wanted to have a television station, so he started one on Channel 33 in Dallas. His studio was located in the garage of a former car dealer. From the rumors that came to me, this particular pastor had lost his credentials with the Assemblies of God denomination for marital infidelity. In his inaugural broadcast he featured a film called *I Wonder Who's Kissing Her Now*, a musical made in 1947. Let's just say it was a movie about seduction and betrayal. His manager said, "I am now going to do the citizens of Dallas a favor. I am going to shut this thing off the air."

The TV station had little or no commercial value, and the man left in charge was more than happy to sign a transfer of the license to the Christian Broadcasting Network, along with the title to whatever equipment was not under lien. I brought in some of my technicians and production crew to Dallas, who in short order got things together so we could go on air.

At the time, I felt that I was coming from a little town in Virginia, and here I was in a highly sophisticated major metropolitan area. Nevertheless, I remembered the statement "When you're taken to a party, you dance with the one who brought you." We had been brought this far by the power of God, and it did not seem appropriate to change our programming to accommodate what turned out to be an erroneous view of sophisticated Texans.

So we signed the station on at noon. Our counselors were in place, our telephones were in place, and everything was operating. As I began taking prayer requests and praying, the Lord gave me a vision of a person with a deep back gash inflamed with suppurating pus. I spoke that word and declared it healed. The television signal from Dallas was being received at that time in Ardmore, Oklahoma. There was a woman sitting on a piano stool in Ardmore whose kidney had been removed. The resulting incision had become infected, and since it was not adequately closed, the surgical cut was oozing pus. When she heard that word, she was knocked to the ground and then came up completely healed.

This was the first of many miracles we heard about in Dallas. Our audience grew dramatically. The blessings multiplied, and we had more than enough resources to grow and expand.

With three major market television stations, I realized that it was time to start developing some substantial programming. The concept was relatively simple. We would air a block of wholesome secular programs up to about seven o'clock at night, and then we would put our religious programs on the air to finish out the day.

Hollywood producers realized that even getting minimum payment for their unused library would be good for business, so I was able to acquire a number of old television series at low prices. The audience available for television in the afternoon was made up primarily of after-school children and teen girls. I did my own focus groups with my teenage daughter Elizabeth and her friends. I would read a list of program titles and would then scale the audience's reaction by the intensity of the oohs and aahs for each program.

I obtained rerun rights for several programs, such as *The Andy Griffith Show*, *The Dick Van Dyke Show*, *The Lucy Show*, *Hogan's Heroes*, and *Gomer Pyle*. This simple concept caught on quickly, and the audience for our fledgling Dallas station went up dramatically.

When I was a youngster, on Saturday afternoons, clutching a dime and a penny in my hand, I would go to the Lyric Theatre in Lexington and watch Westerns. The popular Westerns had gone out of favor with advertisers, so hour-length features such as *Gunsmoke*, *Laramie*, *Laredo*, and *Bonanza* were all available. My program block titled "Saturday Afternoon at the Westerns" became so popular that it scored first place in the ratings.

Doubleday Broadcasting had started a station in Dallas on Channel 39. They built a beautiful studio on Harry Hines Boulevard. They bought state-of-the-art equipment, had a fully equipped remote truck, and committed themselves to millions of dollars in programming costs. Unfortunately for them, they didn't know how to put all of these expensive pieces together in order to make money. In fact, they were losing a million dollars a year and wanted out.

Our Channel 33 was beating them in the ratings. One day the station manager asked me to stop by and see him.

"Would you like to buy our station?" he asked.

"Not really, but here's what I will do," I answered. "I'll give you a tax certificate for the gift for your station and take over your unused film liabilities."

My idea of relieving him of his obligations sounded attractive to the station manager. "I'll call my home office in New York and see if they are interested."

A few days later he called me back. "We'll do it," he said. "I'll have our lawyers draw up the papers."

Once again, the God of miracles had acted on our behalf. We were able to move from that old garage and the broken-down facility at Channel 33 into an ultra modern facility with state-of-the-art equipment, fully equipped offices, a remote truck, and a microwave link to the tower farm with a one-thousand-foot television tower. The station not only had a beautifully furnished lobby but also had a well-equipped lunchroom for our staff to enjoy.

I had been walking with the supernatural God, and I was about to find out that He had many more things ahead for me.

24

MELODRAMA WITH JIM AND TAMMY

DEDE AND I moved the family to Dallas for the summer to perfect the work on Channel 33. I thought we had a furnished house lined up, but it turned out that nobody would rent us a furnished home since we had little children.

In this instance the God I serve performed another one of His miracles. Instead of a house we found a short-term rental of a furnished apartment in what was considered at the time the most prestigious neighborhood in Dallas, at 3525 Turtle Creek Drive, where we leased a spacious two-thousand-square-foot apartment in a twenty-two-story building.

I then began to study serious techniques for the placement of television programs. If you think about it, a program director has before him a blank slate. He then must fill out every hour and every half hour of the program day with specific titles.

The first thing I did was obtain copies of the HUT report, which stands for Households Using Television. In other words, this was the available universe for my programs. Next was to find out who was occupying the homes using television. The advertisers wanted what were called "targeted demographics" or demos. They generally sought to place commercials on programs that women from eighteen to forty-nine were watching. Broadcasting those shows would bring premium prices from ad sales.

Here is the concept I developed: I would begin our broadcast day with programs that attracted young people. Then every hour I would put in programs that would appeal to a slightly older demographic. So during the day there would be a seamless buildup of the audience watching our television station and the age of those who were in the audience.

94

Prime time for an independent station in the evening was from seven to eight o'clock. The networks showed their evening news at 6:30 Eastern Standard Time and began their high-budget network programs from 8:00 to 11:00, so there was a one-hour gap to grab an audience. I had learned that in our home market the majority of television viewers were African American people. So at seven o'clock I put on the very popular comedies, *The Jeffersons* and *Diff'rent Strokes,* which gained an astounding 14 rating, meaning that 14 percent of the entire population of TV-equipped homes had tuned in.

When I returned from Dallas to Tidewater, however, I found a serious roadblock in our programming. The Jim and Tammy Bakker kids' show, which appealed primarily to third- and fourth-grade students, was firmly in place at 6:00 p.m. This meant that the audience I had built up so carefully up to 6:00 then turned the station off—or turned the channel—while the little kids tuned in to watch Jim and Tammy. Then at 7:00, when our serious religious block started, the little kids all tuned out and left us with no audience going into prime time. It was an impossible situation, and I felt like a college football player trying to compete with a broken leg.

I want to say a couple of words about Jim and Tammy Bakker: Jim had told me that he was a rock 'n' roll disc jockey. One day an announcer for WXRI was sick and couldn't make his shift, so I told Jim to go back to the station and begin the afternoon shift.

Jim looked at me like the proverbial deer in headlights. "I don't know how to do that," he said.

"What do you mean you don't know how? You said you were a rock 'n' roll DJ."

"I've never been on the radio," he replied. "I just played records at sock hops."

In hindsight I believe this was a foreshadowing of things to come. We received a phone call complaining that Jim was driving a large Cadillac. Instead of letting that remark pass, Jim went on television and carefully explained that he was being attacked because the blessings of God enabled him to own and drive a Cadillac.

Jim probably has his version of this, but from my perspective at the time, he and Tammy seemed to make continual demands to accommodate their personal needs. Jim could speak in such a way that people felt sorry for him and Tammy, and the good people of Tidewater extended instant compassion toward them. Our staff of dedicated Christians at the time was living a sacrificial life. Jim and Tammy's conduct stood out in stark contrast, and it seemed as if every month or so I had to call a meeting of reconciliation. I began to feel that my calling in life had been reduced to conflict resolution.

Not only was Jim doing the children's program, but he was sharing alternate nights as host of *The 700 Club*. When I moved their children's program from 6:00 in the evening to 2:00 in the afternoon, a firestorm erupted, complete with tears of incrimination. I held fast and made the move.

On a Monday four days before our upcoming telethon in Baltimore, Jim resigned and walked out, leaving me to handle the forthcoming responsibility by myself. We had a gap in our lineup, but God gave me the strength to fill in where there was a need.

As our team continued traveling around the country doing live telethons, I came to realize the truth of the saying by the apostle Paul: "We wrestle not against flesh and blood, but against principalities, against powers, against the rulers of the darkness of this world, against spiritual wickedness in high places."[1] I learned that over each city there was a spiritual presence. In one it might be a spirit of witchcraft; in another, a spirit of lust; in another, a spirit of power. I learned that these demonic spirits had two main goals. First, they desired to inhabit human beings and participate in the fleshly enjoyment of humans—whether gluttony, sexual addiction, drunkenness, or drug addiction. Their other goal was to destroy spiritually or physically human beings who had been created in the image of God.

Before we would go into these places and expose ourselves to hours of live broadcasting, our staff would hold a serious prayer meeting, during which we bound Satan and the forces of evil. Then we would ask the Lord to send the angels to accompany us so that we would have spiritual protection. I'd like to give you a brief example of my introduction to this dark, spiritual world.

The Bible tells us that shortly after creation an angel called Lucifer, who, according to Ezekiel 28:14, was charged with covering the very holiness of God,[2] looked in pride at his own beauty and determined that he could do a better job of running the universe than almighty God. We are told in the Bible that Lucifer was thrown out of heaven because of his rebellion, and he took a third of the angels with him to earth. Lucifer was then called Beelzebub or Satan, which means "adversary."[3] His followers, the fallen angels, were described as unclean spirits or demons.

One night I worked late and got home to our house on the Frederick College grounds at about 8:30. I was eating leftovers from dinner when there was a knock on the kitchen door. I opened the door and found a couple of teenagers. They were part of a wonderful group of young people who had turned our garage into a place of prayer and worship that they called "the coffeehouse." These youngsters said, "Dr. Robertson, we believe a young girl in our group is demon-possessed. Would you come and cast the demons out of her?"

I was tired and hungry, and the last thing in my mind was going out and casting out demons.

"OK, guys, let me finish dinner, and then I'll come out to help her," I said.

When I arrived, I found the young girl lying on the grass between our house and the horse barn.

"What's the matter?" I asked.

"I can't stand being with those people when they pray," she said. "I feel something in my stomach, and I hear a voice saying, 'Get out of here quickly.'"

"Are you sure?"

"Absolutely. I can't stand to be with those people praying."

I knew that this was not a normal reaction and that this indeed was some type of demonic possession. So I told the two fellows who had come with me, "Take hold of her hands, and I want to pray for her."

As I started to pray, she screamed at the top of her voice, "Let me go!"

Our nearest neighbor lived at least a mile away, but I was afraid her shrieking scream would bring the police to us. I then rebuked the demon and said, "Satan, I command you in Jesus' name, come out of her!"

Then, out of that little girl's mouth came these words: "You can't have her, she's mine. We won! We won!"

"Satan, you are a liar," I pushed back. "You have not won! Jesus has won! You must release this girl."

She fought the restraints with almost supernatural strength, but nothing happened. Then I remembered the words of Jesus, who had said, "This kind goeth not out but by prayer."[4]

So I earnestly prayed and said, "Lord, please get this thing out of her." At that moment, the demon left her, and she relaxed and opened her eyes.

"How do you feel?" I asked.

"I feel wonderful," said the girl.

"Would you like to go back to the coffeehouse to pray with your friends?"

"I would like that very much."

We helped her up, and she went back to the prayer meeting restored and in her right mind.

I had spent my first year of high school at the McDonogh Prep School in the countryside not too far from Baltimore Street, a notoriously evil place. Along Baltimore Street was a series of strip clubs, massage parlors, seedy bars, and places of evil beyond imagination.

Then the City of Baltimore decided an urban renewal program was appropriate and tore down all of those places of evil. In their places they built condominiums and a beautiful hotel.

When we arrived in Baltimore for our telethon on Channel 45, we were housed in that beautiful new hotel. I had a nice room with a comfortable double bed, and I lay down for a few minutes of rest before I had to go to the studio. I fell asleep, and then my mind was assailed by the vilest thoughts imaginable. I didn't realize what was happening, but I struggled to get back awake.

Apparently the spirits that had inhabited Baltimore Street remained and were present in my hotel room. I rebuked the spirit and commanded it to leave me, and then I got furious. "Satan, how dare you attack me in this fashion! I am going to get you tonight!" I declared. And get him we did.

We went on air that evening on Channel 45, and as soon as I was on, I gave an invitation to people to find the Lord. And during that time, fourteen hundred people repented of their sins and gave their hearts to Jesus.

I know for a fact that Jesus Christ is more powerful than any devil. He said, "All authority in heaven and on earth has been given to me. Therefore go and make disciples of all nations."[5] Jesus has power over all of the spirit world. No Christian should ever confess the power of Satan.

God has promised that He will bruise Satan under our feet, and for all of us that is the posture that I recommend.

25

TED TURNER FOUNDS PTL AND CNN; JIM BAKKER GOES TO PRISON

WHILE I WAS in Dallas in 1974, I received a call that Ted Turner wanted to meet with me. When he flew in from Atlanta, I picked him up at the airport and drove him to a steakhouse just off the freeway called Lock, Stock & Barrel.

Ted was the owner of a billboard company, Turner Outdoor Advertising, which he had inherited after the tragic suicide of his father. Ted had been a regimental commander in the military at McCallie School a number of years after I attended. The story of his loss of faith included a description of his unanswered cries to God to heal his sister, who had brain damage from encephalitis and died at age seventeen.[1]

Ted had built a TV station on Channel 17 in Atlanta. He also owned the Charlotte station Channel 36, called WRET, which I have already mentioned. Up to that time, our station in Atlanta, Channel 46, had been strictly noncommercial. After our program overhaul I had salesmen on the street in Atlanta selling airtime against Ted. He had come to Dallas to demand that I keep Channel 46 in Atlanta nonprofit.

"Ted, you know I can't do that," I said. "I cannot make my station subservient to your wishes."

"I'm not going to let you raise money on my station in Charlotte to use to compete against me in Atlanta." He even stamped his feet and shouted, "You will do it!"

I did my best to remain calm. "Ted, you are acting like a child. There is no way I can do that."

"If that's the case, I'm taking you off the air."

"Ted, we have a contract."

"I'll break the contract. So sue me." With that he asked, "Will you take me back to the airport?" to which I replied, "Of course."

He then told Sandy Wheeler, the general manager of his television properties, "Call Bakker and tell him he's going on air in Charlotte." And that's exactly what happened.

The next week, Jim took over my set, my audience, and my time period—everything I had built up in Charlotte. He never asked permission and never apologized. He just took over everything we had built. So in my opinion it was Ted Turner who truly started *The PTL Club* television show, not Jim Bakker.

I could easily be reconciled to the loss of our Charlotte affiliate. What grieved me was that my dear friends in Charlotte had been taken away from me.

Jim Bakker seemed to quickly begin building a network called PTL to compete with the Christian Broadcasting Network. He began bidding for our affiliates and in turn forced up the prices I had to pay. My staff grew nervous about this apparent rivalry, but I said very simply, "He can't suspend the laws of economics."

Jim's ambition went far beyond Christian broadcasting. He set up an operation outside of Charlotte called Heritage USA and built a hotel modeled after Opryland in Nashville. He also added a theme park with a lake and waterslide, as well as a series of rental condominiums.[2] And of course he also built a big television studio. All of this has been well documented, as has the fact that he and Tammy were paying themselves sizable salaries.

Because funds were not available from contributions for the next phase of hotel development, Jim began selling accommodations in yet unbuilt properties to those investing in multi-thousand-dollar increments. It was then that the state authorities began to investigate the activities of this flamboyant couple.

I personally questioned whether the sale of a time-share was actually a security. Yet the judicial authorities said it was a security, and it wasn't up to me to challenge their authority, even if I disagreed with them. Under federal securities law, the issuer of the security is held liable for all of the terms that induce an individual to purchase the security. And the seller is held liable for the veracity of each statement that induces a sale.

Failure to register a security is, in my opinion, not a serious offense. However, in the case of PTL, when bankruptcy was looming, the government was able to throw the book at Jim Bakker for breaking a law that he probably didn't even know existed. Bakker was indicted on charges of mail and wire fraud and conspiring to defraud the public.

It's hard to state the impact of this scandal on the Christian world. Jim Bakker was not the leader of a denomination. He was not a member of the National Religious Broadcasters.

Nevertheless, the secular press made him out to be a towering example of evangelical Christianity. The scandal was not merely here in America. I remember seeing a newspaper headline in Hungary, a Communist country at the time, talking about Jim and Tammy Bakker. The press called Jim Bakker a television evangelist, and after his fall all of us who had been honestly trying to use broadcast media to help people spiritually and physically were now under a cloud.

Our revenues at CBN dropped precipitously. I believe the same thing happened to my fellow religious broadcasters. It wouldn't be fair to say that Bakker was the only ministry leader embroiled in scandal in the late '80s; in short the exposure of the improvident excesses of several ministries became a source of discredit upon us all.

When these charges hit, Jim panicked, and in my opinion he did a very unwise thing. He resigned from PTL and allowed the board of directors to appoint Jerry Falwell as head. By doing this, Jim transferred all of the records and accounts of his operation into someone else's hands.

If Jim had stayed in control of PTL, he would have had the protections afforded by the Fourth and Fifth Amendments of the US Constitution. Upon every request for a deposition, his lawyers could have instructed him to plead the Fifth Amendment against self-incrimination. At every document request his lawyers could have begun vigorous litigation in opposition. Instead, Jim left himself open to every unpleasant sanction that the federal and state governments could place upon him.

I remember the case of Scooter Libby, a lawyer for Vice President Dick Cheney. Federal prosecutor Pat Fitzgerald leveled a charge against Scooter Libby that he had leaked the identity of a CIA operative named Valerie Plame.[3]

Fitzgerald already knew that the leaker was a Defense Department official, yet he continued to hammer away at Scooter Libby. Scooter answered his questions in a way that the prosecutor alleged was untruthful. Libby was not convicted of the charge against him, but he was sent to prison for perjury at the hands of a malicious prosecutor.[4] Regrettably, in our legal system prosecuting attorneys are not required to be nice guys. They are only rewarded with getting convictions, so they mislead defendants and do whatever it takes. A defendant without adequate legal defense does not elicit sympathy from a prosecutor, but bloodlust.

When Jim finally went to trial, the prosecutors had a field day. The presiding judge displayed a serious animus against Bakker when he said, "He had no thought whatever of his victims, and those of us who do have a religion are ridiculed LTC as being saps for money-grubbing preachers or priests."[5] The standard penalty for criminal fraud would not exceed five years. Instead, the judge in Jim's case imposed on him an outrageous sentence. As one commentator said to me, "The judge gave Jim forty-five years for overbooking a hotel."

Jim and Tammy had been living large. Now Jim was a convicted felon—a humble, mistreated inmate in a harsh federal prison.

After completing his sentence with appropriate time for parole, Jim emerged a broken and humble man. He has begun a new television ministry and found a lovely new wife after Tammy divorced him. (Tammy died of cancer in 2007.[6])

In 2019 I was able to pray with the new Jim Bakker. I congratulated him on his new work and sincerely prayed for God's blessing on him.

Getting back to the beginning of the story of Ted Turner and the Charlotte television station, Turner sold WRET in 1979—I believe the sale price was twenty million dollars—and used that money to start the first twenty-four-hour television news network, Cable News Network (CNN), which bore an interesting similarity to our letters, CBN, but maybe his choice of call letters was just a coincidence.

Ted took advantage of new satellite technology to send his Atlanta-based station all over the country. He was able to obtain financing from cable titan John Malone. Although CNN went through a rough patch in the early years, Turner Broadcasting System became a success on the New York Stock Exchange, and Ted Turner became a multibillionaire.

26

A Big Deal With RCA

I T HAS BEEN my feeling that the Lord is pleased if our offerings to Him are of the best quality. It was becoming apparent that our entire facility in Portsmouth needed to be upgraded. We needed new color television cameras, banks of updated tape recorders, new studio switchers, a much more powerful transmitter, and an improved antenna.

I asked for a meeting with RCA's head of broadcast equipment sales. The list price of what we needed was five million dollars. We met at the Holiday Inn in Portsmouth and negotiated back and forth, item by item, for hours. At about one o'clock in the morning, after we had worked out the financing terms, we finally got the last concession at 50 percent off list price and shook hands on a $2.5 million package of new equipment.

In 1970, on the tenth anniversary of our first air date, our flagship station was now broadcasting on a thousand-foot tower at 2.25 million watts with a complement of the best conceivable production equipment, which dramatically increased our local audience and showed us the excellence that was to come in the future.

Something much more profound had happened. In our early days our Lord had taught me the proper way to use television for His glory. As we broadcast, telephones were available in our studio. Members of the audience were invited to call in with prayer requests, spiritual testimonies, and answers to prayer. We also solicited questions about troubling theological problems. I told our audience members that we welcomed their prayer requests and reports of answered prayer and that our counselors were there to pray with them, to laugh with them, and to cry with them, if need be. Not only did we share the news, but we also offered solutions to the problems facing people.

This type of programming was anointed with the power of God and became the model of Christian television—not only in the United States but all over the world. We wanted to have the proper equipment and attractive sets. We did not need glitzy surroundings or high-paid actors and expensive scripts. From time to time, if funds were needed, we were able to appeal to an audience that had become very much like a family. The success of this type of programming was evident when in just one recent year we recorded an amazing ninety-six million prayer requests from our audience.

Our guiding principles were contained in three words: integrity, innovation, and excellence.

I have prayed throughout my life for the Lord to give me wisdom, favor, and anointing. During my life He has honored my commitment and never disappointed me.

27

Dario Quiroga's Vegetative State

I HAD INSTALLED AS manager of our radio station, Nuevo Continente, in Bogotá, Colombia, a young bank executive named Dario Quiroga.

Dario contracted a sinus infection that spread to his brain and brought on a life-threatening illness. I heard that he had fallen unconscious and was lying at death's door in a Bogotá hospital. I arranged with Sixto López to meet me in Bogotá. I flew directly from the States, and Sixto came through Panama on to Bogotá. As I recall, we spent the night at the Tequendama Hotel in Bogotá.

We had a late breakfast and began to talk about Dario and his grim outlook. Sixto said to me, "If he is dying, do you suppose we will be interfering with God's will if we go and pray for him?"

"We certainly don't want to interfere with God's will," I said, "so here's the plan: We'll stay here at breakfast and have another cup of tea before we go to the hospital. If he's still alive, we'll take it for a sign that the Lord wants us to pray for his healing." After that second cup of tea, we got in the cab and drove to the hospital.

The nurse on his ward warned us, "Dario has suffered severe brain injuries. If he wakes up from this coma, he will be nothing but a vegetable."

With that dire prognosis, we went to the room where Dario was lying unconscious. I stood on one side of his bed, and Sixto stood on the other. We laid our hands on him and began to rebuke the death angel, commanding it to leave him. Then we fervently prayed and spoke in the name of Jesus that Dario would regain consciousness and be completely healed.

As we said those words, the power of God touched him, and Dario surfaced from his unconscious state. I remember that as we said, "Amen," a voice came out of Dario's mouth that said, "Ah-men."

From then on, Dario was healed entirely and resumed his duties as the manager of Nuevo Continente. The appraisal of his nurse about the extent of his brain damage was overridden by the power of God.

28

QUIET TIME

IN THE MID-1980s I had some CBN business in Atlanta, during which I stayed at my older brother's house. During my visit I noticed that his morning routine mirrored that of millions of Americans. As soon as he woke up, he turned on a radio, and his room was filled with raucous music. I don't recall if it was rock 'n' roll, rhythm and blues, country and western, or classical. The genre is unimportant; all I remember is that it was *loud*. It dominated his thinking. When he got into his car to drive downtown, another radio was on, filled with either news, loud talk, or more music. This in turn set his mood for the day.

God tells us in His Word, "Be still, and know that I am God."[1] We are also told that Jesus Christ, the Son of God, arose early in the morning and went out to a lonely place to pray.[2] He learned the essential truth that all of us, as human beings, need to be quiet before the Lord and to listen to His voice before something else comes in. But think of how our minds are barraged with electronic clutter. Instead of spending time reflecting on important things, we wade through the blogs and tweets and comments of people, many of whom we barely know. In the process our minds never have the chance to "be still."

Young children are unbelievably vulnerable because they have not yet perfected a self-image, which gives them stability. So in today's world if they are criticized or bullied on social media, they can be driven to despair, even to suicide.

I have been intentional about who is given control of my thought processes—especially in the morning.

Think of how most people's mornings are spent. It's a fact that the major television networks' morning shows, such as *Today*, *Good Morning America*, and *Fox & Friends*, are much more lucrative than their prime-time shows. The cost of production of those shows is so much smaller than the evening productions, and the spot availabilities to sell are doubled for morning versus evening. The same goes for radio, where the big audiences are found on what is called "morning drive" and it is assumed that the vast majority of drivers are listening to their car radios.

Subtly, or sometimes not too subtly, our minds are being manipulated by people who often hold unbiblical views or perhaps are lacking a moral compass. How then can we expect an intelligent electorate—either church members or civic leaders—to come out of this maelstrom of conflicting views? Is it any wonder that our nation is so bitterly divided and there seems to be little or no chance of reconciliation?

In my life, whether it was from reading the Bible or being exposed to the InterVarsity Christian Fellowship or other influences that came into my life, I have realized that it is imperative to start my day reading the Bible and listening to God. Only then am I in any way prepared to meet the multiple challenges with which I will be confronted on a daily basis.

At the celebration of my eightieth birthday each of my children was asked to give a word about their father. I was astounded that one thing stood out. It wasn't my gentle, paternal nature; it wasn't my organizational excellence; it wasn't games that we had played together. Instead, one thing stood out. "Whenever we got up in the morning, we found our father reading the Bible and praying." Isn't it amazing that with all of the influences they may have received, this one characteristic of my life was the one they remembered most?

It's very simple. I have made it a habit that before the kids got up and started calling for my attention, before my workday begins, before the phone starts ringing with urgent messages, I take time to be alone with the Lord.

I read a psalm, a chapter of the Proverbs, a portion of one of the Gospels, or one of the letters of the apostle Paul. I read them over and over and ask God what message there is in these Holy Scriptures to guide me through the day.

Then I thank God for all of His blessings. The old song said, "Count your blessings, name them one by one; count your blessings, see what God has done!"[3] I have found this to be a good habit. I thank Him for all of the goodness that He has given in my life. I thank Him for my family. I thank Him for the provisions that I have. I thank Him for my health. I thank Him for the freedom that I enjoy. The Bible says, "Be anxious for nothing, but in everything by prayer and supplication, with thanksgiving, let your requests be made known to God; and the peace of God, which surpasses all understanding, will guard your hearts and minds through Christ Jesus."[4]

I don't diminish in any way the opportunity we have to be distracted. There are any number of screens vying for our attention, offering us a convenient connection to information at the push of a button. When I touch my iPad screen, up come the headlines of the world's press. I touch it again, and I see the weather forecast for the day. A couple more swipes, and I've got the sports news. A couple more, and I have commentary from the *New York Times*, the *Wall Street Journal*, or Bloomberg.

The question is, Whose thoughts will dominate your mind? The Bible says, "Great peace have they which love thy law: and nothing shall offend them."[5] I want my day to start with the peace of God, and when it does, that peace stays with me all day long. If I don't spend time in the early part of the day with the Lord, I feel helpless and disconnected the rest of the day.

Again, I'm not talking about some have-a-little-talk-with-the-Lord kind of prayer life. I am talking about serious study of the Bible and earnest prayer. Jesus has said, "Hitherto have ye asked nothing in my name: ask, and ye shall receive, that your joy may be full."[6] Ask Him, and then be sure you remember what you've asked for so that you can thank Him when you receive it.

I have found that life is filled with joy and excitement because I am in partnership with the living God, and my day belongs to Him and He belongs to me. Out of my quiet times have come ongoing revelations of major ministries, not the least of which is our Operation

Blessing, which has become one of the world's leading organizations for the relief of human suffering.

God once spoke to me the words "Do not fear the future, for I am the future." When we have this assurance, we have no fear because fear has torment.

There's a story in the Bible of two women—one named Martha and one named Mary. The Bible says that Martha was "distracted with much serving."[7] She was bustling around the house, always busy. But Mary was sitting at the feet of Jesus and listening to His words. Martha said, "Lord, do You not care that my sister has left me to serve alone? Therefore tell her to help me."[8] The Lord said, "Martha, you are worried and troubled about many things. But one thing is needed, and Mary has chosen that good part, which will not be taken away from her."[9]

If you can take one thing away from this book, it is this: Get rid of the clutter in your life. Stop doing nonessential things, and stop thinking you are accomplishing something just because you are engaged in a whirl of activities. Instead, spend your time in the presence of the Lord. Ask for His wisdom and guidance, and then receive the blessing that He so desires to give you.

29

A KILLER HURRICANE OBEYS THE VOICE OF GOD

THE HEART OF the Christian gospel is that the all-powerful and loving Creator of this universe yearned to reveal Himself to the human beings that He had made. In order to do so, He sent His Son, who was every bit God, to become a human being to explain to these special creatures how much their Creator loved them and how He wanted them to have eternal life with Him. This God-man walked on earth and showed His disciples the enormous potential they had if they were indwelled by His Holy Spirit.

On one occasion He had rebuked a violent storm at sea, and the storm obeyed His voice. Later on He told His disciples, "Most assuredly, I say to you, he who believes in Me, the works that I do he will do also; and greater works than these he will do, because I go to My Father."[1]

I took this as His promise to me, and when an occasion arose, I took that power and demonstrated it. Here now is the story of another incredible miracle.

Our planet builds up heat during the summer in the tropics and then releases that heat with massive windstorms called hurricanes. The typical track of these hurricanes—when they approach landfall in the United States—is to veer toward the eastern coast of Florida, go up past the Carolinas and coastal Virginia, and from there go out to sea. A category 4 hurricane with winds in excess of 150 miles an hour can wreak havoc in its path.

Back in our earliest days I was named the president of the Tidewater chapter of the Full Gospel Business Men's Fellowship. Our monthly breakfast on Saturday mornings was held in the ballroom on the top floor of the old Monticello Hotel in Norfolk. We had a dais for chapter leaders and the day's speaker. The fellowship members were seated at tables all over the room.

On a September morning in 1961 at about nine in the morning I received word from someone who had been listening to the radio that a massive hurricane named Esther was hurtling up the coast and aimed right at us. I knew a storm of this magnitude would mean the end of the Christian Broadcasting Network not long after it started. A massive hurricane like this one could tear down our self-supporting television tower in Portsmouth and crush the studio building housing the other equipment. We had no insurance and no ability to rebuild. This wasn't time for a polite prayer, but a cry of desperation.

I remember standing on the platform before our chapter members and telling them that this giant storm was on the way. I asked them to pray against it. "Let's stand and point our hands in the direction of this storm," I said, and that's what we did. And then, with all the faith I could muster, I held out my hand and cried out, "I forbid you, hurricane, in the name of Jesus, to come into our area, and I command you to go back to where you came from."

I later learned what happened. This monstrous storm obeyed my voice in Jesus' name, just like the storm on the Sea of Galilee that had obeyed the voice of the Lord Himself. Like a big dumb beast, this monstrous storm ceased its forward motion and slowly turned away from us. I've seen the actual weather track of this storm, and what happened is just as I have said. Hurricane Esther skirted our area, churned in the ocean for quite some time, and slowly moved away from our area.

Not only was the television station spared but also what would later become Operation Blessing, Regent University, and the American Center for Law and Justice. In short if that hurricane had destroyed our little television station back in 1961, all of the initiatives we later birthed would not have happened.

This simple demonstration of God's power not only preserved the work we were doing but actually provided a shield of protection around our home area. For years after this moment, hurricanes that tried to enter our area were repeatedly denied access. I remember one, in fact, that tried to enter our area but was denied, and then it went back out to sea and tried to come in at another angle. The hurricane was denied again and finally went harmlessly out to sea. A television weatherman humorously described the erratic movement as "the Robertson shuffle."

30

GOD'S ACCOUNTING, THE MIRACULOUS GROWTH OF OUR TITHE

O N OCTOBER 1, 1973, we were celebrating the twelfth anniversary of CBN's television broadcasting. Our board of directors met at the old Adolphus Hotel in Dallas. From a financial standpoint this was one of our most significant meetings because I proposed to the board that we establish a program of tithing our gift income to other ministries. With a feeling of elation, we began that practice.

The Bible says, "Give, and it will be given to you. A good measure, pressed down, shaken together and running over, will be poured into your lap."[1] Consider this: after seven years, the tithe of our CBN income exceeded our total gross income in 1973.

And God has been faithful to supply our need despite the circumstances surrounding us. I recall the time that an expert assured me that if I were no longer on the air, we would only experience a minor dip in our contributions, and CBN would be able to continue unscathed. I took this expert at his word, and when I felt led to enter the race for the Republican nomination for the presidency of the United States, I felt that our Lord would be willing to bless our ministry.

How wrong I was in this assumption. And yet God was faithful. Our contributions fell by about 60 percent from what they had been before I left the ministry, and yet at the same time, the income for the commercial arm of our Family Channel had grown by the identical amount that our contributions had declined. So indeed God looked after us despite the fact that I was no longer the television voice of CBN.

Without question God will bless His people, but His way is not exactly the way we want it. We cannot tell Him how to bless us; we can only receive His blessing. As I have walked with Him throughout my life, I have experienced it time and time again.

Over and over our God proved faithful above anything that we could ask for or even think.

31

Rabin's Exhortation: "Be Strong"

As a television broadcaster I have been privileged to interview a number of prominent world leaders. One such occasion happened during the winter of 1974 when I took a group of Christian pilgrims to Israel. While we were settling into our beautiful hotel, located on the Mount of Olives, overlooking Jerusalem's Old City, I traveled to the office of the prime minister, who was then former general Yitzhak Rabin. When he was a brigadier general, Rabin had led the Israel Defense Forces that captured East Jerusalem from Jordan in 1967. Rabin, a newly minted national hero, was later promoted to army chief of staff and then elected prime minister.

When I met with him, the 1973 oil embargo had been imposed upon the world by King Faisal of Saudi Arabia. The price of petroleum had risen at least three times because of this embargo. The economies of the Western nations, including the United States, took a big hit, and blame was placed on Israel.

As I spoke to the prime minister, I felt a strong compassion for this brave leader and his tiny country. When my interview time was coming to a close, I asked one last question: "Mr. Prime Minister, what would you like America to do to help you?"

Rabin thought for a minute and then replied, "Be strong. Be strong."

When I rejoined our group on the Mount of Olives and looked across to Jerusalem and the prominent Dome of the Rock, with its gold-plated roof, I made a vow that regardless of how difficult it might be, I and the ministries associated with me would stand in defense of Israel and the Jewish people. More than forty-five years later I'm pleased to report that I have kept that vow.

In Germany the Nazis had brought a campaign of extermination and genocide against the entire Jewish population of Europe. Many of the ardent Nazis were themselves nominal members of either the Lutheran Church or the Catholic Church. As far back as the Protestant Reformation, Martin Luther had written unimaginable condemnation of Jewish people.[1] It was certainly understandable that the Jews who fled the Holocaust would feel animosity toward Christians.

However, even as a small boy I had been taught God's words to Abraham in Genesis: "I will bless those who bless you, and I will curse him who curses you."[2] I had learned early on to bless the Jews, and my time with Rabin merely intensified that feeling.

Over the years, I've been asked why I'm so friendly toward Israel and the Jewish people. I like to quip, "Well, you see, my boss was a Jewish rabbi."

I realize that the Bible, which is my guide in life, was given to humanity, with the possible exception of Luke, by Jewish writers. I am convinced that the favor I have received over the years has in no small part sprung from my support of God's chosen people.

32

THE MIRACULOUS SHOEBOX

AFTER A DECADE of television ministry our staff had grown dramatically, along with our income. There just wasn't enough room in our small Portsmouth facility to accommodate the needs of our people.

I moved my office, along with our accounting staff, to occupy a floor in a building designated as Pembroke Five in the Pembroke Office Park in Virginia Beach.

One afternoon my chief financial officer and his assistant asked for a meeting, and I joined them in our small conference room. They showed me some figures and said, "We have an urgent need to pay some bills. The amount is $1.5 million."

I looked at them and said, "Fellows, I hate to tell you this, but we don't have $1.5 million. The last time I heard, it was against the law for a private citizen to print money."

My chief financial officer said, "You're in charge, so we'll pray that somehow you can get it." I then drove the half hour back to my home in Portsmouth, where I spent a very troubled evening.

I cried out to the Lord for an answer, and He led me to the fourth chapter of Paul's letter to the Romans where He was talking about the patriarch Abraham, who, though childless, was promised by God that he would be the father of many nations.

I then read these words: "He did not consider his own body, already dead (since he was about a hundred years old), and the deadness of Sarah's womb…but was strengthened in faith, giving glory to God, and being fully convinced that what He had promised He was also able to perform."[1]

I read that phrase again—"being fully convinced that what He had promised He was also able to perform." And then I reread it—"being fully convinced that what He had promised He was also able to per-form." Then I read it again and again. Then I was finally convinced "that what [God] had promised He was also able to perform."

Then I went to sleep, and I woke up the next day, ate breakfast, got in my car, and drove from our home at Frederick College in Portsmouth to the Pembroke Office Park in Virginia Beach. I entered my office, and my secretary, Barbara Johnson, said, "Look what came in the mail."

"What is it?"

"Open it and take a look."

She handed me a shoebox wrapped in brown paper. I held the box and took off the lid. Inside was the most sizable contribution we had ever received. The shoebox was full of New York State Bearer Bonds with a face value of $600,000—and a market value of $500,000. They were sent by a woman in Ohio whom I had never met and of whom I knew nothing.

I went from my office to the conference room to meet with my chief financial officer and his assistant again. I was describing the shoebox and its contents when there was a knock on the door. It was Barbara Johnson.

"Look what came in the mail," she announced for the second time that morning.

"What is it?" I asked.

"You'd better take a look at it."

I looked inside the envelope and saw a letter and a New York Lottery ticket. The letter said, "I am enclosing the winning ticket to the New York State Lottery. I've just won a million dollars, and I want to give it to CBN." I was amazed.

The task before us seemed so daunting. I had no idea how we would raise $1.5 million in less than twenty-four hours. And yet here, without any solicitation whatsoever, were two pieces of mail that contained the money we needed. Believe me, I was fully convinced that what our Lord had promised He was also able to perform. I was holding in my hand the dramatic truth of that section of the Bible.

In the interest of full disclosure, I must confess that the New York

Lottery ticket was not worth a million dollars, but only $15,000. However, within a short period of time the Lord sent in the rest of the million dollars, and we were able to pay our bills.

The prophet Zephaniah said, "Not by might, nor by power, but by my spirit, saith the Lord."[2]

Now that's a verse I love repeating.

33

CANTALOUPE AND COTTAGE CHEESE

IN 1963 PASTOR Ralph Wilkerson bought a former dance hall named Melodyland in Anaheim, California, across Harbor Boulevard from Disneyland. He refurbished the dance hall and termed it Melodyland Christian Center. Ralph brought in noted evangelists such as Kathryn Kuhlman as speakers.

As I recall, Melodyland Christian Center was celebrated all over the West Coast. Ralph decided that he would add the Melodyland School of Theology. He put together a board to manage the school and asked me to be one of the members. In 1975 the School of Theology board of directors scheduled a meeting at the Grand Hotel, also across the street from Disneyland.

Before coming to California for this meeting, I had been trying to find a suitable place to build a headquarters for CBN because we were spread out all over the area. By this time we had bought a couple of old houses adjoining our property. We had offices in a bank building in downtown Portsmouth. We had a warehouse and offices for our printing and mailing operations in Chesapeake, Virginia, and the executive team was occupying the offices in the Pembroke Office Park.

I had tried repeatedly to find an appropriate parcel of land but had been unable to do so. The Development Department of the City of Virginia Beach referred me to the owners of a potential shopping center site that they had called Metroplex. This land was uniquely located on the border of Virginia Beach, Norfolk, Portsmouth, and Chesapeake. A bonus was that a regional airport was about fifteen minutes away. I thought this was an ideal location, but the owners had no desire to break off a six-acre piece of this valuable commercial property.

I was late for my lunch meeting on the top floor of the Grand Hotel, but I was famished, so I slipped into the coffee shop on the ground floor to get a quick bite. California is noted for its delicious, big cantaloupes, so I ordered a half of a cantaloupe with some cottage cheese. I bowed my head to say thanks, and then God began to speak to me. The waitress must have thought I wasn't hungry because I continued to pray at length before I started to eat. Here's what God was telling me before I started eating that modest lunch: "I want you to return home, buy all of the land, build your headquarters, and build a school for My glory."

When I finished paying the bill, I made my way to the top floor and apologized for my tardiness. But I also knew I needed to get on the next plane from Los Angeles back to Norfolk, so I excused myself from the board meeting.

When I arrived, I called my friend John Zimmerman, who was an executive vice president of the local bank that held the mortgage on the property I wanted.

"John, I've come back from California, and I've heard from the Lord," I announced. I could tell I had John's attention.

John was curious. "What did the Lord tell you?"

"He told me to buy all of that Metroplex land and build CBN's headquarters and a school for His glory."

My good Christian friend replied, "Praise the Lord!" But then he had a question that bankers tend to ask. "How do you want to pay for it?"

Of course, neither I nor CBN had any money, so I said, "Nothing down. I'll pay interest only for two years and the balance over twenty years at simple interest."

"How much interest are you willing to pay?"

"I'll pay 8 percent simple."

He told me that there were 142 acres in the parcel under consideration, and the combined price was $2.3 million. "I think we can do it," he said optimistically.

And on December 31, 1975, Dede and I sat in the office of the attorney representing the bank and received the deed for this fabulous piece of property after signing the appropriate notes for the full purchase price.

On New Year's Day a group of our staff joined Dede and me as we marched around this marvelous piece of property and claimed it for the glory of the Lord. This land would eventually become the site of our beautiful headquarters building and a major university, first known as CBN University and later renamed Regent University.

If we hadn't purchased that land when the Lord directed me to, we might have missed out on many of the wonderful things He wanted to accomplish through us for His kingdom.

34

God's Anointing on the First Settlers Is Transferred to CBN

Y MARCHING ORDERS from the Lord were to build a head-quarters and then a school for His glory. Therefore, I hired an architect to design a building that would be suitable to house our studios, our control rooms, our prayer room, and our various offices. The architect I hired turned out a succession of absolutely dreadful-looking structures. One night Dede said, "Do we have to have another ugly building?" The answer was no, we didn't.

I prayed for wisdom. On a Saturday morning I took a piece of paper, and with the Lord's guidance I sketched out the outline of a building in the form of a cross. The wings on either side contained large studios. At the core was a place where we would pray. The prayer room was circular in shape, and behind the circle was a place for equipment and control rooms. Behind the control rooms were a couple of large spaces that could serve as alternate studios or storage areas. In the internal core were multiple stories that were used for offices.

We then engaged the services of architect Archie Davis, who had designed some of the beautiful buildings on the University of North Carolina campus. He designed two decorative columns in front of the building that were to be made out of limestone. Each of them was adorned with a limestone frieze. The roof of the central core was made to resemble Monticello, the home of former President Thomas Jefferson.

I knew a man in Washington named Ray Bates, who was an expert in Colonial architecture. When he saw the design, he said, "Pat, why don't you design the central core to look like the Governor's Palace in Williamsburg?"

I agreed with that, so we changed the design from Monticello to

Georgian Colonial. When the architectural drawing was finally finished, I saw a massive, beautiful structure capped by a towering spire.

As we were transitioning our offices from Portsmouth to Virginia Beach and had prayed many times for the dedication of this piece of property, Phyllis Mackle, the editor of our little newspaper called *The Flame*, began to research the history of Virginia Beach. She discovered that the first English settlers to Virginia had come ashore at a place in the northeast corner of Virginia Beach, where the Atlantic Ocean meets the Chesapeake Bay. They named the spot Cape Henry after the son of the king of England. These settlers had come ashore on April 26, 1607.[1] Their first official act was to plant a cross on the shore and claim this land for the glory of almighty God.

In the modern era the US Department of Interior had erected a cross here in Virginia Beach, at the landing site of Cape Henry, and had placed there a plaque that read "Act 1, Scene 1 of the unfolding drama that became the United States of America."

I felt that this was a powerful example of what the German theologians called *heilige Geschichte*, which means "holy history."[2] I wanted to memorialize that important date, so we gathered our staff at Cape Henry and then reenacted a short drama. We had staff members dress in the costumes of each of the continents, and then they carried from the ocean a seven-foot oak cross that contained a hollow place inside. I had with me, printed on microfiche, the names of our CBN donors who had participated in helping to build our headquarters. As the special cross was being placed upright on the sandy slope overlooking the ocean, I took the names of our donors and placed them inside the cross. I put my hands on the cross, asked our staff to join me in prayer, and then blessed this day and asked that God transfer His blessing from Cape Henry to our new headquarters as we sought to take His gospel all over the world.

As I spoke these words, I received an anointing of power greater than I had ever felt in my entire life. Our Lord had truly connected me with the prayers of our ancestors on the shores of what later became

Virginia Beach, who had prophesied that the gospel of Jesus Christ would be preached in all of the world. I will never forget that moment.

We then took the cross and shipped it twenty-one miles to the site of our new headquarters building, where it remains to this day.

35

THROWING DOWN THE GAUNTLET TO JOHN DEWEY'S FAILURE IN EDUCATION

SINCE THE BUILDING of our new headquarters was quite complex and we needed to save money, I cut out the general contractor and took on these responsibilities myself. The ironworkers crafted enormous girders to support the roof of our huge television studios. The masons put up walls of cinder block, but I wanted to maintain the look of antique brick, so we bought the entire year's production of handmade bricks from Cushwa Brick in Pennsylvania. We then asked the masons to put them up in what is called Flemish bond.

For the limestone columns at the front of the building, there was another story. Without asking me, the limestone company made the caps with what is considered a traditional adornment—egg and dart. When I saw these embellishments, though, I was horrified.

"Are you aware of what they are?" I demanded.

The masons' sub said, "Sure. That's the traditional design of egg and dart."

"I'm sorry," I said, "but those things are pagan fertility symbols that I saw some years ago at the Baalbek temple complex in Lebanon. You've got to fix them."

The only person skilled enough to do such a job was a seventy-year-old mason from Indiana. When he asked me about changing the eggs and darts into pomegranates, I said, "That's a biblical design, so get with it." So they hauled up this older man in a bosun's chair to the top of the forty-foot column, and with a chisel he got rid of the fertility symbols. In their place he carved out some lovely biblical pomegranates.

Our headquarters building, because of its complexity, took a long time to build, but on the eve of the Feast of Tabernacles on October 6, 1979, we had a glorious dedication of this headquarters building.

Billy Graham was our featured speaker and gave a stirring address, declaring that this facility represented a beachhead into the communication of the future.

The Virginia Symphony was there to provide music. My good friend Andraé Crouch played and sang his music. Our staff gathered together in the new prayer room. And under a full moon, pyrotechnic expert Boom-Boom Zambelli launched a memorable display of fireworks. This night was like a fulfillment of a dream, but here again, it was only a taste of what was to come.

As I pointed out earlier, network broadcasting was the exclusive province of CBS, NBC, and ABC. The cost of entry was prohibitive. It was like trying to sit in on a poker game where the price of one blue chip was fifty million dollars. Then I learned that RCA, which owned the NBC network, was launching a satellite called Satcom 1.

I arranged a meeting with RCA to find out the details. I learned that a twenty-four-hour-a-day transponder on the Satcom 1 satellite could be rented for the price of $600,000 a year. This was an astounding opportunity, and I suggested to their sales team that this would open a host of competition to their own network. They told me that they were in charge of furthering the satellite subsidiary, not NBC.

To be on the safe side, I had our accountants study the proposition as thoroughly as possible. We found no downside and signed a contract for an entire transponder on the satellite. The first client for their company was HBO (Home Box Office), the second was Ted Turner's CNN, and the third was CBN.

What would this mean for us? We now had unlimited access to every city in the nation. We could send out our programs live instead of on tape. We could connect regional or even national telethons if we so chose. And, of course, with our news broadcasts on *The 700 Club*, we could furnish our audiences with up-to-date news.

In 1976 we applied to operate our own satellite earth station and purchased from Scientific Atlanta a satellite antenna and transmitter. In February 1977 we became the first Christian ministry in the history of the world to own and operate its own satellite earth station, potentially beaming television programs via satellite to the entire nation.

Then, on a wonderful day, we had our first international broadcast. On this momentous occasion we had cameras on the Mount of Olives, where a couple named Merve and Merla Watson were singing Jewish songs of praise. This broadcast was beamed by satellite to New York, where it was retransmitted to our satellite transponder and then to our earth station.

The Bible tells us that when Jesus returns, His feet will stand on the Mount of Olives, and all nations will behold Him. Our satellite relay was not the second coming of Jesus, but we certainly had the technology in place to show how the prophetic word could be fulfilled.

So now let me take you back to the word the Lord gave me in the Grand Hotel next to Disneyland, the part where He said, "Build a school for My glory."

I had an earned doctorate in jurisprudence from Yale Law School, a master of divinity from Biblical Seminary in New York, and a bachelor's degree from Washington and Lee. That added up to ten years of higher education, but I didn't have a clue about how to start any kind of school. So I waited several years for the Lord's instruction.

One spring day CBN had been asked to provide part of the program at the Christian Booksellers Association (CBA) convention in a Midwest city. At the CBA meeting we went onstage and did a live broadcast of our program.

That afternoon before the broadcast I was sunning beside the hotel pool. I had a yellow pad and a pen and said, "Lord, what kind of school do You want me to build for Your glory?"

He then showed me that our role was to provide the intellectual firepower that would challenge the strongholds that the secular world held over our society. To accomplish that our university would begin as a freestanding graduate school for several academic disciplines. We would have a law school, a government school, a business school, a broadcast school, a divinity school, and a school of education.

With that mandate I went home and contacted a Norfolk lawyer named Bob Boyd, who'd been a founding member of a Methodist school located in Norfolk. Bob showed me some verbiage that had worked well in securing his school's charter, so I was able to draft the necessary articles of incorporation and bylaws for CBN University. I sent my application to the Virginia State Corporation Commission, and within a couple of weeks I received a charter indicating that CBN University had been appropriately registered within the state of Virginia.

I was able to hire a capable dean for our fledgling Communications School. Together we rented some classroom space in a commercial office building on Battlefield Boulevard in Chesapeake. We were offering master's degrees for our students, and somehow we were able to find some brave souls with a pioneer spirit to sign on for our first class. CBN University was launched with seven professors and seventy-seven pioneering students.

I remembered that the Lord had instructed me to build various schools that would challenge the citadels of power in our secular society. The next citadel was education. I was able to hire Dr. Phil Frost, who had been superintendent of education in a small Connecticut town, as dean of the Graduate School of Education. We launched a master-of-education program with a handful of students and a small, but committed, faculty.

I vividly remember the first graduation of the education students. We had just one graduate. She was a determined young lady who marched proudly across the platform to receive her degree. I turned to Phil Frost and said earnestly, "We have just broken the back of secular education in America." But what was I really talking about?

When my children were growing up, my wife and I used flashcards to teach them how to read. With these cards would be a consonant, after which there was a selection of vowels that would form a word, and they could see with the transposition of the lead consonant how new words could be formed.

My principal student was my son, Tim, when he was a preschooler.

I took the consonant *b* and the vowel phrase *at*. So I said to Tim, "The *b* is pronounced *buh*, so say *buh*."

And he said, "*Buh*."

Then I took the phrase *at* and told him it was pronounced *aat*. I then said, "Make the *buh* sound," and he did. And then I said, "Make the *aat* sound," and he did. Now I said, "Put them together," and he said, "*Buh* and *aat*."

And I said, "No...put them together," and he again said, "*Buh* and *aat*." And I said, "No...put them *together*."

And for the third time he said, "*Buh* and *aat*." Finally, on his fourth try, out of his mouth came *bat*. I congratulated him on his victory, and from that moment on he was off and running in language skills. We enrolled him with a lovely lady in Churchland, Virginia, named Mrs. Garrett. She taught first and second grade in her home and was a strong advocate of phonics. In no time Tim was reading like a champ.

My mother wanted to help my children's education, so she gave them the complete set of the children's *World Book Encyclopedia*. Before he had reached his teens, Tim had read every single volume in the set. This was before the days of electronic devices, so on vacation we often played what became known as the Word Game.

One of the participants would start with a letter, and then the next individual would have to add a letter. Anytime a letter was added, the person could challenge if indeed it was forming a word. The object of the game was not to let a word end but to be able to pick up the beginning and carry it on to a successful conclusion.

As we traveled, my children grew more and more literate. Then I encountered public education. Modern educators had given up on phonics and had begun teaching reading by what was called the "look-say method." Children were being taught to look at a picture of a monkey with a long tail that might resemble a *y*. So they would look at the monkey, see the tail, and spell out *y*.

I know that sounds insane, but a lot of things many professional educators do would seem to be insane to a rational person. Of course, under this new method of teaching, many children in major public school districts were considered functionally illiterate when they left third grade. Because these older children could not read the material, they grew bored and rebellious. Many eventually dropped out of school.

A course in phonics called Sing, Spell, Read & Write was brought to my attention. The premise of this course was that children learned reading much better when they could sing the material. Indeed, it proved true. I took a team of young teachers with me, and we went to churches in the inner cities of New York, Philadelphia, Washington, Baltimore, and Chicago, and throughout the South. Using Sing, Spell, Read & Write, we could guarantee literacy in no more than thirty-six lessons, and our students gained a working vocabulary with as many as ten thousand words.

This reading method was revolutionary. I remember one three-year-old boy who stood up in front of a church congregation and proudly read from a local newspaper with complete fluency.

But the professional educators would have no part of it. I remember one article that was written by a secular educator titled "So What If Johnny Can't Read…We Have Him Until He's 18 Years Old."

Then they introduced what was called the new math. They did away with the multiplication table that all of us were forced to memorize when we were young. If a child was asked to give the sum of five plus four, and he said nine, he would be given a bad grade. He was taught instead that the answer was "a little more than eight and not quite ten." So what has been the result of this distorted pedagogy?

We have brought about a generation of young people where many have received social promotion in our public schools but can lack the ability to make intelligent, critical decisions. It's no wonder that some of the self-called Millennial Generation are eagerly embracing socialism and turning their backs on the free enterprise system. More recently educators have been pushing Common Core State Standards, which ultimately mandate the teaching of a progressive quasi-socialist agenda in all schools in America.

The leading figure in the effort to radicalize America's education was a man named John Dewey, who lived from 1859 to 1952. Dewey was a professor at Teachers College at Columbia University and an atheist who was part of the committee that drafted what was called the Humanist Manifesto.

In this manifesto it was stated that there was no such thing as a supernatural God, that there was no validity to an inspired book called the Bible, and that human beings were not unique creations of God but were the product of natural evolution.

Dewey was responsible for helping institute in higher education a practice called tenure, which was intended to protect radical teachers from being summarily fired by conservative school boards. Thousands of graduates of Teachers College at Columbia University went forth into the schools of America having been taught radical views that completely undermined the belief in God and the biblical view of man.

I determined that the School of Education, which I was privileged to found at CBN University, would have as its target the pernicious influence of John Dewey's Teachers College. Although our effort started small, I am pleased to report that the successor of CBN University, Regent University, now offers a master's degree in education as well as a PhD in education. From our school have come the following: one nationally acclaimed Middle School Teacher of the Year, eight hundred Virginia Teachers of the Year, ten college presidents, principals in about 75 percent of the communities in and around Tidewater, and tens of thousands of well-trained teachers who were able to take their places in the schools of America.

Before I leave this chapter, I want to point out another powerful educational force in America, the teachers' union called the National Education Association (NEA). In the 1976 convention of the Democratic Party that nominated Jimmy Carter for president, one-third of the delegates were NEA members. Carter's payoff was the establishment of a federal Department of Education. The initial funding for this department was $10 billion.

At the time I write this book, the annual funds received by the Department of Education have ballooned to $59.9 billion,[1] and any attempt to throttle back this monstrosity is immediately labeled anti-education. In short this means that a radical union violently opposed to standards for teachers has available its own $60 billion government slush fund.

That is a hefty war chest to fight against, which is why I'm grateful that we're doing everything we can at Regent University's School of Education to push back against this tide of secularism.

36

"I Am Sending My Spirit All Over the World"

EACH YEAR IT'S my custom to spend the week between Christmas and New Year's Eve in a time of special prayer. I like to go someplace where I can be alone with a couple of yellow pads of paper. And while I wait on the Lord, I ask for His direction about what I should be doing in the coming year, or what He will be doing with us.

As I was praying during the Christmas week of 1976, the Lord spoke to me and said, "I am sending My Spirit all over the world. Millions of people will respond. I want you to proclaim a simple message of salvation. Do not try to teach complex theological matters. Just preach the simple gospel."

I came back and told the staff what I had learned, and in our New Year's prayer meeting, we formally launched what would be called WorldReach with a staggering goal: to win five hundred million souls to faith in Jesus Christ throughout the world in the years ahead.

One of our people suggested that we light a gas flame on the land in front of our headquarters building to commemorate this decision. I laughingly said that this was an awful waste of money, burning up all that natural gas. But we did it anyhow, and our flame is still burning as I write this book.

God has been true to His word. Many nations have opened up to our broadcasting over the years, which has given us the opportunity to present invitations for members of our audience to profess faith in Jesus Christ.

Over the years, we've engaged two survey firms—one called Ipsos and a firm headed by two of Regent University's Communications professors, Drs. William Brown and Benson Fraser. Year after year we have recorded tens of millions of decisions for Christ, and we give all glory to God for the huge number of people who have responded to the gospel through our programming. In the one year just before I started writing this book, the total has exceeded a staggering one hundred million souls.

The Lord is not done yet. Without question the key to spiritual success is seeing where God is moving and then following in His footsteps.

37

MAXIMUM SECURITY

IN MARCH 1977 I reached my forty-seventh birthday with a strong
desire to do something to help the subculture of our society housed
in federal prisons. By then a former Black Muslim from Uvalde,
Texas, had joined me as cohost on *The 700 Club*. His name was Ben
Kinchlow, and he was a striking six-foot-five-inch somewhat gangly
African American fellow who quickly won the hearts of our viewers.
Ben had a keen insight and a ready wit, so much so that he could have
had an alternate career as a stand-up comic.

A maximum security prison in Raiford, Florida, housed murderers,
rapists, and assorted criminals. Our team was given the privilege of
addressing these men, but we were locked in with them. If there had
been any prison riots, we easily could have been killed. Facing that
kind of situation certainly heightens a person's prayer life. Not only
did I pray to the Lord for protection, but I prayed for a message that
would touch the hearts of these people.

When it came time for us to speak, the men were rowdy. Then Ben
Kinchlow took over. He was hilarious. He told of his experience as a
Black Muslim working for Elijah Mohammad, who instructed Ben to
leave normal citizens alone but if they ever touched him to send them
to the cemetery. As he spoke, the men slapped one another's hands,
they stomped on the floor with delight, and they were ready to hear
the gospel when he turned them over to me.

As I spoke, I talked of a young man who had been railroaded by the
judicial system and falsely accused of a crime He didn't commit. Then
I described the punishment that this innocent young man had had to
endure.

The Lord gave power to each word as I described the cat-o'-nine-
tails tearing the flesh off of the back of Jesus Christ. I could see these

hardened criminals wincing in pain as they felt the suffering of Jesus Christ. It wasn't me who was speaking—it was the Holy Spirit. But these men understood the concept of unjust judges, of somebody taking the rap for them and suffering in their place. When I extended an invitation, hardened criminals, murderers, and rapists came forward to surrender their lives to Jesus Christ.

When they came forward, not only did they shake my hand, but they also hugged me. Later on I heard from the heavyweight boxing champion of the prison, who told me that one of the men who hugged me was such a vicious killer that he was terrified of him.

After we left, a holy hush descended on that prison. The men walked in love with one another for at least a few days. There were no knife fights, no rapes, no physical assaults. They sensed the holiness of the God who had touched their hearts.

Later our producer, John Cardoza, developed a ninety-minute television special called *Maximum Security*, which became the basis of the CBN prison ministry. We gave free spiritual tapes and tape players to a hundred or more prisons.

With this effort before the advent of Chuck Colson's Prison Fellowship, CBN became the largest prison ministry in America, and I'm pleased that God could use us in this way.

38

OPERATION BLESSING AND A
THREE-BY-FIVE CARD FILE

ON A FRIDAY in the fall of 1978 I was sitting in a chair in my living room overlooking the big yard and magnolia tree outside the window. I had my Bible in my lap, and as I asked God for a word for the day, I opened the Bible to the fifty-eighth chapter of the book of the prophet Isaiah.

In this passage the prophet, speaking on behalf of the Lord, said, "Is this the kind of fast I have chosen, only a day for people to humble themselves? Is it only for bowing one's head like a reed and for lying in sackcloth and ashes?"[1]

The Lord said in Isaiah 58:6–7: "Is not this the kind of fasting I have chosen: to loose the chains of injustice and untie the cords of the yoke, to set the oppressed free and break every yoke? Is it not to share your food with the hungry and to provide the poor wanderer with shelter—when you see the naked, to clothe them, and not to turn away from your own flesh and blood?" (NIV). Then the prophet went on with this astounding promise:

> Then your light will break forth like dawn, and your healing will
> quickly appear; then your righteousness will go before you, and the
> glory of the LORD will be your rear guard. Then you will call, and
> the LORD will answer; you will cry for help and he will say here am
> I...The LORD will guide you always; he will satisfy your needs in a
> sun-scorched land and will strengthen your frame. You will be like
> a well-watered garden, like a spring whose waters never fail. Your
> people will rebuild the ancient ruins and will raise up the age-old
> foundations; you will be called Repairer of Broken Walls, Restorer
> of Streets with Dwellings.... I will cause you to ride in triumph on
> the heights of the land.
>
> —ISAIAH 58:8–14, NIV

See Isaiah 58:6–14 to read this passage in its entirety. As I read this section of Scripture, I was amazed. I thought, "I am a New Testament believer, but this is Old Testament. Is it relevant today?"

The answer was yes, and it was becoming clear to me that this was something extremely desirable and represented the most extensive blessing that I understood to date. So I determined in my heart that these blessings would belong to CBN and to me.

Jim Collins, a researcher and business consultant, has studied American corporations that he classified as great. In his 2001 book, *Good to Great: Why Some Companies Make the Leap...and Others Don't*, he set out some of the salient characteristics of these successful companies. One he identified as a "bias toward action."[2]

You've probably heard the clichéd expressions "paralysis by analysis" and "A camel is a horse formed by a committee." They are often used to convey the challenges of a group's inaction and indecision. Conversely, in Spanish the word *ahora* means "now," and the word *ya* means "Do it this second." I'm a *ya* kind of person. I'm biased toward action.

On that Friday I left the house and headed for our studios on Spratley Street in Portsmouth, knowing that we had thirty-six telephone counseling centers nationwide where viewers could call in for various reasons. About fifteen minutes before going on air, I told the team, "Send the word out to our counseling centers that when we go live, we're starting a new program. It's going to be called Operation Blessing."

After we signed on, I told the audience that I wanted to share with them a program that the Lord had just revealed to me: Operation Blessing. I took a blackboard and wrote down what God had asked us to do: feed the hungry, clothe the naked, and house the homeless. Then I listed what God would do in return.

When I finished, I said, "So here's what I am asking you to do. If some of you have extra canned food that you want to give to the poor, give us a call. If some of you need food, give us a call. If some of you can give others a ride to the doctor or the beauty parlor, give us a call. If someone has a need for a ride to one of those places, give us a call."

The idea was to match the abilities of our audience with the needs of our audience. In those days there weren't PCs or laptops. We had to write down all these things on little three-by-five cards. And so Operation Blessing began with a three-by-five card file, albeit a pretty large one.

It wasn't long until our systems became much more sophisticated and the extent of our humanitarian efforts expanded dramatically. We organized a separate charity called Operation Blessing International Relief & Development (OBIRD). We quickly grew from handling small gifts to facilitating massive food distribution. We bought a fleet of tractor trailers to haul produce trucks and refrigerator trucks, calling the fleet the Hunger Strike Force.

We organized hospital teams and sent them to third world countries to assist suffering poor people who had no access to medical care. In times of disaster we commissioned teams of construction workers and volunteers to rebuild homes. We hauled millions of pounds of potatoes and other produce from the farms of America. We learned the nutritional value of brown rice and purchased millions of pounds of it from Arkansas farmers. And we were the recipients of millions of dollars of medicine from pharmaceutical companies in America.

A simple Scripture reading and a box of three-by-five cards grew in time to a CBN subsidiary that has helped about three hundred million people around the world with an estimated four billion dollars' worth of food, medicine, clothing, and clean water.

When Bill Clinton was president, he called a group together to the White House to discuss third world debt relief.[3] The head of the Budget Committee for the House of Representatives was a Republican congressman from Ohio named John Kasich. John's mother was an ardent viewer of our *700 Club* television program and had urged her son to watch, which he did. When Kasich learned of our missionary work overseas, he invited me to come to the White House to be part of this prestigious gathering with President Clinton in attendance.

The problem we would be considering was the crushing burden of debt among third world countries. In many of these nations, vicious dictators had profligately squandered the assets of their countries and amassed large debts. When their democratically elected successors were unable to pay their bills, this left many of these developing nations unable to access international credit markets. The issue before the gathered congregational leaders and administration officials was the cancellation of this colossal amount of third world debt.

When my turn came to speak, I stated that these debts were uncollectible and we would be wise to write them off and give these struggling nations a fresh start. This sentiment was echoed by a majority of those at the meeting.

Shortly thereafter the United States canceled about four hundred million dollars in third world debt,[4] and members of the United Nations followed suit and canceled a remarkable thirty billion dollars in third world debt,[5] which gave many poor nations in Africa that much-needed fresh start.

As we were leaving, President Clinton walked around the room and shook the hands of all who had been there. When he got to me, he took my hand into his and said, "This is the second good thing that we've done together."

I was somewhat taken aback. "Well, what was the first, Mr. President?"

"You remember that rice farmer in Arkansas that I bought a rice mill from China for? I remember when Ben Kinchlow came with the Operation Blessing trucks to pick up the rice."

I then realized this man's enormous appeal to people. President Clinton had a remarkable memory, incredible charm, and a brilliant mind. He worked well with the Republicans. His political adviser had told him, "There are certain things that conservatives want. I suggest you give them everything they are asking for. From then on out they won't oppose your agenda." And that was generally true.

The best example came when he and House of Representatives Speaker Newt Gingrich, a Republican, were able to craft a remarkable change in our welfare laws.[6] If it hadn't been for his sexual proclivities, which became legendary, Bill Clinton might have been remembered by some as one of America's great presidents.

Today Operation Blessing is one of the most efficient charities in America and one of the most effective in the world. From the distant reaches of Western China to the crisis in Tibet and the tornadoes in the American heartland to the earthquakes in suffering Puerto Rico, Operation Blessing teams are at work. As one African leader commented, "Operation Blessing comes with a Bible in one hand and a bag of food in another." I am amazed at what God did by expanding one simple chapter from an Old Testament prophet—He created an organization dedicated to easing the suffering of hurting people that reaches around the world.

39

Moose Smith Out, News In

During the mid-1970s *The 700 Club* program aired daily in the Philippines. In the process CBN became the first religious broadcaster in American history to broadcast overseas with a television program.

Soon after, we put *The 700 Club* on the air in Canada, Taiwan, and the South American countries of Brazil, Chile, and Colombia. We also had a Spanish version of our program that aired in Puerto Rico.

By January 1979 CBN had counseling lines open around the clock. Our sixty *700 Club* counseling centers responded twenty-four hours a day across the nation. We had eight call centers in foreign countries and seventy-five hundred volunteer counselors.

As 1979 came to a close, I called our key program staff together for a special retreat. I asked them to bring me the surveys that had been taken regarding the program preferences of our viewers and potential viewers.

At that time, our main program, *The 700 Club*, featured a bearded young musician from North Carolina named Moose Smith in a band with a piano player, a drummer, a bass player, and a sax player. They played the opening theme, the closing theme, and various transitions in the middle of the show. Our audience surveys showed something very startling.

The younger people despised older hymns and traditional church songs. The older people despised youth-oriented worship songs and the up-tempo rock music of contemporary Christian music. What they both liked were news broadcasts and dramatized testimonies of salvation or miracle healings. These surveys clearly showed that the large sum we were spending on a house band was not helping us hit our target.

After careful deliberation, we let the house band go and determined that we would divide the hour available to us into three sections. We devoted the first twenty minutes to news, the next twenty minutes or so to dramatized testimonies, and the last twenty minutes to answering spiritual questions or providing other items of interest to the audience.

There is no question that our emphasis on hard-hitting news from a Christian perspective set *The 700 Club* apart from the overcrowded world of religious broadcasts. In fact it can be said that this move was groundbreaking.

The apostle Paul gave what I considered clear guidance as to how a ministry should be structured. First of all, he boldly proclaimed that he would not build on another man's foundation.[1] As far as I'm concerned, the Lord Himself is the author of great creativity. It certainly isn't necessary with that source of inspiration to try to poach someone else's ideas.

Secondly, the apostle Paul made it clear that a man should only build on Jesus Christ as the foundation. He taught that all of us build foundations either of gold, silver, and precious stones or of wood, hay, and stubble. Paul taught that all of our work would be tried in the fire, and the wood, hay, and stubble would burn up. The person involved would be saved, but only by the skin of his teeth.[2] So the goal of those of us who are assigned to build and innovate is to be sure that what we are doing glorifies the Lord and that our motives are pure and not underhanded or deceitful.

The Book of Proverbs also teaches us that we can't go it alone. It says, "For by wise counsel you will wage your own war, and in a multitude of counselors *there is* safety."[3]

The Bible tells us that "God resists the proud, but gives grace to the humble."[4] There is a fine line for those who earnestly seek to be led by the Holy Spirit of God and to act on God's direction. Only the fool refuses wise counsel. The secret is for a person to surround himself with wise counselors, for the companion of wise men will become wise.[5]

We in America have had our fair share of presidents who thought they were smarter than their advisers. We read in the Book of 2 Chronicles that Rehoboam, the son of Solomon, faced conflicting advice from two sets of advisers.

The old men who had known his father said to him, "If you will be kind to these people and please them and give them a favorable answer, they will always be your servants."[6] When Rehoboam asked the young men who had grown up with him whether he should ease up on the tax burden on the people, they said, "Now tell them, 'My little finger is thicker than my father's waist....My father scourged you with whips; I will scourge you with scorpions.'"[7]

At that, the people of Israel cried out, "What share do we have in David?"[8] Ten tribes defected because the king took terrible advice. Rehoboam only had Judah and Benjamin remaining and was faced with continual warfare.

Before Jesus Christ was crucified, He took on the form of a servant and washed His disciples' feet. He said, "If I then, your Lord and Teacher, have washed your feet, you also ought to wash one another's feet."[9] The true role of greatness is to be a servant. The more people a person can serve, the greater he becomes.

Our university business school teaches what I call servant leadership. What I have learned as I have walked with the Lord is that He took on the form of a servant, laid aside the splendor of the Godhead, and sacrificed His greatness for me. Therefore, God highly exalted Him.

As I come nearer to the end of my days on earth, I delight in the title "servant of God." There is no greater honorific, in my opinion.

40

I Regret Helping a Former Peanut Farmer Gain the Presidency

Those of us who were alive during the early '60s remember them as an era of national turmoil. In 1963 John F. Kennedy's shocking assassination left the nation stunned.[1] Within five years we witnessed the murder of civil rights leader Dr. Martin Luther King Jr. and of President Kennedy's brother, Bobby Kennedy, in 1968.[2] Adding to the turbulence of the time was the escalation of America's involvement in Vietnam and the protests that accompanied it. In November of 1968 Eisenhower's vice president, Richard Nixon, was swept into the White House by a large margin.[3]

I met with Nixon and found him to be an incredibly astute student of world affairs. I shared with him that in my law school days I had seen a law journal article he had written in my tort casebook. He remembered the article and the precise legal points involved.

Nixon's brilliance was clear, but his presidency was complicated. He was sure that highly placed people in his administration were leaking valuable secrets, so he established what he called the White House Plumbers to try to find the leaks.[4]

People associated with his administration did some bad things. The beginning of the end for Nixon happened when *Washington Post* reporters Bob Woodward and Carl Bernstein wrote their exposé of Watergate based on information from a confidential informant known as Deep Throat.[5] This source turned out to be former FBI deputy director William Mark Felt.[6]

After Richard Nixon resigned the presidency in disgrace and flew off to California, his vice president, a warmhearted former congressman from Michigan named Gerald Ford, was named the new president of the United States.[7]

In the wake of these tumultuous events I wanted to mobilize prayer for America. We produced a program called *It's Time to Pray, America!*, which was syndicated to a large audience across the country. We featured not only President Ford but also leading figures in entertainment, government, and business.

Since American politics typically revolve from Democrat to Republican and vice versa on an eight-year cycle, I could tell that the country was ready to elect a Democrat in the 1976 election. One of the leading candidates was a peanut farmer and former governor of Georgia named Jimmy Carter.[8] He was not only a Southern Baptist Sunday school teacher, but Carter told the world he was a born-again Christian.[9] You had to like that.

I flew to Carter's home in Plains, Georgia, and met for a seated interview around a table on his outdoor terrace. We discussed a wide range of issues and spoke about his Christian faith. I remember tiny gnats called no-see-ums attacking us. This forced me to talk out of one side of my mouth while I blew the gnats away from the other side. When we finished, I thanked Carter, drove back to the regional airport in an adjoining town, and flew back home.

Carter was having success in some of the Southern states, but he had not broken through in any Northern state. I had gotten to know a couple of men who were associated with the United Steelworkers of America. One was an interesting fellow named Francis "Lefty" Scumaci.[10] I told him a born-again Christian was running for the Democratic nomination and it would be nice if the United Steelworkers of America would back him. Under Lefty's urging, the steelworkers did just that. Suddenly the campaign of this Southern governor was validated by a primary win in Pennsylvania,[11] which was considered a Northern industrial state. From there Carter rolled on to a national victory.

Louis Sheldon, a Presbyterian minister from California, was working with our university, and he in turn had become a good friend of Jimmy Carter's. I thought perhaps Carter would be interested in having some strong evangelical Christians in his cabinet. Lou contacted Carter and was told he might be open to a proposal of potential candidates. We put together a list of superb people who were leaders in industry, banking, and government.

Through a friend of mine in the civil service I was able to get my list of potential candidates vetted by the FBI, and they all came out clean. Lou then took the list and flew to Americus, Georgia, and then drove to Plains.

When he knocked on Carter's door, our new president-elect was standing barefoot in blue jeans and welcomed Lou inside. Lou then handed over our carefully drawn-up list. When Carter looked at it, he began to cry. Later when I heard this story, I knew why. I told Lou, "He wasn't crying because he was touched with gratitude. He was crying because the deal was already fixed and the decision regarding his cabinet was not really his."

Unfortunately, I was correct. Jimmy had been taken over by what was called the Trilateral Commission, founded by David Rockefeller in 1973.[12] Carter's final picks included a few Christians, but the bulk of his administration was composed of members of Rockefeller's Trilateral Commission.[13]

What ensued was, in my opinion, one of the worst presidencies in modern history. Carter was so obsessed with minutia that he even kept a list of who got to play on the White House tennis court. I remember reading one commentator who remarked, "Excessive attention to detail may be a worthy attribute for a chicken sexer, but it hardly serves a president of the United States."

During Carter's only term our staunch US ally, the Shah of Iran, called him and said, "The people are rioting. Can you help me?"

Carter's icy response was, "We don't get involved in the internal affairs of other nations."

The Carter administration, following the advice of a four-star general sent from Germany to Iran, decided that the government of Iran should be turned over to a shadowy figure who had been exiled by the Shah. His name was Ruhollah Khomeini. His title, Ayatollah, came from two words, *Ayat Allah*, which means "emissary of Allah."

Soon a vicious theocratic dictatorship descended on that once free land, and more than forty years later our nation is still struggling against this country. The shouts of "Death to America" we hear in Iran to this day began back in 1979 when street thugs under the control of the Ayatollah stormed our embassy and held the personnel captive.[14] Instead of vigorous, swift action, Carter's indecision caused him to retreat to the Rose Garden as a sign of mourning.[15] He did attempt one rescue effort, but that ended in disaster when a helicopter collided with a plane in the Iranian desert.[16]

The Iran hostage situation was not the only time Jimmy Carter displayed what I would call ineptitude. In the African nation of Zimbabwe there had been a vicious fight between two well-armed militias. After a truce was declared, a free election was held, and Methodist Bishop Abel Muzorewa was elected president. President Carter and his adviser, Andrew Young, however, decided not to support that free election. Instead, Carter demanded a second election, in which they supported Robert Mugabe for president.[17] During the ensuing decades Mugabe proved to be a vicious dictator who brought that once prosperous country to a state of desperation. In 2019 Mugabe died at the age of ninety-five.[18]

Added to the folly in Zimbabwe came the incredible assertion by Carter's chief African adviser that the presence of ten thousand Cuban Communist troops in Angola proved a "stabilizing influence."[19]

Carter was so thoroughly discredited before the 1980 election that the former governor of California Ronald Reagan won a resounding victory in the Electoral College, 489 to 49, winning forty-four states in the Union.[20] The Iranians now knew that a man of action was in charge.

On the day of Reagan's inauguration the Iranians released our embassy personnel, and we were able to send in airplanes to take them to Germany and then to the States.[21]

That was great news that we celebrated with the nation on *The 700 Club.*

41

THE BEATLES, THE RONETTES, AND NORTHEAST RADIO

O N FEBRUARY 7, 1964, when I was about thirty-four years old, the so-called British Invasion hit the United States. A music group from Liverpool, England, called the Beatles arrived in New York City and was welcomed by thousands of screaming teenagers.

The Beatles dressed in Eton-style suits and sang remarkably creative, original music. Paul McCartney, John Lennon, George Harrison, and Ringo Starr overwhelmed the music industry, and week after week, one or more of their songs topped the charts.

They were booked with much acclaim on the *Ed Sullivan Show*, where the nationwide television audience was huge. During their stay in New York, a popular deejay for station WBIC on Long Island named Scott Ross recorded one of the first interviews with the Fab Four.[1] Scott was the son of a Scottish minister and a godly mother. While in New York, he met and married Nedra Talley, the youngest member of a singing group called the Ronettes.[2] This group had a smash hit called "Be My Baby" in 1963.[3] In England, the Ronettes were so popular that the promoter placed a group known as the Rolling Stones as their opening act.[4] The Beach Boys listened to the Ronettes to pick up the appropriate rhythm for some of their hit songs.[5] Nedra Ross has been inducted into the Rock & Roll Hall of Fame in Cleveland,[6] where she joined major stars in the industry.

But back to Scott Ross. While he had been seeking God's will for his life, he met Pastor David Minor from Pennsylvania, who taught him many things about biblical values and then contacted me to see if I was interested in hiring this New York disc jockey. When I met Scott, we hit it off. I liked his manner and knew that his experience would be a decided asset to our WXRI staff in Portsmouth.

Scott joined our staff and lived with us in the country until he could rent a place for himself and his young wife, Nedra. Oh, and I need to tell you that Scott was white, and Nedra was a mixture of races: African American, Native American, and Hispanic.

The first day he was on the air, his shift was in the late afternoon. His shift had been previously occupied by a preacher named Dr. C. W. Burpo, who lived in a remote place in the desert of Arizona with a small watering hole and virtually no vegetation.

Burpo had a keen imagination and sold the audience on the idea that while he was on the air from Arizona, he was looking out on a sparkling lake teeming with fish and wildlife and a profusion of fruits and vegetables. One member of our audience actually believed this stuff, hooked up a trailer carrying his yacht, and traveled to Burpo's place to set sail on the beautiful lake.

When Scott got on the air, people began to call to ask where Dr. Burpo was. Scott, in his innocent way, asked, "What's a Burpo?" That brought a great deal of laughter from our staff.

After a few months, Scott brought Nedra down to Portsmouth. Remember, this was a time before federal civil rights legislation. The segregation of the races was in full swing in our area. At the time, I knew absolutely nothing about Nedra's distinguished singing career. All I knew was that my new disc jockey was married to an African American woman living in segregated Portsmouth.

Perhaps I should explain the situation in the South at that time, the mid-1960s. Virginia was in a state of massive resistance to the integration of our schools. Restrooms, restaurants, lunch counters, and of course schools were segregated. Even drinking fountains were segregated.

Certain states had laws against miscegenation—the marriage of white and African American people. There were laws on the books in some states making it a crime to teach an African American person to read or write. I refused to give in to the bigotry of the moment because I felt that spiritually born-again men and women were my brothers and sisters in Christ, and we were all part of God's family.

During this time we had on our payroll a man named Sam Tolbert, who was our vice president of engineering, which made him the highest-ranking African American executive in the state of Virginia. Sometime later, I hired Ben Kinchlow to be the cohost of *The 700 Club*. Ben won the hearts of the audience with his extraordinary intelligence and ready wit. I didn't think of myself as much of a pioneer; I just knew that whatever the prejudices of the day, we were not going to submit to any of them.

Threats were made to me demanding that I fire Scott and send away this "obnoxious interracial couple." My anger rose. I believe the Bible had instructed that whether rich or poor, male or female, African American or white, we all were one in Christ Jesus. I refused to yield to bigotry, and Scott and Nedra became dear friends.

Not too long after this I was approached by an offer to give the CBN five radio stations in upstate New York that had comprised the old Ivy Network. These stations stretched across Route 20 in upstate New York from Albany all the way to Buffalo. They were WGIV, WEIV, WOIV, WMIV, and WBIV.

The control room for this network was located on Connecticut Hill outside of Ithaca, New York. During the winter months, the steep hill where the studio was located was covered with snow and ice. To reach the studio, our people had to park their cars and walk a considerable distance through the driving snow or slippery ice. It was anything but easy.

The Lord sent us some of the most talented radio people in the nation. Larry Black came down from Hartford. Bill Freeman came from Kansas City. Scott Ross moved up from Virginia. And the manager, Andy Anderson, was a native New Yorker. These fellows put together a blend of contemporary Christian music that was as good as anything on the radio anywhere. The sound was fantastic, and we built a loyal following.

There was a technological problem we couldn't solve, however. The stations were located outside of the major metropolitan areas, and the signal we put out did not reach those major populations. It was a great experiment, but the economics were against us.

Scott and Nedra rented a small farm in Freeville, New York, and opened up what could be described as a commune. They grew delicious fruits and vegetables and ministered spiritually to the surrounding neighborhood.

Unfortunately, Scott had somewhat of a temper, and he clashed with Andy Anderson, the manager of the Northeast Radio Network. I reluctantly asked for Scott's resignation. Not too long after that, it was apparent that the Northeast Radio Network was not viable, and we either sold the stations or gave them away. A few months later, I was in Colombia, South America, and I was on my knees praying on a Sunday morning. I said, "God, please save the youth of America. Use me to save the youth that they might turn to You."

The Lord spoke back and said this: "You fired the man that I gave you to save the youth of America. Contact Scott Ross when you get back home."

I contacted Scott and tried to smooth over whatever differences there had been. We made plans for a radio program that would be geared to the youth of America.

I realized that the big rock 'n' roll stations were hurting for weekend talent. We put together a six-hour package using Scott as on-air talent playing a well-chosen selection of pop and contemporary Christian music. We offered this package to top-rated radio stations across the country on a barter basis and found that it was readily accepted.

Without going into more detail, I can only say that the *Scott Ross Show* not only touched people for the glory of God but garnered substantial ratings all across America.

As I write this book, I am pleased to report that Scott Ross is still here with us after fifty years. He and I together have been the hosts of several television specials, the last of which was called *The Plan*, and Scott proved to be a valuable spiritual resource to all of those in our audience.

I'm glad I listened to the Lord and we got things turned around with Scott, who's a great friend.

42

THE LARGEST CHRISTIAN
NATION ON EARTH

BEGINNING IN 1966 the Cultural Revolution under Mao Zedong rocked the nation of China.[1] To those of us in America, China was viewed as an impenetrable black hole under the grip of Communist tyranny. President Richard Nixon broke through in his historic state visit to China in 1972, where he was pictured toasting Chinese leadership in the Great Hall of the People.

Not too long after that, I visited Hong Kong and traveled to what were called the New Territories. My associate, Ben Kinchlow, joined Dede and me in standing at the border of mainland China. As we stared across a fog-covered valley, we joined hands and prayed that God would open that country to the gospel.

A year or so later I was invited to visit China by a government agency known as the "Committee on Friendly Relations." I realized that former President Nixon was an expert on China. I went to see him and ask for his advice.

"You ought to try to meet with the former mayor of Shanghai," he said. "His name is Zhu Rongji. He's an up-and-comer in the Chinese government."

I flew into Beijing, the capital of China, and was warmly welcomed by the Committee on Friendly Relations with the assurance that they would facilitate a meeting with Zhu Rongji, who at that time had become first vice premier of China. I walked into a large hall for this important meeting. In an official setting like this, the participants sat on chairs on a raised platform with an interpreter sitting behind them. Their respective aides were seated on the floor below them in rows facing each other.

I talked with Zhu about the extraordinary growth of the gross domestic product (GDP) of his country and mentioned to him the names of several people who would be mutual acquaintances. Then I explained to him that evangelical Christians in his country were hard-working supporters of his government and that their presence as loyal, hard-working citizens would be a long-range asset to China.

I talked to him about the characteristics of America that led to its remarkable growth. We both realized that the United States' GDP was approximately ten times that of China. I later learned that Zhu had shortly thereafter attended a meeting of a Communist Party Politburo. The interview was published in length in the official Communist newswire, *Xinhua*, which was the equivalent of receiving the official endorsement of one of the party leaders. At that time, I was given the designation as "friend of China." On subsequent visits I was identified as an "old friend of China."

God had clearly opened the door to answer a prayer that we had prayed years before when we looked into what seemed to be impenetrable darkness.

Subsequent to that we were asked to provide theological training for theological students seeking to become ministers in the state-sanctioned Three-Self Church, and our broadcast was officially sanctioned by the Chinese government.

I remember one amusing incident when I was privileged to meet with the head of the Ministry of Poverty Alleviation in China. His words to me and my words to him had to pass through an interpreter. As I was speaking to him, I was praying for wisdom from the Holy Spirit to give me the exact words to say.

I started by asking him a question, "What is your definition of poverty?"

He demurred at first, and then he finally spoke out, "Any food level below two thousand calories a day is considered poverty."

I then explained to him that I headed an organization that was delighted to serve the poor and needy with food, medicine, and education. After hearing that, he replied with a smile, "We can give you twenty-five thousand villages if you would like to take care of them."

When I think of the persecution of Christians in the past and I hear of the persecution of them in the present moment, I marvel at the extraordinary favor that God showed me during my time in China.

In one of my many visits to China I came across a book that described how the gospel was found in the Chinese language. Instead of the letters that we use in our English language alphabet, the Chinese language is portrayed in characters that are called Kanji. These Kanji tell an interesting story. In the early days of mankind, one group of people left the Garden of Eden and moved from the Middle East into China. They formed a pure and wonderful religion with a language based on what we would call the Old Testament. The Chinese language dates at least three thousand years before Christ, whereas Moses lived about fourteen hundred years before Christ.

Consider the stories portrayed by these Chinese Kanji. In the Chinese language, the direction "west" is depicted as two people in a garden (think Adam and Eve). The Kanji for the devil is "a man in a tree speaking lies." The Kanji for an ocean vessel is "eight people in a boat" (think Noah and the ark). The Kanji for happiness is drawn with a picture of "a man in a garden in the presence of the god of heaven," whose name is Shangdi.

The philosopher Confucius, who lived during the Zhou dynasty, wrote that if a man could understand the "border sacrifices," he could rule China.[2] What are the border sacrifices? They refer to a time approximately 2256 BC during the reign of Emperor Shun, who symbolically offered the borders of China to the unknown god, Shangdi.

The Emperor would come with great fanfare, walk up a set of steps, and offer his country to the unknown god who was portrayed not by a figure, but by a scroll in a chair represented only by his name.

I had dinner in Beijing with the Chinese ambassador to the United States, who later became Foreign Minister. He, by the way, was a great Shakespeare scholar. I went over my understanding of the Kanji of his language with him, and I mentioned some of the examples I shared with you plus several others. He verified that my understanding was correct. And then I observed, "Do you understand that Christianity is not an alien religion, but your Chinese beliefs spring from the core narrative from the Christian Old Testament?"

It was clear I had given him something to think about.

The Chinese people venerate Confucius, who is not considered a religious figure but a teacher of morality. In the writings of Confucius, the foremost human emotion is called *li*,[3] which I understand is synonymous with the love urged by Jesus upon His followers.

In one of my early visits to China I went out on the street in the dark, and soon a small group of curious Chinese people gathered around me. Through an interpreter, I told them that I had come from the United States and that the reason for our prosperity was our belief in the God of heaven and His Son, Jesus Christ. Then I explained that if they would receive Jesus as their Savior, they would be welcomed into the kingdom of heaven. It was like a scene out of the New Testament. When these Chinese people heard that, they actually laughed with joy to think that they could become children of God. When an invitation was given to receive Jesus, they reverently bowed their heads and prayed the Sinner's Prayer with me.

When the prayer was over, one member of the group said, "This is illegal. Let us disperse." They dispersed, but not before a number had been welcomed into the kingdom of God.

That experience was merely a microcosm of what was happening all over China. As I write this, there are an estimated 120 million evangelical Christians in China[4] and ten or more million Roman Catholics. If current trends continue, China is on course to become the largest Christian nation on the face of the earth.

The Chinese government remains ostensibly Communist, but I have repeatedly reminded my Chinese hosts that Karl Marx was not Chinese but a German of Jewish ancestry. In discussion with members of the Chinese Communist Party, I found them unable to give any kind of rational defense of Communism or what is called the Hegelian dialectic.

It grieves me to see the hostility that some militarists in the Chinese leadership have been expressing against the United States and their neighbors. We certainly don't embrace Marxist Communism, but I do feel we should embrace our Chinese brothers and sisters who I believe share wholeheartedly in New Testament Christianity.

It remains to be seen what will happen to Christianity in China in the near future. Will there be a crackdown on house churches, or will the church blossom?

We don't know what the future holds, but we do know the God who holds our future.

43

FALSE SHEPHERDS AND
THE TRUE COVERING

THE HOLIEST DAY of the Jewish calendar is called Yom Kippur, the Day of Atonement. What is the biblical basis of such a day and such a name?

In the Jewish temple built by Solomon, there was an area called the holy place, and beyond that, the holy of holies. In the holy of holies was a box called the ark of the covenant. On top of the box was a lid. On the Day of Atonement, the high priests would enter the holy of holies and sprinkle blood on what was called the *capporeth*, or lid of covering. When the blood was applied to this lid, it symbolically shut out the testimony of the tablets of the law that had been placed inside the ark. Because of the lid of covering, the testimony against the people of Israel did not reach God. Therefore, on this day they were "at one" with their Creator.

In the New Testament the apostle Paul described Jesus as our *hilasterion*, which is the Greek translation for the Hebrew word *capporeth*. Unfortunately, the King James Version of the New Testament translates the Greek word *hilasterion* as "propitiation."[1] The fact is, nobody really knew what propitiation was. But Paul's real meaning was that Jesus Christ is our lid of covering. You'll understand why this biblical foundation is needed as you read what happened next.

Amid the joy we were all experiencing during the height of the Charismatic Movement, a countermovement arose in Fort Lauderdale, Florida, that, in my opinion, was controlled by a spirit of witchcraft. It became obvious later on that they didn't understand biblical Greek and biblical Hebrew, nor did they understand that the Bible says Jesus Christ is our covering. Instead, these men began to tell women that their husbands were their covering. They went beyond that, however,

162

to something much more insidious. They said that Christians were nothing but sheep, and sheep needed to be led by a shepherd.

According to them, every Christian needed to be subservient to a shepherd who in turn was supposed to be responsible for their salvation. This doctrine was expanded to reflect a status of master and servant. The shepherds were given the power to dominate the lives of their "sheep." They could approve their marriages, their choice of education, their choice of employment, their selection of a home, and even what type of car they could drive.

As the doctrine progressed, adherents of "shepherding" would gather together in circles and pray curses against those who disagreed with them. So here's what happened to me:

My teenage daughter, Ann, began to show symptoms of influenza. I checked her temperature and found it to be normal. It was clear that she didn't have true influenza, but something else was affecting her. I left her room and went back to my bedroom and sat on the floor facing a floor-mounted television.

As I pondered my daughter's illness, I realized what had happened. The shepherds in Florida had prayed a curse on my daughter that caused her pseudo-illness. I jumped up and shouted, "Satan, you can't do this to me!" and ran back to my daughter's room and said, "Come over here." I laid my hand on her and commanded the spirit of witchcraft to release her and return to where it came from. As that prayer ended, my daughter affirmed with a smile that her headache was gone, and the flu symptoms had left her as well.

A brief word here about my daughter, Ann. She is our youngest child and looks the most like me. She has developed into a wonderful woman with a tremendous sense of humor and a remarkable facility to organize public events. Ann's husband, Gary LeBlanc, has made quite a name for himself with an organization called Mercy Chefs, which is distinguished by providing hot meals to first responders in disasters that have taken place all over America and other parts of the world. Her children have excelled. Her daughter Christy, along with her former husband, won the Western Hemisphere Moot Court

Championship and went on to claim the National Championship in England. Christy is currently serving as a special litigator on the staff of the ACLJ.

Ann's son, Raymond, is set to graduate from Hampden-Sydney College in Virginia with a near-perfect academic record and has been accepted for a special term at Oxford University. Ann's lovely daughter Megan recently married a young Christian man she met while attending King's College in New York City. My forecast is that Megan will become the mother of many wonderful children, but that is yet to be seen.

Demos Shakarian, my longtime friend and president of Full Gospel Business Men's Fellowship International, and I both cared deeply for the people who had been entrusted to our care, and we did everything in our power to point out the evils of "shepherding." Gradually the Charismatic community began to wake up to the dangers of shepherding, and the doctrine fell into obscurity.

I learned one thing, however. The Bible tells us that "...evil comes to one who searches for it."[2] We weren't seeking evil, but even a fight against an evil force, if it goes on too long, can damage a righteous warrior. We clearly need to turn our attention to what is noble and good and not what springs from witchcraft.

44

Washington for Jesus

In the early spring of 1980 when I turned fifty, I was approached by my good friend John Gimenez, pastor of Rock Church in Virginia Beach. If you recall, I had met John during the London meetings of the Full Gospel Business Men's Fellowship International when John was performing with a singing group called The Addicts.

John had been a hard-core heroin user who was in and out of rehab and jailed countless times. He was so bad off that an attendant in a prison hospital laid beside him a loaded .38-caliber revolver in the hopes that he would use it to terminate his drug addiction by ending his life. Fortunately, God took hold of this man and brought him to Virginia Beach, where he and his wife built one of the largest churches in the area.

In 1980 prior to the election, the United States was gripped by what President Jimmy Carter had termed "a crisis of confidence."[1] A pall did hang over the country. John came to me and said, "I feel that God wants to bring Christians together for a massive prayer meeting in our nation's capital."

Then he began to recount to me the people he thought would come to such an event on the National Mall in Washington, DC.

"John," I said, "if you can bring together two thousand churches with only a hundred people each, you will have a crowd of two hundred thousand people. The logistics of such a gathering will be staggering."

"What logistics are you talking about?" he asked.

"We'll have to feed them," I replied.

He thought for a minute and then shot back, "Let 'em fast!"

Having solved the logistical problems, I then asked about the program. John said that he would like to have Bill Bright, the head of Campus Crusade for Christ; Demos Shakarian, president of Full

Gospel Business Men's Fellowship International; and me as program chairmen. We drew up a list of speakers that included Roman Catholic priests and well-known Episcopalian, Presbyterian, Lutheran, Baptist, Methodist, and Pentecostal clergymen. It was a strictly interdenominational group.

Our purpose was decidedly nonpolitical. We were coming together to pray God's blessing on a great nation.

The Washington for Jesus event took place outside in an area between the Washington Monument and the US Capitol. A huge crowd assembled, which I had estimated to be at least five hundred thousand people.[2] No matter what the final tally was, this was the largest prayer meeting in the history of America up to that time. Rain clouds appeared from the west, and yet as we looked in that direction, the clouds parted, and we all stayed dry.

Hour after hour we cried out for God's blessing on this nation. In one amusing incident my associate Ben Kinchlow took the microphone and instructed the massive crowd to raise their hands and faces toward the Capitol Building. Then he commanded the demons to leave the Capitol and set this nation free. We were later told that wide-eyed congressional staffers were looking out the window and seeing this huge crowd pointing at them and casting out demons.

We carried the entire proceeding on CBN, and I am convinced that this massive prayer effort became a turning point in the spiritual and political life of this nation.

I also like the symmetry. Someone pointed out that the date of Washington for Jesus, where we reaffirmed our nation's spiritual heritage, was April 29, 1980, which matched the date of April 29, 1607, when English settlers prayed at Cape Henry for our nation's spiritual founding.[3] It's easy to see God's hand was in that.

45

A ROUNDABOUT TRIP TO TOKYO

IN 1981 I was participating in a short prayer retreat in the mountains of Hot Springs, Virginia. As I was praying, the Lord clearly spoke to me that we should target the nation of Japan for our television ministry. Then the Lord went on to explain what we should do. He said that previous attempts to broadcast in that area had failed because we had devoted too few resources to the effort. In Marine Corps terminology, "You hit the beach with too few troops." God said, "I want you to allocate a sizable amount of money to this effort."

When I was in the marines, I had been the Top Secret Control Officer of the First Marine Division and had traveled from time to time from our division headquarters in Korea to the Dai-Ichi Seimei Building in Tokyo, which was the headquarters of General MacArthur. Before going to Korea, I had been stationed at a marine base known as Camp Otsu, which was just south of the former capital city of Kyoto. In other words I had some experience living in Japan.

During the Korean War, Japan was still suffering from the effects of World War II. By the 1980s, however, Japan was booming and producing high quantities of television sets, which also meant Japan was fully covered by television broadcasts.

I didn't have a clue as to how to begin the effort that the Lord had assigned me. So I waited for direction, which came shortly thereafter. But the Lord surprised me when He said, "I want you to go to Mexico City."

I'm sure if you look at an atlas, you'll find that there's no direct route from Virginia to Tokyo that goes by Mexico City, and yet I told my good friend Stan Ditchfield to pack his bag. We were going to Mexico City.

We arrived at the airport, took a cab, and checked into a hotel in the center of Mexico City. I had absolutely no contacts in the city, but Stan knew a company that did language dubbing from English to

Spanish, so he went to see them and negotiate prices for the dubbing of our programs.

I waited about five days, feeling both bored and frustrated, and decided to check out of the hotel and fly back home. As I walked out of the hotel to get a cab to head to the airport, I met Stan coming up the walkway accompanied by two Japanese men, one of whom was named Watanabe and who happened to be the manager of the Fuji Television Network in Toyko.

The Bible says that "the steps of a *good* man are ordered by the Lord."[1] Once again, He had ordered my steps correctly.

I arranged with Watanabe-San to visit his Toyko network headquarters, and soon after that Stan and I were winging our way across the Pacific to Toyko. During my meeting with Watanabe-San, I explained that I was looking to purchase airtime for our religious programs. In America when a proposal was outrageous, my counterpart would look across the table and tell me that I was out of my mind. The Japanese were too polite to do that, so they whispered to somebody else in Japanese, "Robertson-San is full of it. Would you take care of it for me?"

So Fuji referred me to the giant advertising agency Dentsu. Our deal was much too small for Dentsu, so they shuffled us off to Tatsunoko Productions. This agency was interested in our business, and I told them that I wanted to get mass distribution of a Japanese-language copy of the New Testament because by now I realized that the Japanese had no concept of a holy God, sin, salvation, heaven, or hell. I wanted to use all of the means of communication to sell Japanese-language New Testaments, and we were soon able to find willing partners in grocery stores, drug stores, kiosks, magazine sellers, and booksellers.

Our ad agency explained that American hippies were the *in* thing in Japanese culture, so we arranged TV ads that featured a bearded hippie without a shirt lying on the back of a big Harley motorcycle, trimming his fingernails with a huge buck knife. He then screamed out and threw the knife into the air, at which time it transformed into the title of our New Testament, *Alive Again*.

A few weeks later, though, we were told that hippies were no longer the *in* thing, so I asked, "What's *in* now?"

They replied, "A Japanese girl looking like the Mona Lisa, staring into space as if to ask, 'What is the meaning of life?'"

So the final iteration of our book had a white cover, a friendly face, and a picture of a young Japanese girl looking like the Mona Lisa and staring out into space. With the distribution partners we put together, our New Testament became one of the top ten best-selling books in Japan.

I then asked how we should gain access to Japanese television. I was told that cartoons were very popular and that cartoon shows had high ratings on television stations throughout the country. So our next move was to come up with a cartoon series, which I knew would be expensive.

Our Japanese design staff created a young boy and young girl, along with a robot they called Gizmo. The young boy and girl went up to the attic owned by their great uncle, and in the attic they found a large book that they were able to open. And when they did, they were launched back in time to the Garden of Eden, where they met Adam and Eve when they were being cast out of the garden because of sin. Then they went through the Old Testament battles and the victories of great warriors like King David.

We made fifty-two animated episodes of *Superbook*, where the principal characters were drawn with round eyes and faces that could be from any culture. When we aired *Superbook* on Japanese television, the audience watching was greater than the total number of Christians in the whole country.[2]

We later aired *Superbook* with dubbed-in English language in Hong Kong, where the programs scored number one in the ratings. We saw the same thing as *Superbook* scored number one on the BBC on Sunday mornings in Great Britain.

Our next animated series was named *Flying House*, and once again, our two little people and their sturdy robot traveled through space and appeared with Jesus at the important points of His ministry as outlined in the New Testament.

I was able to bring a couple of our writers from Virginia to Toyko to help perfect the scripts. Once again we made fifty-two episodes that were aired all over the world. I estimate at least five hundred million people have been able to watch these wonderful stories.

Here's another way God used this animated series. At that time, Russia was closed to the Christian faith. Communism in Russia was strictly based on atheism.[3] A copy of our cartoons, however, was smuggled from Finland into Russia by a man named Hannu Haukka.[4] This copy made its way to the home of an executive of the principal Russian television network. He thought the material was so interesting that it should play on Russian television.

In those days, a Russian Bible was so valuable that it could be traded for a cow. So the television executive contacted Finland to see if he could obtain the full set of the fifty-two episodes. We were delighted to comply with this request, and soon our *Superbook* cartoons—dubbed into Russian—were being aired throughout the Soviet Union over a national network.

I wanted to take advantage of this opportunity and sent word that we would like to have a contest for the children to offer them free New Testament Bible excerpts in Russian. I was astounded at the answer by a Communist official. "We'll allow you to have the contest you mentioned," he said, "but you must be sure that you have enough Bibles because we don't want to disappoint the children."

So we started the contest and offered the Bible excerpts to children if they could answer three simple questions: "Who is God?," "Who is Jesus?," and "What is the Bible?"

Soon after that, the mail poured into the Moscow post office, so much so that the postmaster came to our representative and said, "We've got so much mail, we don't know what to do. So here's what we propose. We'll give you all the mail. You keep what's yours and give us back the rest."

Who would have thought that in a Communist country such an opening for religious belief would have taken place? But here again I saw the powerful hand of a miracle-working God.

46

MIDDLE EAST TELEVISION IS BORN

A T THE END of World War II, the country of Lebanon was an absolute paradise. The Lebanese capital of Beirut was known as the Paris of the Middle East.[1] The shining city had beautiful hotels, plenty of shops, and fine restaurants and was known for its excellent banks. Lebanon was famed in the Bible because of its lofty cedars and superb climate.

The Lebanese people had arranged a political system in which Christians and Muslims shared authority, with the presidency being held by a Christian and the office of prime minister being held by a Muslim.[2] All of that began to change when members of the radical Palestine Liberation Organization (PLO) moved from Jordan into Lebanon in the early 1970s.[3] They set up refugee camps in tents outside of Beirut and began open warfare against the existing order in that lovely country.

When Syrians tried to join with the PLO to capture Beirut and northern Lebanon, forces loyal to the Lebanese government set up an enclave in southern Lebanon on the border of Israel. Israel felt that the Lebanese would welcome liberation from the oppression of Syria and the radical acts of the PLO.[4] But when Israeli forces began an artillery barrage against the Syrians in Beirut, they were condemned by the United Nations.[5] The Lebanese people had been given a choice: either side with your friends in Israel and accept freedom, or else accept the control of Syria. Regrettably they chose to side with the Syrians and their Muslim neighbors.

The loyalist leader of Lebanon was Camille Chamoun.[6] He sent his son, Dany, to organize military resistance in the south of the country.[7] Dany Chamoun in turn chose a Major Haddad to set up an independent territory in southern Lebanon. Major Haddad had his forces centered around the town of Marjayoun, which is just north of the border of Israel.[8]

My friend George Otis was looking to begin radio broadcasting in the Middle East and realized that Major Haddad had the authority to grant him a radio license. George approached him, received approval, and started broadcasting a program called "High Adventure."[9]

Later, George received permission from Major Haddad to broadcast on VHF Channel 12 throughout that area. Before long, George realized that the complexity and expense of operating both a radio station and a television station was too much for his small organization to undertake. He wrote me, "I won't hold up the second coming of Jesus by being selfish. I think that the CBN can do a better job of running this station than I can, so I'm willing to give it to you if you will accept it."

I had dreamed for years to have a chance to broadcast in that part of the world—and have a shot at broadcasting into Israel. Now that chance was being given to me. This station in southern Lebanon was in a war zone, however. There was a real possibility that it could be overrun on any given day by either Syrian armed forces or PLO terrorists. Our organization could be seriously embarrassed if we invested a large sum into a venture like this and then suddenly lost it. As much as I wanted to go forward, I had to be certain that God was directing this move.

At the time, Dede and I had begun a practice that I cherished. We would each take a Bible, and she and I would pray silently, and we would ask the Lord to give us a word from the Scripture that would contain the necessary guidance that we needed. So we prayed. I thought something came to me, but when I opened the Bible, it had no relevance whatsoever.

"What did the Lord show you?" I asked Dede.

"Here's what I got," she said, "but I don't understand what it means."

I then took her Bible and looked at the word the Lord had given her. It was Isaiah 29:17–18, which reads, "In a very short time, will not Lebanon be turned into a fertile field and the fertile field seem like a forest? In that day the deaf will hear the words of the scroll, and out of gloom and darkness the eyes of the blind will see" (NIV).

I closed the Bible and said to Dede, "The station is in Lebanon, and God is telling us from Lebanon will go forth the Word of the Lord, and the power of God will open the eyes of the blind."

I called George Otis and said, "Brother, I've heard from the Lord in Isaiah 29. I will accept your gracious offer."

"Would you believe that's the same Scripture that God gave to me when I started this venture?" he said.

"That doesn't surprise me," I replied.

We took the station and upgraded the facilities. We had a communication link all the way to Beirut, and our receiver was located on the tomb of the ancient Hebrew prophet Obadiah. The tower was located at a higher place from the studio. We began broadcasting in Arabic and English, and to a lesser degree in Hebrew. I renamed the station Middle East Television, and we were off and running.

The PLO and the Syrians didn't exactly welcome our efforts. A car bomb was set off outside our studio. I tried to make light of it by quipping, "The terrorists at least showed a certain panache. They didn't just blow up an old Chevrolet. They blew up a relatively new Mercedes." But of course the situation was serious.

Perhaps our most popular TV program was World Class Championship Wrestling, a forerunner to WWE, the professional wrestling shows started by Vince McMahon. The Muslim viewers loved it, and it quickly became the number one show on Saturday nights.

The Syrians also decided that Saturday nights would be a good time to lob an artillery shell at our transmitter, which knocked a wire loose so that our transmitter was dark for a short time. This proved to be a costly mistake on their part because their act aroused particular animosity among the population, which had been needlessly deprived of their favorite World Class Championship Wrestling show.

We obtained other wrestling tapes to put on the air, and frankly, we didn't screen each one. We put one on the air and were horrified to discover that it was not World Class Championship Wrestling but Women's Wrestling. I thought viewers would be incensed, but lo and behold the viewers loved it, and we had no complaints whatsoever.

Our Middle East Television station broadcast a variety of interesting programs that were far superior to anything being shown in the region. Not only were we teaching the gospel, but we were able to get rights to sports programs such as the NFL championship games. Although there had been permission from the Israelis to broadcast in English and Arabic, we had not been cleared for broadcasting in Hebrew. With the advent of cable television, cable systems throughout Israel began carrying our station, and at that time we had no problem translating a number of programs into Hebrew.

Middle East Television became the first of its kind in the Middle East, making our network a trailblazer for other similar efforts that would follow.

47

LAWS OF THE INVISIBLE KINGDOM

As I watched the administration of Jimmy Carter and later the beginning of the Reagan administration, more and more I was asking the Lord to show me the secrets of how His universe worked. What were the principles?

When I was in seminary, I studied *The Progress of Dogma*, by Professor James Orr. I learned about the nature of the Godhead called theology, the nature of Christ called Christology, the nature of man called anthropology, and the nature of salvation broken down under the heading objective and subjective soteriology. But there was a great deal more that I needed to know.

I came to the conclusion that if Jesus Christ is indeed God, then general statements He made without reference to place or date would have the same force as physical laws such as the law of gravity. Using this concept as a guide, I then read the Bible looking for these principles. Lo and behold, there appeared before me a set of principles that I determined would govern all human activity. I identified eight and then later ten.

Of these principles, which I named, the first was called the Law of Use. When coupled with what is called the exponential curve, the Law of Use controls the growth of physical nature, the growth of intelligence, and the growth of organizations. Those who use what they have been given will be given more. Those who do not use what has been given them will lose what has been given them.

Since I enjoyed weightlifting in the gym, I tried this principle. I would lift a given load of weight until I was comfortable with it, then I would add about 10 percent more and lift that until I was comfortable. Then I would add 10 percent more to that until I was comfortable, and then 10 percent more and so on.

On the quad leg press rack, I started with two hundred pounds and then kept going until I reached a point where I could push five hundred pounds with my legs. Then I went on to a record seven hundred pounds, became comfortable with that, moved on to eight hundred pounds, and finally reached a point where my daily workout consisted of thirty repetitions of one thousand pounds each. In short the Lord had set up a principle that applies even to financial matters—compound interest, or what nineteenth-century banker Baron Rothschild termed the Eighth Wonder of the World. Albert Einstein claimed the mystery of compound interest, and America's leading investor, Warren Buffett, has amassed an enormous fortune by arranging an investment strategy that has brought about compound returns of about 25 percent a year. For that, there is even a Rule of 72 by which a person can divide 72 by the annual rate of return to determine how many years it will take for that money to double.[1]

Then I discovered the Law of Reciprocity, which governs all social interaction, and the Law of Greatness, and the Law of Responsibility. I set out the fundamental principles in a draft outline of a book and then called on the assistance of my good friend Bob Slosser, who had been an editor at the *New York Times*, to give the material the finishing touches. *The Secret Kingdom* was a national best seller when it was published in 1982, setting forth a glimpse of the unfathomable wisdom of our God.

The Secret Kingdom lives on and is available today on Amazon.

Dede and me at the groundbreaking of our headquarters

Our radio station didn't start in a stable but in an old garage.

We shamelessly copied *The Tonight Show*.

I asked for 700 but got only 330.

Operation Blessing in action

I operated our only camera…black-and-white.

The blessing of our ancestors is transferred.

Dede and I review a television script.

A bold master plan has been fulfilled.

Sixto López translates in Bogotá for *Momentos de Gozo y Alabanza.*

Our first television station, in Portsmouth, Virginia

A cardboard cross, dry-rotted curtain, and beat-up desk for an early TV show

Scott Ross—God's man to reach the youth of America

The Family Channel was a smash hit!

Early days learning the craft

My secretary, Barbara Johnson, put up with me for forty-five years.

Ben Kinchlow and me on the early set

Billy Graham electrifies the crowd at the grand opening of our CBN headquarters, a beachhead for Christ in the twenty-first century.

George W. Bush told me Billy Graham led him to the Lord.

Jay Sekulow, chief counsel of the American Center for Law and Justice and lead counsel for the president of the United States

A shared joke with former chairman of the Joint Chiefs of Staff Colin Powell

A warm visit with the prime minister of China

Prime Minister Rabin of Israel: "Be strong!"

Archbishop Makarios, spiritual leader of Cyprus

Prime Minister Ariel Sharon entertains me at a special luncheon.

My dear friend Bibi Netanyahu, prime minister of Israel

Former president Nixon, a deeply
flawed man but a brilliant strategist

Rabbi Yechiel Eckstein, a pioneer in
Jewish-Christian friendship

The Left and the Right in one of our
many Regent University debates known
as "the clash of the titans"

Dede and me with the president of the
Philippines

We are signing the deed for the
Metroplex property.

My friend former Israeli prime minister
Ehud Olmert

A hearty laugh in the Oval Office with former president George Bush and former chief of staff James Baker

My ordination council

Strategy before the election

Jay Sekulow, a fierce legal advocate

The Donald and my granddaughter
Abbey

My favorite president talks about sending Ollie North to Iran.

I interviewed the future president at his home in Plains, Georgia.

Looking like a country squire

Ufano performing the piaffe

Nuzzled by my Russian horse, Ziggy

Aristocrat, my Trakehner stallion

A night of miracles at the Araneta Coliseum in Manila, Philippines

Operation Blessing helping people

The Flying Hospital spanned the globe.

We prepare to fly out to test a one-million-watt transmitter in Costa Rica.

Seven hundred thousand in Hyderabad, India

My love affair with the Indian people

Los niños in Latin America

My lovely wife

My growing family

A chubby five-year-old

The dream home!

Gordon and me at his law school graduation

Proud father with his oldest son, Tim

Right tackle, McCallie, 1945

I drove from New York to pick up Dede and our family from her folks' house in Columbus, Ohio.

As a young man I met President Truman.

A marine second lieutenant in front of Robert E. Lee's portrait

My Baptist ordination at Freemason Street Baptist Church with Dr. Lumpkin and my father

My wonderful family

The Allegheny Mountains, where I can sit for inspiration

The old marine can still shoot.

Two thousand pounds...once!

In frozen North Korea with my classmate John Warner, later secretary of the navy

General Shephard, Colonel Bigfoot Brown, and me reviewing the troops in Korea

Preparing to march as combat marines

The young shavetail

MANHATTAN ★ ★ ★ ★ SPORTS FINAL

RUPERT: TAKE IT OR ELSE . . .
Story on page 2

DAILY ◉ NEWS

35¢ NEW YORK'S PICTURE NEWSPAPER® Tuesday, February 9, 1988

DOLE ROLLS IN IOWA, BUT . . .

ROBERTSON BURNS BUSH

Gephardt, Simon and Dukakis lead Dem pack

Story on page 5

THE DOG-BONE ARISTOCRACY MEETS

TAKE A BOW

Clancy, an Irish wolf-hound, gets a grooming in preparation for annual gathering of the dog-dom — the 112th Westminster Kennel Club Show, which opened at Madison Square Garden yesterday. He's one of 2,649 competitors. Show continues today. Critic-at-Large David Hinckley gives it a look. **Page 30**

NICOLE BENGIVENO DAILY NEWS

DAILY NEWS RICH & FAMOUS SWEEPSTAKES - You could win **$1,000,000** -See Page 16 for today's winners

New York Daily News Archive via Getty Images

The press couldn't believe I did it in Iowa.

The *Saturday Evening Post* asks, "What's next for Pat?"

A political rally in New Hampshire

The studio headquarters, almost finished

From Monticello and Colonial Williamsburg

We pray again over the studio headquarters.

We used a lot of steel.

With Gordon and Terry Meeuwsen

Beautiful *700 Club* cohosts

The Shaw Chapel is modeled after St Martin-in-the-Fields at Trafalgar Square in London.

The law school to train future Supreme Court justices

Regent University theater

The miraculous library

A Regent commencement with a confetti bomb

A jam-packed commencement at Regent University

The Bible comes alive at the Mount of Olives, overlooking the Old City.

My news team: Chris, Wendy, and Mike

Our Jerusalem correspondent, Chris Mitchell

Fox interviews me at the war zone in Israel.

Some rockets got through in northern Israel.

Incoming rockets, flak jackets, and me in a leisure suit

48

ONE MIND, ONE VOICE

B Y AUGUST 1982 CBN University had grown to approximately three hundred students studying several important disciplines. I realized, however, that for the university to grow, we would have to have an adequate library and additional classroom spaces. Without these added facilities, the university would be like a teenage child being forced to sleep in a baby bed.

I met with an architectural firm to build a library and a new class-room facility around an open atrium, not unlike what I had seen when I visited my father's office at the US House of Representatives in Washington. I had plans drawn up that were suitable for construction, but then a staff revolt struck me.

I had hired as our chief financial officer a former banking vice president from New York City. He was gifted with a typical banker mentality that saw the glass half empty instead of half full. In truth our CBN finances were somewhat precarious and we were behind in paying some of our bills. This well-meaning gentleman was sure that we were imperiling our finances by trying to operate CBN and pay the bills of a struggling university at the same time.

I knew we had built the university by the direct command of the Almighty and, therefore, God was going to fulfill what He had prom-ised. So I called together a full meeting of our entire staff. They sat in rows on the pull-out bleachers that were part of our main studio.

"I believe that the Lord wants us to build a library and classrooms for CBN University," I began. "If we are all together, we will accom-plish this task successfully. However, even if this is God's will, if we are divided and in opposition, the project will fail."

I also recalled the words that the Lord had spoken at the Tower of

Babel, which was a structure built by sinful people to challenge the authority of God.

God's appraisal of human ability is striking. The Book of Genesis records His words in this manner, with italics added for emphasis: "If as one people speaking the same language they have begun to do this, then *nothing they plan to do will be impossible for them*."[1]

So I said to the assembled staff, "I'm not asking any of you to do any extra work. I'm not asking any of you to give any money. I'm not asking that you be involved in any way, except to pray. But I do ask this: Please don't go around in the halls, behind my back, saying how crazy I am and how much you hate this project. Just keep your mouths shut and watch what the Lord will do." They all nodded in agreement that this wasn't that hard a task for them to accomplish.

Before this day I had already secured the approval of the CBN University Board of Trustees. So by faith I signed a contract with a general contractor to construct a twelve-million-dollar library and classroom building large enough to accommodate one million volumes and classrooms adequate to accommodate one thousand students.

Then the miracle began. After the first month, from totally unexpected sources, we received an extra one million dollars. On the second month, again from unexpected sources, we received another one million dollars. On the third month, from the same unexpected sources, we received another one million dollars. And so it went month after month after month…another one million dollars from unexpected sources…until the end when we had received twelve million dollars. We completed our library building and new classrooms debt-free.

Over and over I remind the staff at Regent University today that if they remain in harmony with one another, nothing they propose to do will be impossible for them.

49

Don't Ask Me, Ask God

I N THE EARLY '80s it was clear that not only did the Japanese lack literacy in the Bible, but the youth of America were growing up biblically illiterate as well. We had big black Bibles full of text written in stilted and hard-to-understand King James English. It's amusing to think that a number of ministers at the time would fill their sermons with translating the old English into language we speak today. One particular piece of confusion was the use of the phrase "Holy Ghost" to describe the Holy Spirit. I wanted very much to have a user-friendly Bible.

Dick Thomas was our CBN vice president in charge of marketing. Together we set out to focus-test every item of our proposed Bible. We tested the color of the cover, the typeface of the cover and interior text, the name of the book, and especially the translation that we were going to use. We chose the title *The Book*.

I felt that we also needed to produce a prime-time television special that we could show all across the country. We commissioned the Gallup organization to survey the American public to discover "what one question you would ask God if you could." We then tabulated the results, and taking the top ten questions, our producer, Warren Marcus, put together dramatic vignettes under the title *Don't Ask Me, Ask God*. He also assembled an A-list of well-known actors, each of whom was paid five thousand dollars for his or her appearance and clearance for our lifetime use. We had Michael J. Fox, Vincent Price, Ruth Buzzi, and Norman Fell, among others.

The first question was, "Will man ever live at peace with his fellow man?" We dramatized a battle scene in our studio that featured a white soldier and a black soldier who had been gripped by racial animosity until they died in each other's arms on the battlefield.

We had Vincent Price in a horror scene. We had a touching scene about heaven depicting a father burying his son's pet goldfish and discussing whether or not there were flies in heaven. I was serving as host on the program with a lovely lady from Hollywood named Anita Gillette. This program garnered a 10 national rating and became one of the highest-rated TV specials of all time.[1]

After the last showing of *Don't Ask Me, Ask God*, we opened our telephone lines for questions and received more calls than had come in through the entire run of our big production. It showed me that people in our world were desperately anxious to be in touch with their Creator and to learn the reality of His destiny for them.

Then, in the late '90s, we set a goal to improve biblical literacy in America and to get a portion of the Bible into ten million homes across our nation. It was called "The Book of Hope Campaign." Dick Thomas had been replaced by Tom Knox, who was CBN's senior vice president of marketing. He had worked as a sales manager for the satellite company known as Dish TV. Tom linked up with a very creative CBN individual named Edie Wasserberg who had a marvelous facility for writing prose, music, and ad copy.

We worked with Tyndale to publish *The Book* in the New Living Translation. We also printed over ten million portions of scripture called *The Book of Hope*. CBN distributed them to homes in fifty major cities across America using our network of affiliate churches. We supported it with a marvelous TV promotion campaign and a song that Edie had written called "Take Me to the Book." Recording artists MC Hammer, Smokey Robinson, Chaka Khan, Andraé Crouch, and Ricky Skaggs were just a few of the celebrities who participated in the recording. We had endorsements from sports figures, entertainment celebrities, and government officials.

We delivered over ten million portions of scriptures, and a survey conducted before and after the campaign determined that biblical literacy in America had increased.

50

SPIRITUAL BLITZES
AROUND THE WORLD

DURING 1983 CBN programs enjoyed dramatic growth. We went on air in Chile, Costa Rica, the Dominican Republic, Ecuador, El Salvador, Guatemala, Honduras, and Peru. At the beginning of 1984 CBN programming was on the air in sixty-six countries.

I had observed that Hollywood's major film studios, when introducing new features, would use a concept called four-walling. They would open a major film by renting screens in every theater in a town. If anyone in that town wanted to go to the movies, they were much more likely to see their new release. I thought this technique would prove effective overseas, so here's how we proceeded.

If we decided to broadcast in a country such as Nigeria, we would air a week or even a month of special programs at night on as many of their TV stations as we could buy time on. We would then support the television broadcasts with massive radio commercials and, where appropriate, newspaper advertisements. We also had film teams with 16mm projectors travel throughout the rural areas, accompanied by one or more people to bring a Christian message.

When a month had elapsed in the target country, there would be almost no segment of the population that had not heard the gospel of Jesus Christ. Since most of our television broadcasts contained a simple invitation for recipients to turn their lives to the Lord, we finished these blitzes with the good news that millions of people had turned their hearts to the Lord and had become born-again Christians.

Later in 1984 I put together a book called *Answers to 200 of Life's Most Probing Questions*, which drew from those questions featured in our national survey and then was amplified by theological questions that people were raising. This book became a national best seller and to my knowledge was the number one religious book of the year.

Despite what you may have heard about the carnal, irreligious nature of people, we discovered an overwhelming spiritual hunger that God Himself had brought about in the world. I was delighted to be able to direct a ministry dedicated to fulfilling the deep cry of the hearts of people around the world.

But there are always detractors and people putting roadblocks in your way, such as the American Civil Liberties Union, or ACLU.

51

TAKING ON THE ACLU

AFTER I FINISHED law school, I was shocked to see successive Supreme Court decisions—many of which were engineered by the ACLU—eroding the moral pillars of our society. The ACLU had been founded by a radical named Roger Baldwin to defend convicted Bolsheviks whose sole objective had been the overthrow of our government.[1] There seemed to be no way to stop this liberal steamroller. In successive rulings, the Supreme Court deemed as unconstitutional prayer in public schools,[2] reading the Bible in public schools,[3] and other religious exercises.

The 1936 Constitution of the Soviet Union stated, "The church in the U.S.S.R. is separated from the state, and the school from the church."[4] The term "separation of church and state" appears nowhere in the US Constitution. However, one Supreme Court judge, Hugo Black, who had himself been a member of the Ku Klux Klan and was a rabid anti-Catholic,[5] seized on a letter that Thomas Jefferson wrote in 1802 to the Danbury Baptist Association that assured the Baptists that there was a wall of separation to prohibit the secular government from interfering with church affairs.[6] Justice Black and the Supreme Court affirmed that the Constitution had established a wall of separation between the state and the Court would not permit the slightest breach.[7]

Of course, Thomas Jefferson was not part of the drafting of the Constitution, and Justice Black took Jefferson's remark out of context. Nevertheless, Supreme Court jurisprudence had been dominated by the thought that any form of theistic thinking violates the Constitution. This in turn explains the bitter fight that emerges in Congress every time a conservative is nominated for the Supreme Court.

Here's why this issue is personal to me. Back in 1788, Orange County,

Virginia, sent two delegates to the Virginia Ratifying Convention where delegates ratified the US Constitution. One was James Gordon, and the other was James Madison.[8]

James Gordon was my father's grandfather five generations removed. My father's ancestors were the Baptists in Virginia who had lobbied Thomas Jefferson to pass the Statute of Religious Freedom in Virginia.

To put it mildly, my father was an expert on the Bill of Rights and the Constitution, especially the First Amendment, and also the meaning of the phrase "establishment of religion." He was incensed at the 1962 Supreme Court ruling that banned prayer in the public schools, and he appeared before a Senate committee headed by Senator Sam Ervin of North Carolina to protest that Supreme Court ban on prayer in the schools. Years later when I read his statement, I found that I had personally echoed every sentiment that my father expressed in his appearance before that committee.

Over the years, I felt something welling up within me to resist the legal bulldozer that was destroying the very heart of our freedom. I founded an organization called the National Legal Foundation and engaged a brilliant lawyer named Jay Sekulow to try an important school prayer case called *Board of Education of Westside Community Schools v. Mergens*. An 8-to-1 decision written by a noted liberal judge established the right of students to pray voluntarily in schools as a Constitutional right.[9]

Unfortunately the National Legal Foundation didn't survive, and I had to go back to the drawing board. One morning I was on my knees in my bedroom praying about the situation when word came to me that Jerry Falwell was planning to establish a legal arm. With no disrespect to Jerry, I knew that he did not have a trained legal background and that the burden to resist the ACLU had been given to me.

As I prayed, I opened my Bible and my eyes fell upon the words of Jesus, who said, "A person can receive only what is given them from heaven.... Every plant that my heavenly Father has not planted will be pulled up by the roots."[10] As I realized that the legal arm to be formed was given to me by my heavenly Father, I formed the ACLJ.

Jay Sekulow was the ideal man to become chief counsel of this organization, but Jay was working with Moishe Rosen, the founder of Jews for Jesus, and a subsidiary organization called CASE, which stood for Christian Advocates Serving Evangelism. After several false starts with other people, I approached Jay. When Moishe Rosen gave his blessing, Jay joined the ACLJ as chief counsel.[11]

Since that time the ACLJ has become one of America's leading appellate law firms with numerous victories before the Supreme Court and district courts and circuit courts as well. Briefs by the ACLJ are so well regarded by the Supreme Court that *certiorari* (agreement to hear the case) is granted in a majority of our cases.

Indeed the word that the Lord gave me while I was on my knees in my bedroom praying about the opportunity to serve our Lord in this vital capacity has come to pass.

And that's been very gratifying.

52

"Are You Going to Run for President?"

As I pointed out earlier in this book, I was born into a family involved in public service. Two of my collateral ancestors are descendants from Nathaniel Harrison: William Henry Harrison and Benjamin Harrison, who were both presidents of the United States. My father went to Congress when I was two years old and served for thirty-four years, first as a member of the House of Representatives for fourteen years, and then for twenty years as a member of the US Senate.

Politics has long fascinated me, and until I was fifty-five, I considered myself a member of the Democratic Party, as was my father before me. The profound shift leftward in the Democratic Party led me to join the Republican Party in the mid-1980s.

I have something in my nature that cries out to create things, and one of my creations was called the Freedom Council, which formed as a 501(c)(3) tax-exempt organization to train people for political action. Within the Freedom Council there are established state and local chapters and significant training. Each precinct represents a cohesive neighborhood but also a unit for political action.

I also joined and was later made president of an organization called the Council for National Policy. This organization was intended specifically to counterbalance the effects of the Rockefeller-dominated Council on Foreign Relations and its sister organization, the Trilateral Commission. The Council for National Policy included a number of conservative leaders and some officials in President Ronald Reagan's administration.

Up until this time, the concerns of evangelical Christians had not been given a voice in national politics. On the left were the ACLU, the labor unions, and those who favored a collectivist form of government. From those with a conservative worldview, we found a ready audience to join us in the Freedom Council, and the organization grew dramatically.

I was with Ronald Reagan when he spoke to a large gathering of evangelical Christians in Texas. I knew members of his cabinet. Reagan's tax policies were brilliant, and I was a fan of his muscular foreign policy that said, "We win, they lose."[1] I even had the privilege of drafting part of the speech he gave to the meeting of the National Religious Broadcasters in Washington. So as the 1988 presidential election loomed after President Reagan's second term, I was asking myself: "Who will follow him?" I had never served in public office, but somehow I felt that my fervent embrace of Reagan's policies might qualify me as a potential successor. In meeting after meeting I learned the longing of evangelical Christians to be governed by laws and policies set down by someone who shared their biblical worldview. It was my custom after speaking to groups like the Freedom Council to open the floor for questions. Invariably, I would be asked, "Are you going to run for president?"

My answer was simple: "What do you think?" In each instance, there was a roar of approval.

Again, how could a minister and broadcaster who'd never held public office possibly compete for this job? Of course, some might say that leaving the ministry to enter politics should be considered a demotion. That view is humorous but not lacking in realism.

So I told myself that I would lay before the Lord a challenge. If three million registered Republican voters signed petitions agreeing to support my candidacy, I would do it.

On October 1, 1986, I formed a political exploratory committee called Americans for Robertson. At the same time, I closed down the Freedom Council. From other sources I obtained names and lists from various sources, and before long, we had the three million names that I had been requesting. But I knew that wasn't enough.

Later that fall, a mighty hurricane came barreling out of the Atlantic and headed straight for our city. I got on my knees in my bathroom and said to the Lord, "If I can't move a hurricane, I certainly can't move a nation. I will now command that hurricane to leave our shores and go back into the Atlantic. But if it hits us, I'm out of this race and will leave it to others." I was so confident that the hurricane would hit us that I went to bed and slept like a baby, knowing that I was out of the race.

I woke up the next morning and looked out. The sky was clear, the birds were singing, the sun was shining, and there was no evidence of a hurricane. It had missed our area and moved harmlessly into the Atlantic. Unfortunately for me, I was back in the race.

The political map of America is divided into approximately 175,000 units called precincts. Each precinct represents a neighborhood. Political parties are organized by precinct. The leadership of a political party is chosen by a series of votes that go upward from precinct to county to congressional district and then statewide. Depending on the rules, delegates are selected by this process to attend a national convention, at which a specified majority of delegates then decide upon the name of the party candidate to run in the general election for president.

My task, therefore, was to organize the precincts and work up the ladder to gain the appropriate number of delegates. To gain control of a party precinct is ridiculously simple because hardly anybody ever attends a precinct caucus. Therefore, it's possible for a husband and wife to be the only attendees at a precinct caucus with the ability to vote each other into positions of responsibility. Even up the line, the attendance at county and congressional district caucuses is low. So in states that elect by caucus, a dedicated group of Christians can gain significant control.

I campaigned in at least thirty-three states. I quickly learned that the prize awarded to the winner of the presidential sweepstakes is so enormous that unscrupulous people will use any means possible to win. And for a novice like me politics was indeed a contact sport. Previously through the Freedom Council, I had traveled to Michigan and joined a group of young conservatives who were laughing at the plan they had conceived to win the delegates from the state.

I was able to win to my side an unbelievably gifted political strategist named Marlene Elwell. With Marlene, I covered the length and breadth of that great state. And in meeting after meeting I gained delegate strength. Marlene took me to the Upper Peninsula, where none of the candidates had visited. The Upper Peninsula turned out to be a happy hunting ground for delegates. Unfortunately, I grew complacent and didn't take every opportunity to press the fight to the end.

My state chairman came to see me, and as we talked, it was decided that we would be gracious and let the opposition have the chairmanship of the state party convention instead of the man we favored, Harry Veryser. This proved a fatal mistake. When the vote count from Michigan was announced, the George Bush campaign jumped on television and declared victory. In truth, my delegates had won, but only by a slim majority. Since I was late to announce, the networks didn't believe me and declared Bush a winner of Michigan.[2]

At the state convention, the chairman from the other side ruled that a number of my delegates were disqualified, and their credentials were denied. Our delegates walked out in protest, but that protest was meaningless. And when the votes were finally counted, a Bush delegation went to the national convention, not a Robertson delegation.

Later on, Bush rewarded the leader of his Michigan forces, Peter Secchia, by appointing him as the US Ambassador to Italy.[3]

The first serious contest leading to the presidency is held in Iowa in early winter. George Bush had beaten Ronald Reagan in Iowa eight years before,[4] and this may have been one of the reasons that Ronald Reagan chose him as his vice presidential running mate.

Marlene Elwell did a masterful job for me in Iowa. The first big contest in Iowa is held on the campus of Iowa State in Ames, Iowa. The party straw ballot has no official meaning, but it is a good indicator of what might come next. The registration fees from the Ames event became a major fundraising factor in the parties' overall budgets. When the votes were tallied, I had beaten a sitting vice president by an astounding multiple.[5] I remember looking into Bush's face. He was absolutely downcast and overwhelmed. I was told his campaign manager, Rich Bond, was so furious that he put my picture under his desk so that he could wipe his feet on it.

When the official Iowa caucuses were completed, Senator Bob Dole of Kansas was the winner, I was second, and sitting Vice President George Bush was third. Headlines all over the country proclaimed that Robertson beat Bush. There were even political cartoons talking about "the burning Bush." Marlene had done her job, and God's people had come through.

A cold-hearted analysis of Iowa politics, however, will reveal that a much larger audience attends the state basketball championships than show up for the political caucuses. Out of three million people, caucus attendance hovered around 110,000.[6]

When Jimmy Carter won Iowa, his handlers rushed him to New York, where he appeared on all of the major morning talk shows. When I was interviewed for my second-place finish in Iowa, I was insulted by Tom Brokaw of NBC News, who referred to me as a "televangelist," a put-down for sure. I soon realized that a win in Iowa was ephemeral unless it was backed up by big money and a big national organization.

Nonetheless, I was going to stay in the race.

53

WHEN FAILURE IS NOT A FAILURE

NEW HAMPSHIRE PROVED to be something entirely different during the 1988 presidential primary season. New Hampshire, the state with the first primary, was a bastion of individual liberty and personal freedom. The state motto is "Live Free or Die." But southern New Hampshire had changed dramatically as citizens from liberal Massachusetts began to move across the border and settle in small New Hampshire towns.[1]

The major newspaper in New Hampshire was the *New Hampshire Union Leader*, published in the state's largest city, Manchester. The only television station was WMUR, also in Manchester. The big network stations were in Boston, and the Boston television advertising rates were vastly higher since they covered a large metropolitan audience as well as their small audience in New Hampshire.

Despite all of the media hype to the contrary, politics is still a numbers game. In most elections, the candidate who acquires the largest number of votes is usually the winner. The number of votes needed to win is in turn decided by the turnout of registered voters on Election Day.

I calculated that in a crowded field in a Republican Party election, fifty thousand votes would probably gain a candidate a first-place win. I didn't have a lot of money available to buy television advertising on the Boston stations or WMUR. Therefore, to build up a grassroots network, I relied on my state field director, who repeatedly promised me that the precincts had been organized with enough strength to gather the votes I thought we needed.

I did everything possible to garner the voters' attention, including a sparring match with a professional middleweight boxer, a demonstration of my shooting prowess at the Ruger gun factory, an ice-fishing contest with my son Gordon, and so on. My campaign drew large crowds all over the state. I even went north to the famous Dixville Notch, whose hotel employees usually are the first to report election results shortly after midnight on the day of the election.

Only after it was all over did I learn that my state field director had been lying to me over and over again. In fact, this person had done none of the work promised and had no organization in place whatsoever.

I also realized that the people in New Hampshire idolized Ronald Reagan. They had beautiful posters showing the handsome actor in a cowboy hat with the inscription, "This is Reagan Country." Since George Bush had been Reagan's vice president, the New Hampshire people identified Bush with Reagan, which made him almost unbeatable. When election day came, I learned the awful truth. I had gained only a handful of votes and ran a humiliating fifth in the primary, even losing to Pete du Pont, former governor of Delaware.[2]

Before the votes were cast, I did learn something about the manager of George Bush's campaign, Lee Atwater. On frequent occasions, Bush operatives under Lee Atwater's direction would call hotels where my campaign had booked luncheons or dinners and cancel the event. One took a hacksaw and cut the telephone line into our headquarters. Bush campaign operatives also called news outlets and pretended to be calling for my campaign, and then they would change the time appointed for one of our press conferences. Worst of all, the Bush people got to Marc Nuttle, my national campaign manager, and talked him into removing the one most effective television spot that showed a consensus of experts declaring that my economic program was far more effective than the one advocated by George Bush. I think it was fair to say that I felt like an innocent lamb being set upon by wolves.

When a list of the final primary and caucus delegates was compiled, it was clear that my totals didn't come close to winning. On the plus side, though, I had won party caucuses in Alaska, Hawaii, and Nevada. I won the primary in Washington State. I was second in North and South Dakota, Iowa, Kansas, Minnesota, Maine, and Texas. Overall

I came in third and in the process defeated Donald Rumsfeld, who later became the Secretary of Defense in President George W. Bush's administration; four-star General Al Haig, who had been President Nixon's chief of staff; Jack Kemp, the popular congressman who would later become Secretary of Housing and Urban Development; and Pete du Pont. In the Olympics, a runner who wins the bronze medal is never described in the press as a failed runner, but the mainstream media at the time urgently hoped I would never appear on the national stage again and always labeled my presidential efforts as a failed campaign.

God never told me whether I would win because He knew better. If He had told me that I was going to lose badly, I wouldn't have made the effort. But something good did come out of my run for the presidency that the Lord saw far in advance. Through my efforts, tens of thousands of evangelical Christians became trained in political tactics. I believe my campaign helped people see that public service should be considered an honorable thing, not something dirty that Christians should not get involved in.

During the 1990s evangelical Christians joined together in an organization I founded called the Christian Coalition of America, which played a dominant role in the Republican Party and had been responsible for the election of George W. Bush.[3] Although I was no longer with The Christian Coalition and it had severely diminished in scope, the role of Evangelicals in Donald Trump's victory coalition sixteen years later was of inestimable value as well.

I'm thrilled that as this book is being written, evangelical Christians have continued to play a significant role, not only in recent presidential elections but in the appointment of judges and the strategic planning of vital policy issues.

After I declared my campaign at an end, I played the role of good soldier and endorsed the nominee of the party, George Bush. I took my delegates with me to the Republican Convention in New Orleans, and we participated in a joyous time preparing for the general election, which we thought George Bush was sure to win over Democratic nominee Michael Dukakis.

As one of the significant candidates, I was given a prime-time speaking slot and delivered what many thought was a memorable address. Bush had the preferred spot at the end of the convention and gave a speech written by Peggy Noonan, a gifted speechwriter who also wrote Ronald Reagan's address at the fortieth anniversary of D-Day in Normandy, France, which featured the line "These are the boys of Pointe du Hoc. These are the men who took the cliffs."[4] Peggy also wrote Reagan's speech commemorating the explosion of the Space Shuttle Challenger with the line "They prepared for their journey and waved goodbye and 'slipped the surly bonds of Earth' to 'touch the face of God.'"[5]

Few remember the things Bush had to say during his convention speech, but one stood out. It was taken from teenage words of scorn, "Read my lips." In his speech Bush uttered Peggy Noonan's famous line, "And the Congress will push me to raise taxes and I'll say 'no.' And they'll push, and I'll say 'no,' and they'll push again, and I'll say to them, 'Read my lips: no new taxes.'"[6]

That line brought the house down at the convention and resonated throughout the consciousness of the nation. Later in the Bush presidency, though, Democrats were holding hostage the major points of the Bush legislative agenda. They agreed to pass parts of his program, but only if he would acquiesce to what seems to be a continued Democratic legislative agenda—an increase in taxes.[7] When Bush gave way on that issue, the Democrats had him, and in the next general election, he was defeated by a young governor from Arkansas named Bill Clinton.

But before Bill Clinton took office, I'll talk about the interactions I had with President Bush 41 and then later with President Bush 43.

54

TWO MESSAGES FOR TWO PRESIDENTS

URING GEORGE BUSH's term in 1991, I was praying and the Lord gave me a message, "Tell your president that he is going to lead America to a great victory in the Middle East, and when it is over, he will be hailed as a war hero."

On a Monday I called John Sununu, who was chief of staff for Bush after serving as governor of New Hampshire. "John, I have a word for your man," I said. "Do you suppose you can fit me in?"

"Can you make it Wednesday of this week?"

"You set the time, and I'll be there."

I arrived at the White House and learned that talks had broken down in Geneva between Jim Baker, the president's emissary, and Tariq Aziz, Iraq's foreign minister.[1] The timing was perfect when I was led into the Oval Office.

"Mr. President, I have a word from the Lord for you," I said. "You are going to lead a powerful coalition that will win a great victory over Saddam Hussein and Iraq, and you will be hailed as a war hero."

When I delivered those words, he came around the desk to thank me. I extended my hands and said, "May I pray for you?"

He took my hands, bowed his head, and we prayed together for God's blessing on this enterprise. He then left the Oval Office and went into the Cabinet Room and laid out the plan to liberate the nation of Kuwait from the aggression of Saddam Hussein's Iraqi forces.

The next day I received a handwritten letter from President Bush, thanking me for this time together. Then the following day, I received a handwritten letter from Barbara Bush, who spoke of the fact that her husband, George, had commented on my visit and my prayer, and she thanked me for my kindness.

Indeed, after this war Bush's favorability rating reached 89 percent,[2] and he later addressed Congress as a conquering hero. Regrettably, he felt that his mandate from the United Nations only extended to removing Iraq from Kuwait. In truth, the combined forces under General Norman Schwarzkopf had not only defeated the Iraq army but had a large group of the Republican Guards surrounded and facing annihilation.[3] It made excellent publicity to say that this war was over in a hundred days, but it would have been much better for the United States and the world if we had removed Saddam Hussein from office and given the Iraqi people the ability to have democratic elections with honest leaders.

As a footnote, when George W. Bush became president, he felt duty-bound to complete the task begun by his father. He received erroneous information that Saddam Hussein had amassed vast quantities of weapons of mass destruction and was working on a nuclear bomb. At that time, I had the privilege of interviewing a nuclear scientist who had been called "Saddam's Bomb Maker." This gentleman told me clearly that Saddam did *not* possess the technology to enrich uranium, much less to build a nuclear bomb.

If I knew this as a television broadcaster, surely the CIA must have had the same information. Yet the CIA and the State Department allowed General Colin Powell to go before the United Nations to deliver a speech containing patently erroneous material.[4]

George H. W. Bush was a man of unusual restraint. Unfortunately, his son lacked the wise advisers who had ably served his father.

As I prayed in late 2002 and early 2003 about what looked like another war, the Lord spoke to me that this conflict would be "bloody and messy." I managed a brief meeting with George W. Bush in Nashville, Tennessee, and shared with him the word that God had given me for his father, which came to pass so wonderfully.

President Bush asked, "What word do you have for me?"

"This war will be bloody and messy. You had better prepare the American people for what is going to happen."

I don't think he liked hearing that. President Bush then replied with a statement that reeked of cynicism, "I can't sell it if I tell them that."

Sell it, he did. The war began with an invasion starting on March 30, 2003. There were no weapons of mass destruction found. A force of American soldiers caught Saddam Hussein in a hole in the ground.[5] The Iraqis brought him to trial and executed him.

With the death of their leader, the Iraqi troops were looking for a new command to permit them to continue to serve in the army and make a living. George W. Bush chose as head of the Provisional forces in Iraq a man named Paul Bremer, who determined that he would purge Iraq of all former members of the Ba'ath Party. He also dismissed from the army all of the former officers and key enlisted men.[6]

Bremer reportedly virtually never left the Green Zone in Baghdad and, therefore, never mingled with the Iraqi people. In his wake were thousands of highly trained troops who found the only way to gain a living was through fighting a civil war. The tragic fight that ensued between Shiite and Sunni Muslims led to the takeover years later of large portions of Iraq by a group known as ISIS.[7]

As I am writing this book, the nation of Iran is threatening the United States and is showing every sign of asserting hegemony over the post-Hussein Iraq. As was in the case of Korea, once again our civilian leadership in Washington has proved either incapable or unwilling to order US foreign policy in a fashion that would one day support the long-range best interests of the American people.

55

Like a Prairie Fire

WHEN ALL OF the politics in 1988 had come to an end, I was physically and mentally drained. But beyond fatigue, something else was wrong. I lacked the sweet presence of the Lord in my life, and I did not feel the anointing of His Spirit.

For years Dede and I had a habit of praying together on New Year's Eve for God's special direction. As we prayed together this time around, she handed me a book written by Mother Basilea Schlink, the founder of an order of women known as the Evangelical Sisterhood of Mary.

Mother Basilea had written a little booklet that said that the most painful wounds we have in life are those aimed at our character. She pointed out that forgiveness is the only way out of wounds that we have incurred.

During my campaign most of my fellow candidates had left me alone because in their hearts they felt that they might become the recipients of my supporters after my campaign was over. The nation's press had no such compunction. I was the butt of scorn and ridicule beyond belief.

Having been a Golden Gloves boxer, I longed to get the editor of the *Washington Post* into a ring so that I could punch his lights out. But you will recognize that such sentiments are hardly Christlike, and I had to repent and forgive those who had offended me. And this I did with all sincerity. So much so that I can truly say now that it's almost impossible for me to hold a grudge against anybody, regardless of what they have done.

And as I came to this prayer for forgiveness and contrition, the presence of the Lord came back into my life in great power. Whole new vistas opened up for the future.

During the summer of 1989 Dede and I took a much-needed

vacation to Europe. We flew into Vienna, Austria, and rented a car and drove west to southern Germany and a place called Dachau, a concentration camp where I saw the horrors that members of God's chosen race were forced to endure under the hands of the Nazis.

Then we traveled down into Bavaria, where, on a lovely summer evening, we sat in an outdoor café beside a lovely little brook under the shadow of a famous mountain known as Zugspitze.

Before we left for Europe, I was contacted by Billy McCormack, who had been the Louisiana state representative for my presidential campaign. "Pat, you have expended millions of dollars and trained thousands of people in political skill," he said. "If you get out now, all of that will be lost."

Billy had a point. At that time, my prayer was straightforward: "Lord, is there something else that You want me to do? If so, please give me direction."

So as I sat in that lovely open-air Bavarian restaurant, I was playing with some names of what to call an organization. Jerry Falwell had started something called the Moral Majority. This name had been misinterpreted by large numbers of people who took it to imply that if they didn't join up, they were not moral. I wanted my organization's name to convey that it was open to all those who considered themselves Christian and were interested in uniting for political action.

I knew the word *coalition* implies many people moving together voluntarily. So I settled on the name Christian Coalition. I would need help with this new organization and remembered a young man I had met at a meeting during the time of the Bush inauguration in January. A group called Young Americans for Freedom had graciously named me "Man of the Year," and I was asked to address their gathering at a hotel in northern Virginia. During the meeting, I sat next to a bright young man from Atlanta named Ralph Reed. I was quite impressed with his knowledge of political strategy and current affairs.

When I returned from Europe, I contacted Ralph to see if he might be interested in becoming the executive director of the Christian Coalition. As I remember, I donated $20,000 of my own money and the mailing list from my campaign to the Christian Coalition. Ralph's advice upon accepting the call was illuminating. "Let's not start spending any money until we get revenue coming in," he said.

So we rented a modest office in nearby Chesapeake and sent out a mailing to the donors on my list with news that we were continuing to work to further the goals that I had enunciated during my campaign.

The response was heartening, and in a short time the Christian Coalition had $200,000 in the bank, which allowed us to begin building a national organization and the necessary infrastructure.

Shortly thereafter, I heard that Lee Atwater, the campaign manager for George Bush, had developed brain cancer and was in critical condition. He welcomed my visit to his hospital room. When I saw him, he apologized for the dirty tricks that he and his team had played on me during the campaign. Of course, I was more than willing to forgive him. It was my joy to lead Lee in a prayer of repentance in which he received Jesus Christ as his Lord and Savior.

I then told Lee what we were planning with the Christian Coalition. "Jim Baker and I were the campaign managers for George Bush, but we are both out of politics now," Lee said. "There is no one from the Reagan team in the field at this moment. So if you announce the Christian Coalition, it will sweep like a prairie fire and be an immediate success."

Lee turned out to be absolutely right, and the Christian Coalition soon became one of the most effective grassroots political action groups in the nation.

Our young executive director, Ralph Reed, was a bit more flamboyant than I when he spoke these words to some reporter: "I paint my face and travel at night. You don't know it's over until you're in a body bag."[1]

The Christian Coalition had four long-range goals: the establishment of conservatives in charge of one or more of the major political parties, a majority of conservatives in one or more of the houses of Congress, a conservative president, and a conservative majority of federal judges.

I presumed that most of those goals had been met, and with that, the work of the Christian Coalition had come to an end.

During the election of George W. Bush the Christian Coalition printed and distributed about seventy million voter guides and, in the process, exhausted our resources. Unfortunately George W. made no show of gratitude for the work of the Christian Coalition whatsoever.

Since we had achieved the goals that had been established, I resigned as president of the organization. Although the Christian Coalition has served a vital purpose in the history of our nation, it was time to see my participation with it come to an end.

56

I Get to Play Cupid

CHARLES BLAIR WAS a gifted pastor who headed a megachurch in Denver called Calvary Temple.[1] He was also one of the kindest and most gracious people I have had the privilege to meet. Unfortunately his development officer, whose name was Wendell Nance, suggested that he and the church finance several worthwhile projects, including a nursing home, by selling bonds. Nance began a program whereby interest on one set of bonds was paid for by the sale of additional bonds.[2]

In common parlance, this is known as a Ponzi scheme. State and federal laws governing the sale of securities are very precise. Incorrect information given out in the sale of these securities can bring heavy penalties. Unfortunately, the three entities that had sold the securities went bankrupt, and a number of the elderly parishioners who had purchased the securities lost a portion of their life savings.

Charles Blair affirmed that he was not aware of the details surrounding this entire operation, but unfortunately for him, he had signed off on a number of the transactions, and his name appeared as an officer of several of the entities.

In the legal action that ensued, his claim of lack of knowledge was not taken seriously. The presiding judge found him guilty of securities fraud. The prosecutors wanted him to go to jail, but the presiding judge placed him on probation, provided that he could raise the money to pay back the defrauded bondholders. Charles raised some money and paid back a portion. Even after a debt-reduction program, he was still about $1.5 million short of paying off 100 percent of what was owed.[3] It's hard to imagine the emotional and spiritual grief that this fine servant of the Lord endured. But endure he did, and Charles went on to establish a worthy charity to help Christians in Ethiopia.

I reached out to encourage Charles, and he in turn invited me to speak to his congregation at their Sunday service. In the advertisement for that meeting, he said the speaker was a graduate of Yale Law School. A fellow Yale graduate, David Nelson, and his wife, Barbara, came to Calvary Chapel that Sunday to hear me speak.

The Nelsons had five wonderful children, and their younger daughter, Lisa, had enrolled as a student at the all-women Sweet Briar College near Lynchburg, Virginia. In my earlier college years I had carried on a sincere romance with one of the students at Sweet Briar College to whom I gave my fraternity pin.

In her role in planning the spiritual life emphasis, Lisa was given a limited budget at Sweet Briar for this event. She figured, for her religious emphasis weekend, that her budget would accommodate a local minister from Portsmouth, Virginia, a couple of hundred miles away. So she wrote and asked me if I would visit Sweet Briar for a weekend and lead their spiritual weekend exercises. I accepted. Then my secretary, Barbara Johnson, said, "Why don't you take your son Tim along with you?"

At the time, Tim was a student at the University of Virginia in Charlottesville and was possibly lost in the "haze" that is not uncommon at UVA. When he heard that I wanted him to go with me to Sweet Briar, he complained bitterly that the Sweet Briar girls weren't any fun.

"Fun or not, you're going," I said. "I'll come by your dorm, pick you up, and your mother and I will drive you over to Sweet Briar." So we arrived at his dorm and took our reluctant son in our car and drove down the road a short distance—around seventy miles—to the Sweet Briar campus.

The services began the following day. When my turn came to speak to the young women, I spoke on the love of God and invited them to receive His love. I also told them about the baptism of the Holy Spirit and asked them to kneel at the front of the room to receive this blessing. A large number of these lovely young ladies responded, and suddenly I saw my reluctant son with his hands on their heads, praying that God would fill them with His power. For me, it was a wonderful experience. For Tim, it was transformational.

He remarked over and over again how "sweet" those girls were and what a wonderful time he had had. He and Lisa Nelson hit it off right away. They even bonded over the mutual experiences of having health-conscious parents who insisted on giving them sandwiches with whole wheat bread instead of white bread when they were young.

After a few months, Tim invited Lisa to come and visit with us over a weekend, and I remember being awakened at 1:00 a.m. by a knock on our bedroom door. These young people had come to tell us the good news...they had decided to get married.

I've often said that Lisa is my "designer daughter-in-law," meaning that if I had been able to design the perfect wife for my son and the perfect mother for my grandchildren, I know of no way that I could have improved on what the Lord had already done with this lovely girl.

Together Tim and Lisa have five children and eleven grandchildren, all of whom are exceptional in their dispositions and deeply committed to the things of the Lord.

Without question being God's instrument in putting together a marvelous family can be one of the most important things that any of us can do.

57

PLAYING IN THE BIG LEAGUES

WHEN OUR BROADCASTING at CBN began, the big stations were affiliates of three major commercial networks and one educational network. The signals of these metropolitan stations did not reach remote mountain areas. Local entrepreneurs realized that by building a high tower in their area, they could access the urban television signals and then feed that signal by cable throughout a local area. The term was CATV, which stood for Community Antenna Television. A number of these local CATV systems were put together in states like Pennsylvania and other rural areas.

In Colorado, a cowboy named Bob Magness started a number of CATV systems that he combined. Soon the cable entrepreneurs realized the big audiences were in the cities, so if they could run cable throughout a city, they could offer a variety of programs not available to the TV viewers from over-the-air network shows.

With the advent of satellite broadcasting, a number of broadcasters put together what were called channels of unique television programs, which were then offered to cable systems. Over the years, specialty programs were created, featuring topics such as history, geography, weather, food, exercise, etc. Each cable offering was sold to the local operator for a negotiated price based on the number of subscribers that the cable system had available.

We put together a grouping of wholesome entertainment programs combined with the religious programs that we had been featuring on our owned-and-operated television stations. This eventually became known as the Family Channel.

Each community cable system needed permission from the city fathers to hang their wires—or put them underground—throughout the city. If a cable operator could show their respective city government that they were going to carry a wholesome religious channel, they were guaranteed favorable treatment. In 1977 we became the first direct-to-cable, satellite-delivered television channel in America.[1]

Our first affiliate was a cable system in Owensboro, Kentucky. I would like to take credit for this brilliant stroke, but I think the credit belongs to our God who always knew what the future held. The human instrument was Stan Ditchfield's assistant, Scott Hessick, who had been placed in charge of our cable television interests. The audience grew so fast that when we reached five million subscribers, Scott proudly proclaimed that he had doubled his payroll when he added a secretary.

There were two income streams for the satellite channels. One was from the subscriber fees paid by each cable system, and the other was from sales revenue that could be garnered from advertisers. With a rapidly growing base of subscribers and a dual-income stream, it was not long before this "side enterprise" of ours had become quite attractive financially.

After a few years the number of subscribing households connected to the Family Channel totaled eighty million,[2] and we were one of the ten largest cable broadcasters in America.

Just as an aside, I should mention a satellite channel called ESPN. This twenty-four-hour sports network had secured rights to a large number of sporting events that enabled cable operators to charge their customers premium prices to view popular sporting events. ESPN was not charging ten or twenty cents per subscriber, but it was able to get four or five dollars per subscriber because sports fans wanted to watch college football, college basketball, pro football, and major league baseball games...the list of sports was endless.

When we first began the Family Channel, the CBN financial department was diverting our cable revenue to pay bills for other activities. If our cable network was being denied legitimate revenue, then we would be unable to purchase the programs necessary to keep it viable. So I set up a policy whereby the cable revenues would be segregated and a set amount would be paid to the parent company, but no more.

At that time, my son Tim negotiated a joint venture for major Hollywood motion pictures with MGM/UA that would have made available to us 150 movies per year for a ten-year window. This could have been the foundation for an entire television network that would have been worth millions of dollars. This venture was a brilliant coup, and Tim was quite excited that this opportunity was available.

To his amazement, two senior executives at CBN said, "We can't do that because those things are too 'worldly.'" The decision was never brought to me, and, unfortunately, these two men were able to kill the deal of the century, which would have benefited our ministry enormously. But that's the kind of struggle that ensues during an attempt to marry a ministry with a business.

However, the Lord was about to do a wonderful thing. When the television evangelist scandals broke nationwide, our income had dropped substantially. When later God called me to get involved in public life and go off the air, the funds that were lost from contributions to CBN were matched virtually dollar for dollar by the revenue from the Family Channel.

According to the rules of the Internal Revenue Service, a tax-exempt charity can lose its tax-exempt status if a sizable portion of its revenues is considered unrelated business income. Our CBN Board of Directors felt that the time had come to spin the Family Channel into a separate business corporation so that its revenues would not affect the tax status of CBN.

The Lord gave me the wisdom to establish a structure that satisfied government regulations, fulfilled the wishes of our board, and brought enormous benefit to both CBN and later Regent University, which owned shares. We obtained appraisals of valuations from two outstanding firms and took the highest one. We then established a class of convertible debentures (unsecured loan certificates issued by a company and backed by general credit rather than by specified assets) paying 6 percent interest and convertible into majority shares of a new corporation that we called International Family Entertainment (IFE). The board wanted me to be in control of the new company, so I bought—with my own funds—shares of stock that had supermajority voting rights. That stock was then placed in a charitable trust to the benefit of CBN.

To validate this transaction, I was able to sell 17 percent of the company to John Malone's Tele-Communications for a price that I believe was forty-five million dollars in notes and stock. John Malone was the most powerful figure in cable television at the time, and he in turn arranged for the fledgling young company to have affiliate relations with all of the cable systems that he controlled.

Funds from this transaction were also used to sponsor a massive evangelistic thrust in various countries around the world.

Later the CBN Board realized that we were donating six million dollars a year to Regent University, so the board proposed that we donate one hundred million dollars in convertible debentures paying 6 percent interest directly to Regent University, which in turn provided the university with a sizable endowment and guaranteed annual income.

At the inception of the corporation, our initial board included Lou Isakoff, our attorney; my son Tim; and me. Not too long after IFE was launched, Dede said, "I think that we should take it public." When we went public, our board at that time included former US Senator Bill Armstrong, a former associate of financier George Soros named Bob Wallace, entrepreneur Lowell Morse, my son Tim, and myself. We were in agreement that a public offering would be appropriate, so we engaged Donaldson, Lufkin & Jenrette (DLJ) as the lead underwriter, to be joined by Merrill Lynch and Smith Barney.

We set an offering of $150 million and priced the stock at fifteen dollars a share. After what is called a road show to potential investors, we were pleased that the offering was oversubscribed, and we had a nice reserve to build our network.

Typically stock is supposed to rise after an initial public offering. If it dips on the first day, it is hard to regain momentum. Unfortunately for us, Fidelity Investments had bought a big block of our stock on the offering and then dumped it before the first day was over. That killed our momentum but not the quality of what we were doing.

We were able to assemble a terrific group of marketers and programmers, as well as a sales team in New York headed by the former sales manager of CNN. Tim, whom I had made CEO of the company, and his crew came up with a delightful promotion called Food for Thought. Every month, a gourmet delight was sent to potential advertisers from their friends at IFE. The promotion was eagerly awaited by the advertisers, who responded with gratitude.

The small team at IFE was doing a splendid job. Then something happened. We learned that the British company that owned MTM Enterprises (started by Mary Tyler Moore) was up for sale. We were able to negotiate a price that they recommended to their principal shareholder in the British company TVS.

The British company had a lavish studio in the west of England and maintained a lovely office across from Buckingham Palace. We hired the former head of Steven Spielberg's Amblin Entertainment, Tony Thomopoulos, to try to bring some semblance of order to the west coast operation of our British subsidiary.

My firm conviction was that our destiny lay in the creation of television channels. I wanted to buy a library of cartoons so that we could have a cartoon channel. I also thought that we would do well to set up a soap opera channel with much of the broadcast material that was available for us. I also wanted to have a channel to sell products and began some discussion concerning the acquisition of the sales company known as QVC.

Uppermost in my mind was the thought that executive talent should be concerned with major projects and not diverted to the minutia of running small businesses. At that time, though, three members of our staff did a survey on the benefits of what is called "live entertainment." They presented our board with a proposal to acquire such live entertainment as the Ice Capades and the Dixie Stampede. Their graphs and statistical analysis were persuasive, but my feeling was that the future for us lay in television channels. It's not that the live entertainment was a bad investment, but it only resulted in a tiny fraction of the economic benefit that more channels would have yielded to us.

As Chairman of IFE, I could see this wonderful company was, frankly, topping out. Hollywood producers were now charging as much as one million dollars per episode for the rental of their off-network programs. I saw potential trouble down the road.

I decided there was one action I could take—I could put the company up for sale at a high price to maximize its full economic potential. And that is exactly what I did.

When the word got out, the suitors came calling. I had a call from Michael Eisner, the head of Disney. I was called by the head of Viacom, followed by the head of NBC. And particular interest was shown by Haim Saban and Rupert Murdoch of News Corp. Normal pricing for entertainment stock such as ours was eight or nine times EBITDA, which stands for earnings before interest, tax, depreciation, and amortization.

As I was driving one night, I received a call from Rupert Murdoch, who offered me two hundred million dollars for my controlling shares. That was a tempting offer, but I knew that if I sold out at that much of a premium, I would leave behind the investors who had faith in our company and were hoping that they would see their own stock rise in the event of a sale of the corporation. So I regrettably turned down Rupert's generous offer so that we could all wait for the sale of the entire company.

After much back and forth negotiation, I settled on a price from News Corp and Haim Saban of $1.9 billion for our cable company in July 1997.[3] Instead of eight or nine times EBITDA, the amount I negotiated was more like *eighteen times* EBITDA. Everybody was a winner in that transaction, including Regent University, which received a $147.5 million endowment, which grew to $300 million, from the sale of its 4.2 million shares in IFE. My son Tim profited handsomely from the sale of his shares. He wisely invested in real estate, which added to his resources. These days, he's able to indulge two passions—one is being a father to five children (Laura, Elizabeth,

Willis, Cally, and Abby), and two is being a wonderful grandfather to ten grandchildren, all of whom are deeply spiritual Christians. Tim is also an active member of Alpha, a spiritual fellowship formed by London-based Anglican Pastor Nicky Gumbel.

In an amazing twist to this drama, Haim Saban added some cartoon features to the overall assets of IFE and then sold the company to Michael Eisner and Disney for five billion dollars,[4] which made Haim Saban a billionaire and increased Rupert Murdoch's wealth by a substantial amount. In all this, our Lord led every step of the way, and I can only marvel at what He has done with the initial seventy dollars I had when He led me to start CBN.

When the payout came from the brokers, my charitable trust received $103 million. For most people, that would represent a fortune. Before that transaction, the Lord had spoken to me with these words, "A financial crash is coming. Only the securities of your government will be safe." If I had heeded those words and bought thirty-year treasuries yielding 6 percent, my annual income from the trust would have been enormous. I recall the words of the poet Robert Browning: "Ah, but a man's reach should exceed his grasp, or what's a heaven for?"[5]

I had been traveling in the company of cable billionaires and must confess that this was a time when I wasn't listening to the Lord. Time and time again, I invested in business ventures that easily would have put me in the billionaire category, but each time something unusual happened to prevent me from doing so.

I formed a corporation called Forest Friend Timber Company and gained a concession in the center of Zaire of two million acres of choice hardwood timber that had been appraised for at least five hundred million dollars. Before I could move ahead, warlord Laurent Kabila gained power and canceled the concession.

I formed a Cypress corporation called Zvesda Media, and in partnership with ITAR-TASS, gained the only direct satellite-to-home license for all of Russia. Shortly thereafter, the Russian financial market collapsed, and financial backers refused to go forward.

I helped start a company in China called Zhaodaola that gained approval from the China Securities Regulatory Commission to list on the GEMS Market in Hong Kong. But just before we got going, the internet bubble burst, and financing was no longer available. When I first entered the Chinese internet market, there were only about 1.5 million users. As I write this book, it's my understanding that the number has exploded to 840 million users.[6] One company that was started at the same time as Zhaodaola is called Baidu. Today's market cap of Baidu on the New York Stock Exchange is $41.59 billion. If I had only weathered the storm, my interests in Zhaodaola would have exceeded $20 billion.

I also bought a fifty-thousand-barrel oil refinery in Los Angeles and a hundred miles of pipeline throughout Los Angeles and all the way to San Diego. As we were ready to fire up the refinery to begin operations, a federal judge issued a restraining order and said that we needed to comply with what is called "New Source Review," which required an additional investment of tens of millions of dollars that we did not have. That refinery could have been expanded to handle one hundred thousand barrels a day, which would have brought its value to between one billion and two billion dollars.

I was given a verbal promise to enable my company to take possession of the Tenke Fungurume Concession in Zaire, which is probably the largest copper cobalt mine in the world. I found a South African company to pay a billion dollars for the necessary infrastructure. Unfortunately at that time, a European consortium offered what I believe were bribes totaling $250 million to gain control of that concession and take it away from me.

Finally, I had been able to buy shares in a Canadian company called Hurricane Hydrocarbons, which was producing five hundred thousand barrels of crude oil a day in Kazakhstan. Hurricane Hydrocarbons was so badly mismanaged that it went bankrupt and was unable to export its products because it lacked refining capacity. The receiver of the company approached me with an offer to take voting control of the company. I refused to do that. Shortly thereafter, they hired a new president who issued shares of their stock to the Kazakh refinery, and with the merged operations came out of bankruptcy.

The merged company was later sold to the Chinese for a price in excess of four billion dollars.[7] By then, instead of being the controlling shareholder, I had sold all of my shares.

The failure of all of these tantalizing opportunities would have brought grief to any normal person. But somehow I realized that God did not want me as a billionaire investor. He wanted me as a humble servant who depended on Him and wanted to walk in His ways.

So with my face to the sun and the wind at my back, I looked eagerly forward to God's next adventure for me.

It turned out there were more than a few to come.

58

Two Miracles Close to Home

I would like to digress at this moment to give you two examples of the wondrous way that our Lord works in our lives.

The Bible tells us that the patriarch Abraham had placed his beloved son on an altar and was preparing to sacrifice him when his eye looked up and saw a ram caught in a thicket. He then proclaimed the name of God as *Jehovah Jireh*, which means "the one who sees ahead."

I want to tell you about a time in my life when God saw a looming catastrophe coming toward me and put people in place to avert that catastrophe. And then I want to tell you about a time when God arranged for me to unexpectedly appear in a specific city to protect and pray for my precious granddaughter.

First, my story.

The human heart is divided into four sections. The two bottom sections are called ventricles. The two top sections are referred to as the atrium. This incredible muscle pumps somewhere between forty and seventy-two beats per minute every minute, every hour, every day, every month, every year of our life. In a healthy heart, the atrium pumps a large quantity of blood through the ventricles, from which blood is nourished and oxygenated and then sent coursing throughout our bodies.

As I grew older, my ventricles were working fine, but my atrium was not pumping as it should. Instead, it began to quiver. The term for this medical condition is atrial fibrillation or AFib. When AFib occurs, the person with the condition loses strength and drags through life. When this condition happened to me, I was forced to perform on television in such an exhausted state that I had to grip a podium to stand upright.

Modern cardiologists and doctors known as cardiac electrophysiologists have developed a technique called cardioversion, which shocks the atrium into what is known as normal or sinus rhythm. One time, my cardiac electrophysiologist, Dr. Ian Woollett, arranged for my admission to Sentara Heart Hospital in Norfolk. I was to be given cardioversion, a procedure that works as follows.

The patient is required to fast from any food or liquids for at least six hours. Then he is admitted to a bed in the hospital, where his vitals are checked by the attending cardiologist and also by the attending anesthesiologist. Electric plates are placed on the chest and back and are hooked up to an electronic pulse machine.

After all of the preliminary tests have been performed, the anesthesiologist injects a white substance into one of the veins of the patient's arm. The substance is known as propofol, or what is also called "milk of amnesia." (Propofol, as you might recognize, was the sleep medicine that brought about Michael Jackson's death.)

Once the patient falls into a restful sleep, the cardioversion machine is activated, and the patient's chest is hit with about six hundred joules of electric current, which serves to shock his heart back into what is called sinus rhythm. In my case, the cardioversion was a blessed relief because suddenly my strength came back and I felt normal.

Every couple of months, though, my heart would go back into atrial fibrillation, and I would be forced to repeat the cardioversion procedure. The hospital machine that performed the cardioversion was used on me so often that we laughingly called it the "Pat zapper."

After about my ninth or tenth cardioversion, Dr. Woollett said to me, "What you've got is a progressive illness, and you don't want to continue these episodes much longer."

"What is the solution?" I asked.

"I can put a pacemaker in, which will keep you from having atrial fibrillation."

"Do you know how to do it?"

"I've done about thirteen hundred of them, so I can take care of yours."

The downside of having a pacemaker is that your heart is completely dependent on electricity. If for some reason the power fails, your pacemaker will stop, and you will drop dead. I was assured that the modern pacemakers were ruggedly built and had ample backup. So I went back to the Sentara Heart Hospital, was put back under anesthesia, and then Dr. Woollett cut a flap out of my chest and inserted a small metal device about the size of a box of matches. From that device, two wires were then inserted into my heart. The flap was sewn up, and now I was operating on battery power.

When a person has atrial fibrillation, it's possible that blood will pool in his heart, and clots will form in that blood. If these clots dislodge and are carried to the brain, a serious stroke can occur. As a result, patients with atrial fibrillation are always given a blood thinner. My first blood thinner was called Coumadin, which has the same chemical composition as rat poison.[1] Coumadin requires the patient to have a finger prick once a week to ensure that the composition of his blood is within prescribed limits. I later went on a more modern blood thinner called Xarelto, which required no finger stick and periodic monitoring.

With the advent of my pacemaker, I asked Dr. Woollett if I could stop taking the blood thinner. We discussed my condition, and I told him that I had removed what was called the atrial appendage (a little extension that was the thickness of a pencil and a harboring ground for blood clots). Therefore, he determined that with the pacemaker I could skip the blood thinner.

I thought I was on my merry way, but I'm reminded of the commercial that says that the first sign of a stroke is a stroke. Our gracious God saw serious trouble ahead for me, so He started moving pieces in place to take care of the danger facing His servant.

On the morning of February 2, 2018, my daughter-in-law Katharyn felt a nudge from God to visit Dede. Before driving, she received a text about a traffic jam from my grandson, so she drove a different route. On the way, she had green lights at every intersection, which seldom happens. When she arrived at the house, she discovered that my dedicated housekeeper, Jeanette Harris, had observed an abnormality in my speech and actions and had contacted my head of security and CBN VP, Chris Mitchell, as well as my secretary, G. G. Conklin. When Katharyn arrived and spoke to me, she concurred that I was possibly undergoing a stroke.

According to the laws in place in our city, an ambulance has to transport a patient to the nearest hospital. The nearest hospital to my house is Sentara Leigh Hospital in the Kempsville District of Virginia Beach. Leigh is a fine hospital, but at the time lacked a stroke center. Gordon and Chris talked by phone, and Gordon ordered Chris to skip the ambulance and take me directly to Sentara Norfolk General, which had a fully functioning stroke center.

So Katharyn and Chris Mitchell hurried me out of the house and into Chris' car. As I sat down in the car, I became unconscious, and Chris, who is a certified chief of police, took the wheel of the car, turned on the siren and flashers, and drove fast down the interstate toward the stroke center.

G. G. Conklin had also called ahead so that the hospital was prepared to receive me with a stretcher for an immediate MRI. Before the hospital could proceed with the appropriate treatment, they had to have permission, and Gordon walked into the hospital stroke center just in time to give permission according to my advance directives and my medical power of attorney.

After an MRI, it was determined that there was a blood clot shutting off the pathway to vital nerves. I have read that brain cells, when starved of the necessary blood flow, will lose an astonishing 1.9 million neurons and 14 billion synapses per minute due to ischemic cerebrovascular disruption.[2] If a stroke is left untreated for several hours, the stroke victim can be permanently paralyzed, lose the ability to speak, or end up with the cognition of a little child.

At the stroke center, it was determined that I was not on any blood thinner and could be injected with a powerful new blood thinner called TPA. Before the TPA was injected, my doctor, who happened to be on a TV monitor at the foot of my bed, asked me to raise my arm. This I was unable to do. He asked me to raise my leg, and I couldn't do that.

I couldn't perform the simplest physical feats, and my speech was unintelligible. Then I became unconscious, at which time a needle was inserted into my neck that sent TPA throughout my brain and the rest of my body. The blood clot was dissolved, and I woke up fully conscious and in control of my faculties. Gordon, Chris, and G. G. witnessed the dramatic change as I exited the CT scan and moved my limbs one by one at the doctor's command.

The total time from the onset of my stroke to the time of the TPA injection was an hour and twenty minutes. If I had been left untreated for maybe one more hour, I wouldn't be writing this book, I wouldn't be able to host a television program, and I wouldn't be able to lead a university. Instead, I would be permanently disabled.

But our Lord had something more for me to do and set in place the necessary answers, even before any of us thought such answers were needed.

And now to my second miracle story in my family.

When my daughter Elizabeth was growing up, she developed a remarkable affinity for spiritual things.

As Elizabeth was looking for a potential college, she was impressed with Southern Methodist University (SMU), which was located in the Highland Park area of Dallas. She enrolled as a freshman, lived in the university dormitory, later joined the Pi Phi sorority, and soon became a recognized leader among the sorority members.

After she received a baccalaureate degree, she decided to enhance her future opportunities by entering the SMU School of Business, where she earned a Master of Business Administration. During that time, she met and fell in love with a six feet, five inches tall fellow student from Nashville, Tennessee. Charlie Robinson was a remarkably affable young man who later proved to be an ideal husband and father.

Elizabeth and Charlie had two children, one whose name is Catherine and who was a member of Phi Beta Kappa at the University of Virginia. Catherine initially was a much-loved public schoolteacher and later married a wonderful guy from the University of Virginia named Emmett Nelms.

Elizabeth and Charlie named their second child Charles Robinson III, but they laughingly call him "Three-Sticks." Young Charlie was a whiz at finance and easily graduated near the top of his class at the McIntire School of Commerce at the University of Virginia.

With these two remarkable children, Elizabeth and Charlie thought they had their family firmly established. Then the Lord sent them a third child whose name is Emily.

I was traveling to Los Angeles and stopped in Dallas to visit our TV station there. I was trying to slip in and out without a great deal of notice when the phone at Channel 39 brought me a call from my daughter Elizabeth. She said, "I thought you were in Virginia. Where are you?" I said, "I'm at the TV station here on Harry Hines Boulevard in Dallas." She hurriedly said, "I'm just up the street at the hospital where Emily has been taken for testing—she's running a 103-degree fever, and they can't figure out what's wrong. I need you to pray for her." I responded, "I'll be right there!" I jumped in the car and drove the short distance up the hill from our TV studio to the hospital.

When I arrived, the nurse was bringing Emily back after hours of testing. She was hooked up to IV tubes, burning with fever, and screaming at the top of her lungs. As to be expected, Elizabeth was crying too. I took one look at Elizabeth and in faith said, "Elizabeth, she's going to be fine. Stop crying." I immediately laid hands on Emily's head and began praying for God Almighty to heal her.

Almost instantly, little Emily stopped screaming. The fever began to subside, and she fell asleep. The doctors were incredulous and insisted she stay in the hospital until the tests came back. They waited for three days. The results came in confirming the doctors' worst fears—viral meningitis and encephalitis. Yet Emily miraculously showed no symptoms whatsoever, so she was released. Three days earlier the Lord had answered my prayer, and His power entered that little baby.

At that time, God placed a bond between Emily and me. Since then, this child has grown up into womanhood as someone who has been specially chosen by our Lord. God has incredible plans for Emily, who was the recipient of one of God's extraordinary miracles when He brought me halfway across the country to a place only about a mile away from where my dear granddaughter was critically ill. I was able to be on the scene to be the instrument of healing that God used to give her to the world.

59

WHAT THE PRESS REFUSES TO DISTINGUISH

SHORTLY AFTER I graduated from seminary, I was in a time of prayer when I asked the Lord what role in the church He had for me. He indicated that my role was that of an apostle. Throughout the years, it has been my privilege to lay the foundation for churches all over the world, for business corporations, and for a major educational institution. I have done those tasks as the apostle Paul requires—"in demonstration of the Spirit and of power."[1] Allow me to share some background to help you understand what I mean.

At the time of Martin Luther there was a rebellion against the Catholic Church, which was aptly described by Lord Acton's famous dictum, "Power tends to corrupt and absolute power corrupts absolutely."[2] Luther taught that salvation was by faith alone, not by observing the sacraments of the Catholic Church. Luther's message was taken from the words of the apostle Paul, who said his role in life was to preach the gospel throughout the world. The Greek word for *gospel* is *euaggelion*, which is translated "good news."[3] The English variant of that Greek word is *evangel*. Someone who preaches good news is called an evangelist.

The apostle Paul taught that there is only one intercessor between God and man—"Christ Jesus."[4] Teachers were important, as were pastors, but a Christian believer did not need an earthly intercessor (or go-between) between himself and God. The term that came into use was *priesthood of all believers*,[5] and the church followed the teaching of the apostle Peter, who said, "But you are a chosen generation, a royal priesthood, a holy nation, His own special people, that you may proclaim the praises of Him who called you out of darkness into His marvelous light."[6]

In these evangelical churches a new class of leaders arose. There was a pastor who was the spiritual leader. Elders were chosen for their ability to understand correct doctrine. Deacons cared for the material needs of the church and its employees. Trustees were responsible for financial relations between the church and the community in which it was located. Evangelists were sent out to lead unbelievers to faith in Jesus. And church members were set apart to go to foreign lands to provide physical and spiritual care for those in more primitive societies.

Then a new phenomenon arose called the Charismatic Movement, which was birthed by the Lord to recapture the supernatural life of the members of the early church. The root word, *xaris*, is the Greek word meaning "grace."[7] The *xarismata* have often been called gifts, but they are expressions of the power of the Holy Spirit.

When the Holy Spirit was sent by Jesus and His Father to the church, He had two functions. On the one hand, He reproduced the miracle ministry of Jesus. On the other hand, He reproduced the life of Jesus. The Bible tells us that when Jesus was saying goodbye to His disciples, He breathed on them and said, "Receive the Holy Spirit."[8] Later He told them, "But you shall receive power when the Holy Spirit has come upon you; and you shall be witnesses to Me in Jerusalem, and in all Judea and Samaria, and to the end of the earth."[9] On the day of Pentecost the disciples were filled with the Spirit so that they could reproduce the miracles of Jesus.

Christian believers have been confused by these two manifestations of God's Spirit. Here is an example that might illustrate what I'm saying. If I take a glass of water and drink it, I will be in relation to water, and the water will be in me. It could be said that I have had an indwelling of water. If, on the other hand, I drive from my headquarters to the Atlantic Ocean and dive in, I will be in relation to water, but it will be an entirely different experience. I will be immersed or baptized in the water.

So it is with the two manifestations of the Holy Spirit. One is the indwelling Spirit, which comes to the believer to reproduce nine characteristics of Jesus called the "fruit of the Spirit" in Galatians 5:22–23, which are all derivative of three cardinal graces—faith, hope, and love.

With the baptism of the Spirit, however, the believer is equipped with supernatural weapons for service, of which there are nine in three groupings: supernatural utterance, supernatural revelation, and supernatural power.

These charismata are not to be considered resident gifts but temporary manifestations of the Holy Spirit. To one there might be a message in tongues, and to another an interpretation of tongues. To one there might be a prophetic word. To another there might be a revelation of something to take place in the future, which is called a word of wisdom. To another a revelation of something occurring contemporaneously that is not available to the senses of sight, sound, taste, and touch. This is called a word of knowledge. To another a manifestation of supernatural faith. To another the ability to bestow physical healing called gifts of healing. Those who enter into these wonderful works of God's Spirit are known by the name Charismatic.

Charismatics can have the same ministry officials as other Evangelicals. But in their midst God has given special enablement to people who are called apostles, prophets, pastors, evangelists, and teachers. These are the ministry offices given to establish and build up the Lord's church.

The role of apostle is given to a person who has been gifted to lay the foundation for churches and other Christian ministries. The prophets receive revelation from the Holy Spirit Himself that they can share with their fellow believers. The pastor is in charge of a local congregation to care for the spiritual, physical, and financial needs of his people. The evangelist has a unique calling and anointing to make God's plan of salvation clear to those who themselves are not believers.

The Pew Research Center estimated that in 2011 the number of Charismatics in the world was 584 million, a quarter of the world's largest faith, Christianity.[10] At the current rate of growth the number of Charismatics in the world should reach the billion mark by 2030.

The belief in the power of the Holy Spirit has become dominant in what is known as the Global South—Asia, Africa, Latin America, and the Caribbean. Even in China, the thrust of the Three-Self Church is Charismatic. Just think about it: by far, the fastest-growing religious belief in the world belongs to the people who believe in the gifts and the power of the Holy Spirit of God.

With that as a background, let me turn now to the press in America. As with all professions, some journalists do their jobs well, while others are sloppy and lazy. It has been my personal experience over the years that much of the press is biased against religious belief, especially the evangelical and Charismatic varieties. In my opinion Billy Graham and Oral Roberts were the most influential evangelical figures in the last fifty or sixty years. Yet it seems the press of America had little to no interest or intention of studying a religious movement that was changing the world.

I'm not aware of any who have researched the charismata or grace enablements (which are commonly known as gifts of the Spirit or the spiritual offices in the church). They have no hesitation whatsoever in assigning pastors or television broadcasters the title "TV evangelist" or "televangelist," which deep in their hearts they know is an insult.

Many in the national media and cultural elites label all evangelical Christians as uneducated, backward, and easily led. If you think I'm exaggerating, let me share a story that stands out as one of the most egregious examples of this bias. It took place at the confirmation of Clarence Thomas for a seat on the Supreme Court back in 1991. Senator Arlen Specter from Pennsylvania, who was in the class behind me in law school, was given the task of shepherding the Thomas nomination through the Judiciary Committee and ultimately the full Senate.

I interviewed Arlen on my television program and asked how we could help, and he said, "Have your viewers call their senator." I put the telephone number of the US Capitol on the screen and urged my viewers to exercise their civic duty and call their senators. The response from our wonderful people was overwhelming. They not only jammed the Capitol Hill switchboard but they also shut down telephone service throughout the capital of the United States.

A reporter from the *Washington Post* was assigned to study this extraordinary phenomenon and wrote a major story with these words: "The shutdown in the Washington, D.C., telephone service was caused by the audience of 'television evangelist' Pat Robertson. We know that his following is *poor, uneducated, and easy to command*" (emphasis added).

I showed this blatant insult on television and urged my audience to call the editor of the paper to complain. The writer of this slander showed absolutely no remorse, but under blistering criticism was reported to have said that he had researched this statement and found overwhelming agreement. Indeed the nation's press is in agreement that people of faith are dumb, uneducated yahoos, who, if they had half a brain, could not believe in a creator God. This same sentiment was echoed by Hillary Clinton when she ran for president, claiming that half of Donald Trump's supporters belonged in a "basket of deplorables."[11]

The Bible says, "Why do the nations rage, and the people plot a vain thing?...He who sits in the heavens shall laugh; The Lord shall hold them in derision."[12]

I can assure you that the blessing of God is descending upon His chosen people, and certain judgment will be the destiny of those who have set themselves out to destroy God's work on earth. However, I am encouraged to see that more and more publishing houses, books, magazines, and television programs are incorporating spiritual truth. I was told recently by the dean of our School of Psychology that secular psychology is now finding an openness to spiritual reality, and the Regent University School of Nursing is finding that there is a great openness to training nurses to give spiritual comfort to the patients they treat in hospitals.

60

The Flying Hospital
Captivates Nations

From Angola to Zambia, from the Central African Republic to Mozambique, I have met with many presidents, rebel generals, and prime ministers. I have conducted humanitarian missions, evangelistic efforts, and agricultural projects. As I worked in Africa, I became aware of a dreadful disease affecting a large number of Africans. A variant of the tsetse fly was biting people and with each bite inserting an egg that grew into a worm that found its home around the eye cavity of the recipient. Some of these worms were quite long, and each one caused the afflicted person to go blind. The term was "river blindness," and it's hard to imagine a worse fate for a healthy adult human.

I wanted to do something to eliminate this blight and learned that we could spray the breeding ground of the flies as a possible way of eradicating the problem. We hired Evergreen International Aviation, a helicopter company, to spray certain rivers and their surrounding banks. Delford Smith, the owner of Evergreen, was a devout Christian from Washington State.

Up to this time in the early '90s CBN had been sending out teams of medical missionaries. Unfortunately these teams were unable to carry with them the supplies and equipment they needed for first-class medical care. Noticing this, Dede said to me with a lot of wisdom, "All we are doing is practicing Band-Aid medicine." In the countries where our teams were operating, there were not adequate hospital facilities, so we turned our thoughts toward finding ways to transport this level of care.

My new friend at Evergreen Aviation asked me, "Have you ever thought of using an airplane as a flying hospital?"

Of course, I had never thought any such thing, so I said, "What did you have in mind?"

"The Lockheed L-1011 has been a workhorse for the aviation industry, but they are being phased out. I think you could get one cheap and retrofit it as a hospital."

The L-1011 was a three-engine airliner with the third engine mounted high on the tail. Its avionics at the time were highly advanced and employed a technique called "fly by wire." In the fall of 1994 we were able to locate a relatively new L-1011 that could be purchased for the low price of three million dollars.

Our medical team contacted Lockheed and enlisted their support in retrofitting this airplane. Precise drawings were made to include the necessary structural adjustments to create a true hospital. When the work was finished, the plane was an absolute marvel.

At the front of the plane, we had first-class seating for about thirty people and in-house television. Doctors in the target countries could sit in this mini-theater and watch operations being performed aboard the Flying Hospital or watch an instructional video about advanced medical techniques. Onboard we had three fully equipped surgical suites for major surgery and six or so additional suites for minor surgeries. In the center of the plane were a number of spaces for patients to recover after surgery.

Lockheed reinforced the fuselage to accommodate massive surgical lights needed in the surgical suites, and at the rear of the plane was a place for the physicians to scrub before surgery, along with an autoclave to sterilize instruments. We brought in state-of-the-art surgical equipment so the doctors traveling with the plane could perform complex neurosurgery and procedures such as hip replacements. The most significant demand was for cataract surgery, and our eye doctors performed thousands of operations for cataracts and for a condition called strabismus, or cross-eyes.

In the hold of the plane, we were able to store enough medicine to care for the needs of as many as two hundred thousand people and to replenish the medical stores that were needed to care for the patients on board the plane.

I knew that when this specially fitted L-1011 landed in a country that this plane would be greeted by heads of state. We showed our Flying Hospital at the Paris Air Show, and President Nazarbayev of Kazakhstan stopped by to inspect the plane. When we flew into Kazakhstan, his wife welcomed us with a lavish reception.

It turned out that during the Cold War, the Russians had experimented with nuclear devices in Kazakhstan, and there was an unusually large number of people in that country who were blind because of cataracts.[1] I told the doctor in charge that we could obtain interocular lenses for ninety dollars to cure this condition. She replied, "We can buy them for fifty dollars, but we don't have the fifty dollars."

We were amazed to find that in this Russian-speaking territory our *The 700 Club* program was highly popular. As our team walked down the street, people tried to heap beautiful fruit on us as a show of their love and appreciation. Here again, it was clear to me that the God I serve had not left Himself without a witness, even in the far corners of a distant land.

We flew the Flying Hospital to many nations with remarkable results, but the most extraordinary use of this tremendous machine was by a local charity called Operation Smile headed by a plastic surgeon, Dr. Bill Magee, and his wife, Kathy. Bill took the Flying Hospital to about one hundred countries where they held clinics and raised support. He later told me that every one of those installations had taken root and proved an integral part of their popular ministry, which centered on repairing cleft palates and mandible (lower jaw) surgery of people who, without this surgery, would have faced life disfigured.

Regrettably the Flying Hospital came into conflict with Federal Aviation Administration regulations. A typical airliner of this size was flown commercially about ten thousand hours a year. Each year the government demanded a thorough overall inspection called a C check. We were operating our L-1011 at only a fraction of the typical commercial use, and so we petitioned the FAA for a waiver of their rules.

Unfortunately, the government agency was unyielding and demanded that we spend millions of dollars on an unnecessary annual C check, or else the FAA would ground the plane.

These extra and unanticipated expenses of operating this magnificent humanitarian device were more than we could afford. With great sadness of heart, I was forced to place our Flying Hospital alongside other out-of-service airplanes at an Arizona desert "boneyard."

All I can say is what a shame.

61

GOD'S VISITATION IN RECIFE, LIMA, AND MANILA

THE TYPICAL EVANGELISTIC crusade involves a ministry team, a skilled choir leader, the recruitment of hundreds of choir members and thousands of counselors, and a large amount of publicity. I have had several occasions to go out and hold evangelistic meetings where I had absolutely none of those things, and sometimes I was called upon to stand on a platform in front of a large crowd all by myself. I believe three such meetings would be helpful to talk about at this point in this book.

The city of Recife is on the far eastern coast of Brazil. We took our Flying Hospital to Recife to set up physical healing for the thousands of ill people who needed our help. The medical work took place in the daytime, and our staff determined that during one of the nights, we would hold a mass rally to tell the people about Jesus. I was the designated speaker for the night in question, so that afternoon I prepared the appropriate remarks to deliver to the audience.

The spirit of Carnivale before the Lenten season seems to have permeated the Brazilian consciousness. The excesses of Mardi Gras spill over into the personal lives and marital relations of many of the Brazilian people. As I was preparing what to say to the crowd that would come for our meeting, I laid out—in precise detail—biblical warnings against fornication and adultery.

While I was thinking about this message, the Spirit of God reminded me of the nature of Jesus. God's Word said, "The Spirit of the Lord is on me, because he has anointed me to proclaim good news to the poor. He has sent me to proclaim freedom for the prisoners and recovery of sight for the blind."[1]

The Lord said to me very plainly, "Are you planning to preach good news to the poor?"

"No, Lord," I replied. "I'm going to preach harsh judgment to the poor."

"I would prefer good news, not bad news," He said.

So when I stood on the platform before an estimated forty thousand people gathered together in Recife, I only had liberty to tell them the good news that Jesus Christ had died for them and that He had risen from the dead, and that He was coming again. And that if they received Him as their Savior, they would be part of the heavenly kingdom.

The Spirit of God fell gloriously upon the audience, and at least twenty thousand people responded to the message of God's love. I have to admit that the God of the Bible knows a great deal more about human nature than any of His servants ever will.

In another instance I was invited to go to Peru and to hold an evangelistic meeting in the capital of Lima. At the time, we were not broadcasting in Peru, and I thought none of the Peruvian people would know who I was or what I represented. Yet my host had the audacity to arrange an event in a soccer stadium that was the largest arena in the entire city. I thought that I would be speaking to a handful of people, so I went reluctantly.

I'll never forget walking up the steps to the place where I was to speak. That stadium was absolutely immense, and I was on the podium all by myself. But as I looked around the packed stadium and explained the simple gospel once again, tens of thousands of people accepted the Lord.

Then I told them that I wanted to pray for their healing and asked them to join hands with one another and to pray for the person to their right and the person to their left. As we all prayed together, the Spirit of God descended on that colossal arena. Thousands of the sick were wonderfully healed.

As I was speaking, the Lord gave what turned out to be a prophetic word. I declared that God wanted to bless Peru, and I believed that His presence would come upon the country and reward them for their faithfulness to Him. Later on, I learned that they had discovered a vast reservoir of oil in the Amazon, and many of the people attributed this remarkable discovery to God's blessing.

Not only had that huge arena been packed with people, but as I was leaving, I discovered that about twenty thousand people had remained standing outside because they could not be admitted into the main stadium. I stopped by the fence where they were and prayed for them.

There's one other instance twelve thousand miles away from South America. I was invited to speak at the famous Araneta Coliseum in Manila, the capital of the Philippines. This time the Lord did not have to correct my message because—I had no message at all!

We had at least one hundred security personnel, the necessary singer, the choir, and the musical instruments. We had a full-blown evangelistic event going on, but I had nothing to say. I waited on the Lord and heard nothing. When I arose to the microphone, I still had nothing. So I said, "Let's just praise the Lord!"

And the people began to praise the Lord and sing and clap and rejoice. In that atmosphere of praise, the Lord began to touch people with healing. As I prayed and rejoiced, the Lord gave me words of knowledge describing physical conditions in the audience. As I spoke, they were healed. All over that auditorium, there were dramatic healings. I tried to bring some sort of coherent message to describe what was happening, but nothing came—just wave after wave of healing power and miracles. I learned precisely the meaning of the phrase "the Lord inhabits the praise of His people."

I don't know exactly how many people were healed that evening, but I'm sure that it exceeded twenty thousand. I can say with great certainty that it's fun to serve the Lord. I have known heartache, but I also have seen the fullness of joy in the presence of my heavenly Father.

The hunger for the Lord is so intense throughout the world that it became clear to me that all that's needed to put on a good evangelistic rally is the presence of God—no band, no choir, no elaborate advertising, only God Himself.

62

A Land of Riches Despoiled

I was in my office on a spring afternoon when the receptionist called to tell me that a young man was in the lobby with a message for me from the president of Zaire. I asked one of my security officers to check out the young man and then escort him up to my office. When he arrived, the young man said that he was bringing me an invitation from President Mobutu of Zaire to be his guest at his place in the south of France.

I strongly suspected a hoax, so I thanked the young man and then contacted the Embassy of Zaire in Washington to determine whether the invitation was valid. It turned out to be the truth, and not long after, I received a formal invitation on official letterhead of the Embassy of Zaire.

I decided that this invitation undoubtedly represented a significant opportunity for evangelism, so I made plans to fly with a film crew to France. President Mobutu received us warmly and came straight to the point.

"I'm afraid that the growing number of Roman Catholics in my country may lead to interference by the Vatican," he said. "I would like to see more of my countrymen become Evangelicals, and I would like to offer you an invitation to put your television programs on our national network for free."

Since CBN was always looking for broadcast opportunities all over the world, Mobutu's invitation was hardly one I could refuse.

Before I left, President Mobutu followed up with an invitation to visit his country and see firsthand his television facilities. He told me of a proposed trip from Paris to Kinshasa, the capital of Zaire. I was to be his guest on the trip as well as his guest in the capital of the country.

A few years before this when I was seeking God's will for my life, I had stopped at Fort Washington, Pennsylvania, at the headquarters of the World Evangelization Crusade (WEC), headed by missionary statesman Norman Grubb. I offered to serve as a missionary under WEC. For some reason, I conceived that my task upon entering Africa would be to paddle upriver in a dugout canoe, swatting mosquitos and talking to handfuls of villagers about the Lord. Fortunately Norman Grubb, who was sensitive to the moving of the Holy Spirit, rejected my offer of service.

It may seem a bit ironic, but when I did enter Africa for the first time, it was not in a dugout canoe but in the luxuriously appointed 727 jetliner belonging to the president of Zaire. To say the least, my Lord has a delightful sense of humor.

The land of Zaire, now known as the Democratic Republic of the Congo, is the host of unimagined riches. It has one of the world's largest deposits of copper and cobalt.[1] It has one of the largest deposits of what are known as "rare earths." It has a profusion of forests containing some of the world's choicest hardwoods. Its farms can produce dozens of varieties of tropical fruit.

The problem for Zaire is its colonial past. For much of the twentieth century until its independence in 1960, Zaire was known as the Belgian Congo and was under the domination of cruel taskmasters who held this great nation as the private property of King Leopold II of Belgium.[2]

King Leopold was anything but an enlightened ruler. Out of a population of close to fifty million people, only five thousand had college degrees, and few, if any, had been equipped to manage small enterprises, much less the affairs of a nation. King Leopold seemingly ignored the vast treasures available in Zaire but instead concentrated on rubber. He set onerous requirements for rubber production from the natives. Those who did not meet the standards were often maimed by having arms or legs cut off.[3]

The Congolese leader who negotiated freedom from Belgium was named Patrice Lumumba. From all indications, this young man was destined to be an outstanding leader. The CIA, however, feared that Lumumba had Communist sympathies and would pull his new nation into the orbit of the Soviet Union. Although there is no hard proof of this, it's suspected that the CIA conspired with conservative elements in the Congo to have Lumumba assassinated.

In his place the CIA chose an army lieutenant colonel named Mobuto Sese Seko to head the country. In the resulting chaos, the mineral-rich province of Katanga under a man named Moïse Tshombe broke free from the country, and it appeared that the entire nation might be in danger of dissolution. Consequently, the United States moved forcibly in 1964 to bolster Mobutu's power and to consolidate his hold over the entire nation.

Regrettably Mobutu and his cronies seemed more interested in enriching themselves and acquiring impressive real estate in Europe than alleviating the desperate plight of the suffering citizens of their nation.[4]

While in Zaire at the invitation of President Mobutu, I was introduced to all of the cabinet members and then was given a private escort to tour the entire nation.

On a subsequent trip I offered President Mobutu my services to conduct an analysis of various parts of his economy to see if we could, in some way, assist his nation.

For all its unimaginable wealth Zaire was dreadfully mismanaged. They had a hydroelectric plant on the Congo River that was large enough to supply electric power for the entire country. Unfortunately the power lines had been impaired and electrical service was spotty.

I went to the giant copper and cobalt facility called Gécamines. This was a huge facility, and yet a large portion of it had been shut down because the people in charge had excavated a giant cavity that they failed to backfill. As a result, there was a mine collapse that destroyed a multimillion-dollar crusher. The mine had dozens of expensive twenty-ton trucks that were standing idle because the drivers had failed to service the air filters and the motors on these expensive vehicles had burned out from lack of maintenance.

I surveyed their river traffic, which was essential to bringing agricultural products from the rural communities into the metropolitan areas where the buyers were located. The vital river traffic almost came to a halt for a couple of reasons. Intense vegetation, which should have been cleared, was allowed to proliferate and choke the motors of the vital river craft. So, once again, I was shown dozens of valuable motor-driven watercraft cast aside because of poor maintenance.

At many places I met people desperate for help and hungry for leadership. None was available because the economy was in shambles and credit facilities were no longer available.

I remember one meeting with the principal heads of the financial structure of the nation of Zaire. At that meeting, I took out of my pocket a number of one-hundred-dollar bills and placed these in the hands of each participant. I then asked them, "Do you know what you have in your hand?"

And they said, "A hundred-dollar bill."

"No, you hold in your hand the wealth of the world. Here is how it works. If you, in one year, can double that hundred dollars, it becomes two hundred. Doubled again, it becomes four hundred. Doubled again, it becomes eight hundred. At the end of twenty years it becomes fifty million dollars. At the end of twenty-five years it becomes $1.4 billion. At the end of fifty years, it is measured in terms of quadrillions, and your hundred dollars has become more than all of the money in the world."

My audience was astounded. Then I added this: "On the other hand, this same principle will work against you. If you continue to inflate your currency, in a very short time your debt will be overwhelming and your currency will be worthless."

Almost to a man they replied, "We can't stop inflating the currency, or we won't have enough money to pay our bills." So inflate they did.

When I first arrived in Zaire, their currency was trading at about four to the dollar. In several years, one dollar could purchase about a million of the Zaire currency. I warned them that runaway inflation would lead to rioting in the streets. And sure enough, rioting came in a devastating fashion. The workers went on a rampage and did at least a billion dollars' worth of damage to the places where they had been employed. The soldiers who had not been paid had their weapons, of course, so they were able to roam the streets and prey on the unfortunate civilians. Naturally, those at the top were able to maintain a comfortable standard of living.

The government had arranged to have their currency printed in Brazil. Those in charge had a second set of currency printed for themselves, which they distributed to their friends. It was the type of tragedy that can happen to any nation when its rulers place their personal gain ahead of the needs of their people.

Before all of this happened, President Mobutu and I developed a strong friendship. At one time, we were in the chapel dedicated to his late wife, known as Maman Mobutu. As he thought about her, he was convulsed with sobs. I put my arm around him and began to pray for the Lord to extend His love to this man. I was able to be his friend and through our friendship see hundreds of thousands of his wonderful countrymen receive Jesus Christ as Savior.

President Mobutu contracted cancer and left the country for treatment. He died of prostate cancer in 1997.[5] In his absence, a warlord named Laurent Kabila seized control of the government,[6] and there ensued a period of economic and political collapse that continues to this day.

The nation of Zaire has been the scene of two terrible tragedies that have caused suffering far beyond the borders of this African nation, one of which is Ebola, which is discussed further below, and the other is AIDS. Although there are many theories about the origin of the disease called AIDS, one theory—and it is only a theory—is as follows. The World Health Organization attempted to create a vaccine that would either prevent or cure polio by using blood from monkeys and then injecting this untried vaccine into about two hundred thousand of the natives.[7] For the first time in history, pathogens from monkeys were injected into the bloodstreams of human beings.

From what I can understand, it was then transmitted from person to person by the exchange of bodily fluids. The resulting disease in humans was called Acquired Immune Deficiency Syndrome, or AIDS. In other words, this particular virus compromised the immune system of its victims and left them open to a host of other diseases, including cancer and wasting illness.

Fortunately, some who have the HIV virus that causes AIDs have not been subjected to the disease, as such. Medical science is working diligently, and hundreds of millions of dollars are being spent on curing a disease that, to the best of my understanding, may have been caused by well-meaning researchers using innocent Africans as guinea pigs.

The other disease that originated in Zaire is Ebola, which is the name of a river in Zaire where this disease first became prevalent. It's my understanding that this terrible disease was vectored by bats that lived in caves and the disease was contracted by those who had been exploring these caves.

The Ebola virus is virulent beyond imagination and causes a breakdown of vital organs. The sufferer begins to hemorrhage from every orifice of his or her body. Recovery from this horrible disease is almost unknown, although one worker from Franklin Graham's Samaritan's Purse was able to survive, but only after heroic intervention and a quarantined trip from Liberia to ultra modern hospital care in Texas.

When I learned of the outbreak, I flew some medicine to Kinshasa. My two regular pilots flew only as far as Cape Verde and refused to go into the area where Ebola was present. I was forced to hire two more hardy pilots to take us all the way in.

When I returned to Zaire, I learned that the problem facing most of the natives was not the Ebola virus but what they called diarrhea rouge, which was caused by an intestinal parasite that led to wasting and death-inducing bloody diarrhea. Fortunately we had available the antibiotics necessary to cure this condition, which we distributed freely.

I was also able to send a small plane loaded with crucially needed medicine to the city of Kikwit, which is southeast of the capital of Kinshasa. Thank goodness effective quarantine meant the dreaded Ebola virus did not persist, but one ugly fact emerged. The aid organizations assembled to fight Ebola provided adequate funds for European and Western Hemisphere doctors. They refused funds, however, to purchase hazmat suits for the Zairian doctors laboring mightily to prolong the lives of those suffering from the Ebola virus. I thought that this blatant display of racism was unworthy of any medical personnel. So with funds from CBN, we purchased the necessary hazmat suits to protect the health of the native doctors.

It was the least we could do.

63

A Firsthand Look at War-Torn Afghanistan

Afghanistan was formerly ruled by Mohammad Zahir Shah, the country's last king, who was deposed on July 17, 1973.[1] It's my understanding that King Shah was a dedicated Muslim and took action against the single evangelical church in the country, which he ordered bulldozed. The pastor of that church was Christy Wilson, a noted Bible teacher. In 1979, six years later, the Soviet Union invaded Afghanistan and took control of its government.[2]

Several years after that I visited that troubled country with one of our camera operators. I found that the brutality of the Soviets against the Afghan people was intense. One particularly barbaric practice was to drop attractive toys on the streets for little Afghan children to pick up. These toys were built with hidden explosives.[3] When they exploded, the children lost their hands, a number of their fingers, and other parts of their bodies.

I visited a hospital in Quetta on the Afghan border and saw unimaginable suffering. One young teenager had been shot in the lower leg by Soviet soldiers. Medical personnel were unable to treat his wound properly, and his leg became gangrenous. There were no facilities for amputation, and when I saw him, his leg was purple in color and shriveled up like a prune. He was forced to lie in a hot hospital room without pain medication and without proper nourishment.

In a ward adjoining him was another Afghan man who'd been wounded in his back. The bullet was lodged in a critical nexus of nerves; doctors were unable to remove it without causing paralysis. His destiny was to lie on his back in terrible agony, hour after hour and day after day, with inadequate nutrition, few or no painkillers, and nothing to ease his mind.

I remember sitting on a rug on a tent floor with a group of freedom fighters called mujahideen. They discussed with me their plans to attack their Russian captors. I had brought with me some metal reflective devices that grew sufficiently hot in the sun to provide rudimentary cooking.

I was handing out these solar cookers when a large Pathan warrior strode up to me. He was wearing the full uniform, which included a wool coat and two crossed bandoliers of ammunition on his chest. He began speaking in animated Dari.

I asked the interpreter what he was saying, and the answer was straightforward: "Don't give us toys. Give us rifles and bullets to kill Russians."

I, of course, didn't have weapons with me, but I noticed the extraordinary spirit that these Afghans displayed. These brave fighters were willing to risk their lives to gain freedom for their nation, but they were using old Lee-Enfield rifles and going up against the sophisticated Russian Mil Mi-24 Hind Helicopter. The Afghans were being slaughtered, and throughout the nation was a trail of blood and poverty that war had caused.

Some of you may have seen the amusing motion picture called *Charlie Wilson's War*. Charlie was a young Congressman from Texas who realized that Afghanistan was a proving ground of the global war between the United States and Russia. Charlie finagled a sizable appropriation from his congressional allies and used these funds to buy Stinger missiles. Armed with these Stingers, the Mujahideen fighters were blowing up every Russian attack helicopter or fighter plane that came against them.

The Soviet battle losses mounted to such a degree that they became intolerable, and Russia turned tail and fled the scene of battle. Without question, Afghanistan proved the end of the myth of Soviet invincibility and ultimately led to the rise of Mikhail Gorbachev and what came to be known as *glasnost*, or openness.

Unfortunately, Afghanistan did not return to a system of individual liberty. Instead, an ultra fundamentalist group called the Taliban took power with the aid of the Mujahideen, which the United States had trained and equipped in the fight against the Soviet Union.

To this day, Afghanistan remains a problem for the free world. The country was a base for Osama bin Laden as well as other terrorist groups seeking to harm the United States. Afghanistan is a deeply divided tribal society and has remained this way since the days of Alexander the Great.

In the modern era, policymakers are faced with a dilemma. The principal cash crop of Afghanistan is opium,[4] and the country has been one of the major sources of opiate drugs that have destroyed our young people. We could easily eradicate the opium poppies, but there are many reasons, some not so benign, that we don't do so.

If Afghanistan falls to extreme Islam, it will become a breeding ground for terror all over the world. There is no way that the American taxpayers will support a series of corrupt governments in that nation.

So what are we to do? I don't have a good answer to that question because it seems that any course our nation takes in regard to Afghanistan will prove to be erroneous.

64

VICTORY OVER FEAR

THE BIBLE TELLS us that when Satan rebelled against almighty God, he took one-third of the angels in heaven with him during this revolt.[1] Later Scriptures say that Satan came to earth and took the fallen angels with him.[2] These fallen creatures are called evil spirits or demons. What do they wish to do?

First and foremost, they wish to destroy human beings made in the image of God, so they delight in entering into the consciousness of human beings to turn them away from God—to cause fear, suspicion, and some mental illness, and do all kinds of damage to human beings.

Second, these evil spirits (or demons) want to experience human passion, so they will inhabit people and cause conditions of evil. They delight in sexual pleasure, gluttony, and physical sensation. It's possible for an individual with a demon resident to have excessive greed, become an alcoholic, or become a sex addict.

In treating human beings with issues like these, psychotherapy and other medicinal techniques can be effective. But demon possession has to be treated with an exorcism, meaning the demon has to be cast out in the name of Jesus.

Right about now I know some people are saying, "Well, if a Christian has the Spirit of God within him, how can he possibly have a demon?"

Various conditions are described in the Bible, including being demonized, being possessed, and being controlled by a demonic power. If a person has the Holy Spirit of God within them, then the Holy Spirit is in ultimate control of that person's life.

Nevertheless, that individual can voluntarily welcome a demon, for example, by looking at pornography, undergoing a regimen of heavy drinking, or doing something of that nature. In the process that person can welcome an evil presence into their life. That does not mean that

Satan controls the individual, but it does mean that that person will be influenced by demonic presence.

I remember hearing one godly minister say to me, "I am filled with the Holy Spirit, and I cannot even have a peewee demon inside of me." That was an interesting statement, but it doesn't reflect the reality of what happens in peoples' lives.

I have encountered demonic oppression and demonic resistance on many occasions. I have come up against demon powers, and I have come up against weak demonic influence. Now I would like to give you a personal example of something that happened to me in the nation of India.

I happened to be in southern India on a Saturday at the invitation of my good friend Dr. D. G. S. Dhinakaran, who had established a broad base of support throughout India.[3] He was a highly respected individual, and his meetings were attended by hundreds of thousands of Indian people. D. G. S. graciously offered me the Saturday speaking engagement for his crusade in the area of Hyderabad, India.

Dede and I had a hotel room in Hyderabad, and when I awoke that morning, I realized that I had been seized by an extraordinary lassitude. I didn't want to do anything. I felt tired, but it couldn't have been jet lag since I'd been in the country for several days. I didn't know what was causing this malaise, so I asked the Lord, "What's wrong with me? Why am I so tired this morning? Please give me an answer."

And the Lord spoke very clearly: "It is a spirit of fear."

What would I have to be afraid of? Nothing. I'd spoken at evangelistic meetings many, many times over the years. But I was in India, and the Indian people have a great deal to be afraid of. Just think of some of the things that weighed upon the Indian consciousness in 1994. The situation has improved since, but when this trip took place, many resources had not yet been put in place to help them.

In the Hindu religion there is a belief in approximately three hundred thousand different gods, and most of these gods are not portrayed as friendly but as evil. Imagine an average Indian who embraced the Hindu faith being subject to three hundred thousand malevolent deities.

But that isn't the only thing that caused fear in the Indian people. At the time I was there, they didn't have any kind of social safety net, so if they lost their jobs, they literally had no source of income. And if there was no source of income, then there was no way to buy food. And if there was no food, they would starve to death. That was a real and present danger.

In those days, there would be dead bodies lying in the streets to be picked up every morning by teams that came out to retrieve and incinerate the bodies. For those with serious diseases, the hospitals were inadequate and didn't have the necessary medicine. These poor Indians were forced to suffer because there was no relief from their pain and suffering.

In addition to that, there was the caste system. One caste with members known as *Dalits* were the lower-caste people, and in those days they were called the *untouchables*.[4] In the Hindu religion, the dark-skinned people were viewed as being under the foot of Brahma and therefore were untouchable to the rest of society, leaving several hundred million people as social outcasts.[5]

In fact, if even the shadow of an untouchable would fall upon a higher-caste Brahmin Indian, that higher-caste person had to be ritually cleansed, and the Dalit would be beaten severely for allowing his shadow to fall upon one of the higher-caste Indians.[6] It was a terrible social system to be part of. This aspect of the caste system has been somewhat alleviated in recent years, but when I was there in the '80s, these were among the major concerns of lower-caste Indians.

Before I got ready to leave my hotel room to speak, I dealt with this spirit of fear. I said, "In the name of Jesus, you spirit of fear, loose me." And that spirit immediately left.

There are levels of power in the demonic realm. As Ephesians 6:12 points out, there are regional demonic forces, there are rulers, there are principalities, and there is an entire structure of power with Satan himself at the head. There are demonic rulers in charge of cities, states, and nations.

You will recall the biblical account of Daniel being approached by an angel while he was fasting.[7] The angel told Daniel that when he began to fast and pray about twenty-one days earlier, he (the angel) had tried to come to him but was hindered by the Prince of Persia. But Michael, the mighty angel who looks over Israel, came to fight against this demonic being. This in turn enabled the messenger angel to bring Daniel a communication from the Lord saying that he was highly regarded and his prayers had been heard. This account clearly shows that there was a struggle in the heavenlies between Michael, a powerful archangel, and a demon called the Prince of Persia.

I think one of the lies Satan has imposed upon people is to ignore the existence of the spiritual realm. We are told that Satan isn't a real being and doesn't exist, or that he's merely an influence, nothing more or less than a state of mind. None of this is remotely true. These creatures are real, and they do have enormous influence. Fortunately, because they are just that—creatures—they cannot read our minds or thoughts. They can, however, try to influence our minds.

Jesus said that if you're going to despoil a strong man's house, you first must bind the strong man.[8] Before going into a territory, a Spirit-filled Christian must, out of necessity, take the power of Jesus to bind the strong man. I might add that it's important that the person doing the binding is in touch with the power of God and is filled with pure power and not fake.

Consider the story told in Acts about the seven sons of a sorcerer named Sceva, who had seen the apostle Paul casting out demons.[9] So they came upon a demon-possessed man and said to the demon in the man, "In the name of Jesus whom Paul preaches, I command you to come out."[10]

According to the Bible, the demon replied, "Jesus I know, and Paul I know about, but who are you?"[11] And then the demonic man jumped upon the sons of Sceva, and they fled naked from the place where they had been using their so-called magic.

Scripture tells us that when Jesus was on the Sea of Galilee, he approached an area known as Gadara.[12] As He began to move up a hillside in Gadara, a man came running to Him. The Bible tells us that this man had been possessed by Satan. He had been bound with chains but had such enormous strength that he broke the chains apart. He was naked up in the mountains, screaming out in pain, and cutting himself while wandering about like an outcast from all society. When he came to Jesus, he fell at Jesus' feet, and the demons within him said, "We know who You are. You are the Son of God. Don't cast us into the pit before the time."

"What is your name?" Jesus asked.

And the demon replied, "Our name is Legion."

A legion amounts to ten cohorts in the Roman army, or about five thousand people. Along with the support forces, a legion can have as many as eleven thousand people or more. So this demon was saying that there were at least five thousand demons inhabiting this one man, and yet they bowed before Jesus and acknowledged that He was the Son of God. They were then praying to Jesus not to be sent to the pit before the time because they realized judgment was coming upon them, and they were not going to be given any second chance because they were condemned to eternal damnation in hell. They didn't want to leave any sooner than they had to.

In an interesting turn of events, Jesus answered their prayer and granted their request. He let them go into a herd of swine feeding on the hillside. The demons rushed into the swine, which in turn became crazy, running down the slopes of the hill of Gadara and into the Sea of Galilee, where they drowned.

It's incredible not only that the demons asked for permission but that the townspeople came to Jesus and asked that He please leave. They didn't want any further destruction of property, so Jesus answered their request as well. But the crazed man who was now in his right mind asked to accompany Jesus, and Jesus told him He didn't want him to do so, but to go back and tell the people in his hometown what God had done for him.

Jesus answered the prayer of the demons and answered the prayer of the townspeople, but He refused to answer the prayer of the demoniac. In any event this story is a magnificent example of what happens when Jesus Christ takes authority over demons.

Going back to my time in India, I realized the enormous power of the name of Jesus to control demonic power. These demons had actually come into my consciousness to take away my strength and my joy that morning. The minute I commanded them to leave, they left me. A spirit of fear is not a strong demon and is one that will acknowledge the name of Jesus very readily. There was no fight involved, and the demon left me immediately. My fatigue and strange feeling of lassitude departed as well. I was completely fine.

That evening I spoke to an incredibly large group numbering somewhere between 500,000 and 750,000 people. They were sitting on the grass of a polo field in that part of India. From a platform in their midst, I presented the glorious gospel of Jesus Christ to them. I finished with an invitation to receive Jesus, and then I led them in prayer.

The prayer was a simple prayer, not complicated at all. But it was one that acknowledged that Jesus Christ was the Son of God, that He had died for their sins, that He had risen again, that He was coming again, and that if they received Him as Savior, He would cleanse them from their sins and give them a place in God's eternal kingdom. They prayed that prayer with me reverently, and an estimated three hundred thousand gave their hearts to Jesus Christ.

When I was done giving the invitation, I told them I wanted to pray that they might be set free from a spirit of fear. When I prayed, they again reverently bowed their heads to join with me in prayer.

"In the name of Jesus Christ of Nazareth, I cast out a spirit of fear from these people," I prayed.

Suddenly they began to shout for joy as this burden lifted from them and they felt the fear leave them. The enormity of the oppression they had suffered left as well, and they raised their hands and rejoiced and shouted with praise all over that field.

Thousands and thousands of people were set free. God wasn't trying to make me subject to some kind of demon power, but He wanted to show me what I was dealing with when I stood on a platform on that field to minister to hundreds of thousands of people. As a result of the revelation He had shown to me, these people were now set free from terrible oppression.

I want to say again what Jesus Christ said about Himself. As He was leaving this earth, He took His disciples to Himself, and He said, "All authority in heaven and on earth has been given to me."[13]

Now one translation of the word for "authority" is *power*. There are two words in Greek that have been translated to *power* in the English version of the New Testament. One is *exousia*, which means authority.[14] An example would be the authority that the president of the United States has over our country's nuclear weapons. The president doesn't have to be built like Arnold Schwarzenegger or even a mighty warrior who's eight feet tall. He could be a short individual, but because of his office, he has been given the authority over the nuclear arsenal of America as well as all the ships and planes in the US military. In other words, the president of the United States has the power and authority to incinerate large parts of the earth.

So when Jesus was saying, "I have all authority [*exousia*] over all the world," He was saying, "My father has given Me authority over demons. I have authority over principalities and powers. I have authority over all the rulers of the earth. I am in charge of everything—all authority in heaven and earth. Whatever is in the stars; whatever is in the solar system; whatever is on this planet; whatever animals; whatever creatures; and whatever spiritual beings, whether they are angels or demons; they have all been given to Me, the Son of God." It is an awesome grant of authority that is held by our Savior.

The other Greek word for *power* is *dunamis*, which is where we get the word *dynamite*,[15] which describes the explosives that we use in many commercial and military activities. Jesus also has dynamite, and He said, "But you will receive power [*dunamis*] when the Holy Spirit comes on you; and you will be my witnesses."[16]

So He was essentially saying, "When the Holy Spirit comes upon you, you will have explosive power in yourself. You can overcome demons. You can have power to speak the word in My name, and that word will come about." But more than anything, because of His grant of authority, Christians filled with His Spirit have *exousia* and have authority over demons. There is no amount of demonic force that can overwhelm a child of God.

I have encountered demonic presences over and over again, and I know for a fact that the strong man can be bound. The phrase that I use is simple: "I bind you, Satan, and the forces of evil."

It's not just Satan himself, but it's those who work for him. And the word is, "I bind you in the name of Jesus Christ." Once Satan is bound, you can despoil his house. If he is not bound, he is free to come against you in various unpleasant ways.

This is why Christians should always be alert. We are told by the apostle Peter to "be sober, be vigilant; because your adversary the devil walks about like a roaring lion, seeking whom he may devour."[17] The New Testament writers did not minimize in any way the power of Satan. And Martin Luther, in that great hymn "A Mighty Fortress Is Our God," says, "His craft and power are great, and armed with cruel hate, on earth is not his equal."[18] That sentiment is exactly correct. It would be a terrible mistake to minimize the power of Satan or the power of the satanic forces. But we need to know that if we join together with other Christians, we have power that can control the strong man.

Year after year, as I have entered various territories and various environments, I have seen the enormous power of Satan. But I have also seen the even more enormous power of Jesus. I am fully persuaded that the name of Jesus is more than sufficient to control Satan, to bind the strong man, and to despoil his house. I would advise everyone who reads this book to understand the power that our Lord has. There is no force anywhere in the world that can contend with the Lord Jesus.

I would advise people not to give place to the devil. Don't be saying, "Old slue-foot caused me to do this," or, "The devil caused me to do that." And please don't think that you can control demonic power by serenading it. Some people believe that by singing, "There's power in the blood," they can overcome demons.

You don't overcome demons by singing but by giving a clear command in the name of Jesus and being activated by the Holy Spirit. The devil wants obedience and wants someone to give him praise. If with your mouth you confess Satan's power, then you are giving him the opportunity to hurt you, destroy you, or take down your noblest goals and ambitions.

I would strongly advise your confession to be: "This is the day that the Lord has made, and I will rejoice and be glad in it. In the Lord's power, all things are possible. Therefore, in His name, I will go forth knowing that my Savior has all authority in heaven and earth. He has given me that grant of authority that I in turn can use to have victory over the enemy of my soul."

And then go on with your day and your activities, victorious and knowing that no demon has control over you or how you act.

65

The Greatest Virtue

W<small>E ARE TOLD</small> in the Bible that in the early days of creation almighty God created a powerful being known as Lucifer or the Light One.[1] As I mentioned before, he was known as an anointed cherub who covered the very holiness of God.[2]

According to the prophet Ezekiel, he walked on stones of fire in the most sacred part of God's creation.[3] This extraordinarily privileged creation, however, began to contemplate his own beauty and compare himself to his Creator. Instead of being grateful for his status, he began to be resentful toward his Creator. We read that he was perfect in all his ways until iniquity was found in him.[4]

What was his iniquity? He convinced himself that he could do a better job running the entire creation than the Creator Himself could do,[5] a deep-seated pride reflected in the song popularized by Frank Sinatra, "My Way."

If pride, therefore, is the greatest sin, then love is not the reverse of pride. Instead, I would submit that the greatest virtue is not love but rather humility, whereby the creature is totally submitted to the power and authority of the Creator.

There are many examples of verses in the Bible that amplify this reasoning:

+ "Therefore humble yourselves under the mighty hand of God, that He may exalt you in due time."[6]

+ "God resists the proud, but gives grace to the humble."[7]

+ "The fear of the LORD *is* the beginning of wisdom, And the knowledge of the Holy One *is* understanding."[8]

+ "I am the LORD, that is My name; and My glory I will not give to another."[9]

I have taken as my own personal guide the word that Jesus spoke to His disciples: "...When you have done all those things which you are commanded, say, 'We are unprofitable servants. We have done what was our duty to do.'"[10] I made a firm and straightforward rule for myself: I gave the Lord credit for all the good things that I was able to accomplish, and I personally took the blame for all the bad. Here is how some of this played out in my personal life.

After our first television station was firmly on the air and CBN had begun to grow across the nation, it was obvious to me that we had an exceptional staff. Our camera operators, audio people, and directors were excellent. In short I felt the work that we were doing put us in a class ahead of many of our peers in religious broadcasting.

Along with all of these realizations came a sickening pride. I brought this sin before the Lord and was given over to heartfelt contrition. The Lord gently reminded me with these words: "There are many more able people than you in this land, but only you would heed My call. I will use you for My purposes because *I have not time to train another.*"

I called our entire staff together and confessed the feeling of pride that had come into my heart, a pride that I thought most of them shared. We did not merely say prayers that day. We got on our knees and cried to God to ask for His forgiveness because we realized that our attitude was an abomination in His sight. Together we asked the Lord to make our hearts right so we could move forward in a spirit of humility that would please Him.

I also thought of the story of Nebuchadnezzar, who in his prime was the most powerful ruler on the face of the earth. As Nebuchadnezzar was walking about the fabulous Hanging Gardens of Babylon, he thought, "Is not this the great Babylon I have built as the royal residence, by my mighty power and for the glory of my majesty?"[11]

At that time a watcher from heaven came down and said to him, "The Most High is sovereign over all kingdoms on earth and gives them to anyone he wishes."[12]

At that very moment Nebuchadnezzar was given the mind of an animal. He was forced to live outdoors in a field and eat grass like an ox until he humbled himself and recognized that God Almighty rules in the affairs of the nations, and He can put in charge whomever He deems fit.

As I now look around a beautiful campus with lovely Georgian Colonial buildings at our Virginia Beach headquarters of CBN and Regent University, it would be so easy to have a sense of pride. If such a thought crosses my mind, I rebuke it as evil and quickly turn my mind toward God's power, not the work of my hands. I don't dare let myself fall into the trap that broke King Nebuchadnezzar.

My actions in the early days of CBN as we were putting together stations on the East Coast may seem comical today, but they were very real then. I made what I considered to be an agreement with the Lord. If He would help me put this network together on the East Coast, every day I would put my face on the ground and humble myself before Him. I did that day after day, week after week, month after month, and year after year.

God in turn fulfilled the desires of my heart. It's clear that the safest posture for a human being is with his or her face to the ground because no one wants to take that position away from them. Only when a person is lifted up with honors will he or she come under the attack of those who are jealous or resentful.

The Bible says that although Jesus was God Himself, He did not feel that equality with the Father was something to be grasped.[13] Instead, He took on the form of a man and became obedient unto death. On the evening before His crucifixion, Jesus shared the Passover meal with His disciples. After they had eaten, He laid aside His outer garments, wrapped a towel around Himself, took a basin of water, and began to wash the feet of His disciples. He said to them, "If I then, *your* Lord and Teacher, have washed your feet, you also ought to wash one another's feet."[14]

Before that, when He found them arguing as to who was the greatest, He made it clear that the greatest was the one who was the servant of all.[15] True leaders are those who are humble and who feel that their calling is to serve their fellow workers, not dominate them.

The apostle Paul wrote that because of the abundance of the revelations given to him, "Therefore, in order to keep me from being conceited, I was given a thorn in my flesh, a messenger of Satan, to torment me. Three times I pleaded with the Lord to take it away from me. But he said to me, 'My grace is sufficient for you, for my power is made perfect in weakness.'"[16] So the apostle went on to say, "For when I am weak, then I am strong."[17]

Many commentators have debated what precisely was Paul's thorn in the flesh. Some say it was a chronic eye disease because he mentioned in one letter that the people loved him so much that they were glad to give their eyes for him. Some have suggested that he may have had a disfiguring skin disease because he wrote in one case, "My trial which was in my flesh you did not despise."[18]

Frankly I prefer to take Paul at his word when he said his problem was "a messenger of Satan, to torment me."[19] In other words, there was a demon spirit who was constantly alongside to harass him. When he went into a town, there was opposition stirred up against him. He was arrested, beaten, repeatedly whipped, flogged with rods, shipwrecked, and spent a night and a day in ocean waters. It doesn't take any genius to see him as an ill-clad wanderer, horribly beaten and abused.

I am certainly no apostle Paul, but our Lord made sure that I had an external source to ensure my continued humility. The *Virginian-Pilot* newspaper, based in Norfolk, had been owned by a Colonel Samuel Slover. His nephew (whom I understand he adopted) was a man named Frank Batten, who added to the *Virginian-Pilot* several other dailies and several ad-filled newspapers called Shoppers. His company was called Landmark Communications, and through it Frank Batten became one of the wealthiest men in Virginia and certainly the most affluent in our local area. Among his honors, he was named chairman of the Virginia Associated Press. Despite his vast wealth, Frank Batten unfortunately suffered a number of debilitating injuries, spent many days in and out of doctors' offices and hospitals, and ultimately passed away.[20]

There seemed to be no effort made to rein in the newspaper staff that delighted in attacking me personally. The managing editor of the *Virginian-Pilot* never lost an opportunity to run stories and photographs that were terribly hostile to me.

They hired a so-called investigative reporter, who followed me on the campaign trail when I was running for president in 1988 and wrote ongoing inaccurate stories about what I was doing. And another journalist on their staff—according to his own brother who was a dedicated Christian—was a committed atheist whose goal was to humiliate and embarrass a prominent Christian so that he, the journalist, would feel justified in his atheism.

Words fail me to describe the vicious reporting of this so-called journalist or the headlines that the managing editor permitted. In retrospect I have to be grateful for this "thorn in the flesh" because the more these journalists humbled me, the more thoroughly God blessed me. The Bible tells us that "no chastening seems to be joyful for the present, but painful; nevertheless, afterward it yields the peaceable fruits of righteousness to those who have been trained by it."[21]

As I write this, I have been gratified to see Frank Batten's Christian son, Frank Batten Jr., whose wife is also a dedicated Christian, take the reins of this local daily after his father's passing. Frank Batten Jr. is an investment genius who invested in a software company called Red Hat, which went public and made him a billionaire.[22] He has disposed of various assets of his estate at remarkable prices and can be considered one of the outstanding business successes of this generation.

I know it may seem absurd, but at this point in my life, I'm much more comfortable being attacked and insulted than I am being complimented. Trying to live up to fulsome praise is quite demanding, whereas trying to respond to withering criticism takes little or no effort.

I can say that because I rely on the Lord to fight my battles for me.

66

HE WHO CAUSES EVERYTHING TO BE

ONE TIME WHEN I was reading the psalms, I came upon the last part of Psalm 91, which I believe perfectly describes my lifetime relationship with my heavenly Father, the supernatural God.

To follow up on what I said earlier, the God of the Christians and Jews has a name, but His name is not easily defined like Baal, Astarte, Marduk, Dagon, or Molech. When He met with Moses, God identified Himself with the verb "to be" when He said, "I AM THAT I AM."[1]

In our English Bible, the term is LORD, but that is not an accurate translation of the Hebrew. His Hebrew name is a four-letter Tetragrammaton: YHWH. Some translators have taken the vowels from the Hebrew word for *Lord* (Adonai) and have made the name of God translate to Yehowah or Jehovah. This is why we have hymns such as "Guide Us, O Thou Great Jehovah."

The Hebrew language, however, is expressive, and various tenses of verbs have expanded meaning. A better translation of YHWH is to add the vowels "a" and "e," which makes the name *Yahweh*. In the Hebrew *hiphil* tense, the thrust is causation. So if *Yahweh* is the *hiphil* tense, then the meaning of the name *Yahweh* is literally "He who causes everything to be." And that to me is the proper name of the God we serve. One thing is for certain: it would never be Allah, which is either the name of a tribal deity of the Arabian Peninsula or a derivation of the Phoenician Baal.

So when we are told to love Yahweh, our God, with all our heart, soul, and mind, we are loving the One who created everything in the world—"He who causes everything to be."

At the conclusion of Psalm 91 I found a series of declarations of what our Majestic Deity affirmed He would do. I call them the "I wills" of God. The import is stunning. Our God affirms to each of us who love Him in this manner: "Because he has set his love upon Me, therefore I will deliver him."[2]

I can truthfully say that I have set my love upon the powerful Being who created the universe. I'm not often given to tears, but when I think of the love of God and the sacrifice of Jesus Christ for me, tears come to my eyes. Therefore, here are—for those of us who have set our love upon the Lord—the extraordinary declarations of what our God will do for us:

First, He says, "I will rescue him."[3]

I have experienced many instances where the supernatural God reached down and rescued me from spiritual danger, from financial danger, from physical danger, while flying an airplane, when falling asleep at the wheel of a car, and in encounters with wild animals. "He who causes everything to be" has reached down and rescued His servant.

Secondly, the Lord says, "I will protect him."[4]

In this book I have chronicled demon attacks and slanderous assaults. I have chronicled as far back as grade school how larger boys came to protect me. The God of heaven has proclaimed that He will protect the one who has set his love upon Him. If that describes you, the "I wills" of God are for you as well as for me.

Thirdly, our Lord says, "He will call on me, and I will answer him."[5]

How many times have I related in this book the instances when almighty God answered me? I was once ridiculed for saying that I had heard from God. I answered my accuser with these words, "If you had worked for a company for thirty years, don't you think it would be surprising if during that time you had not heard once from your boss?"

In the fourth "I will," "He who causes everything to be" declares, "I will be with him in trouble."[6]

None of us knows when trouble will come. None of us knows of upcoming sickness or disease. I'll give you one example of when trouble came unexpectedly upon me.

I was flying in the right seat of a Piper Navajo that was nearly out of gas when we encountered a vicious thunderstorm. Then most of our electronic equipment went out. We were flying over the mountains of Costa Rica, and the minimum approach altitude was nine thousand feet. The only instrument working in our little Navajo was the DME (or distance measuring equipment), so we had to estimate the flight path to the nearest mountain and then make a left turn into what we hoped would be the airport.

We flew at the minimum required altitude in the blinding rain, and then we turned left at what we hoped would be the appropriate place. We could not see the airport because the officials there had turned off the lights. To this day I don't know how it happened, but the lights did come back on. Perhaps there was a sensor at the airport that responded to an approaching aircraft. We were like a tiny wood chip in a turbulent sea that was pitch-black and surrounded by mountains. And yet the choice before us was to try to land at the airport or to fly over the mountains and crash in the ocean. You know what trouble is when you get into a situation like that.

But remember that the God who was the recipient of my love had said, "I will be with you in trouble." And He was there. We landed the plane safely at the San Jose Airport and marveled at our own stupidity in putting ourselves in such a precarious position. But "He who causes everything to be" had us under control because He promised "I will be with you in trouble."

I was shaken, but on the next day we enjoyed a Christmas festival and then traveled to a small area outside of San Jose called Paraíso (Paradise), where we were able to inspect a million-watt AM radio station that we had hoped to use to broadcast the gospel all over Central and South America. Radio Paradise had a nice sound to it. Fortunately for me, my time to visit the real paradise hadn't quite come.

The fifth "I will" says, "I will deliver him."[7]

Here again, our Lord stood beside me. As I have pointed out, I am a very experienced rider and was riding high-level dressage. One day I decided to take a long, leisurely ride around the property on a fifteen-year-old perfectly trained dressage horse. I was so relaxed that I didn't bother to take a helmet.

After I was returning to the barn, I rode past the fence around my house. At that time, my dog came running down a small hill barking furiously. My horse shied, and I lost a stirrup, and then he took off on a crazy gallop. I pulled on the reins as hard as I could but was unable to stop this fear-crazed animal. I tried to pull him in toward the fence, but he resisted and kept galloping, then jumped a ditch, and then took off toward some trees.

I had only one foot in a stirrup and had lost my balance. I was then thrown to the ground. I hit hard and broke eight of my ribs, snapped the bone in my thumb, and ruptured my spleen. Without knowing it, I was quickly bleeding to death.

When CBN's vice president and chief of CBN's police department raced up to where I was lying on the ground, I assured him that I was absolutely fine, but he wasn't buying it. "No, you're going to the hospital right now," he said.

Soon I found myself in an ambulance on the way to the Norfolk Sentara Hospital. The only thing that hurt was my thumb, and I assured them that the rest of me was fine. In the operating room, though, they stopped my internal bleeding and removed one-third of my damaged spleen.

That incident with the horse was far and away the worst accident I have ever experienced. But it could have been worse. If I had hit my head without the protection of a helmet, my life probably would have ended.

I am grateful to say that I healed very quickly. My ribs came together perfectly, the blood I lost was restored, and my broken thumb was set correctly. Although I suffered severe damage, our Lord "delivered" me from this near tragedy.

In the sixth "I will," the God who "causes everything to be" also assures those who love Him that they will receive honor.[8]

Despite times of humiliation, I can say that our Lord fulfilled His promise to me abundantly. The National Religious Broadcasters named me "Broadcaster of the Year." My picture has appeared on the cover of

Time, The Saturday Evening Post, and *U.S. News & World Report*. Our *The 700 Club* broadcast has been repeatedly named the Best News Talk Program in America by the National Religious Broadcasters. And I received a Lifetime Achievement Award in Hollywood from *Movieguide*, an organization that reviews movies from a Christian perspective. *Christian Century* magazine named me the Religious Broadcaster of the Year, and the Virginia Broadcast News Association named me Virginian of the Year. Despite all of these titles, I still prefer Servant of the Lord.

In the seventh, our Lord promises that He will satisfy us with a long life.[9]

I am now ninety years old. My mother died when she was sixty, so I have outlived her by thirty years. My brother died when he was seventy-six, so I have outlived him by fourteen years. My father died when he was eighty-three, so I have outlived him by seven years. And there are those around me who insist that I will exceed the lifetime of Moses, who died at 120. We shall see what the Lord has in store. Maybe this isn't my final memoir!

And finally, in the eighth "I will," the Lord promises to those who love Him that He will show them His salvation.[10]

The Bible tells us that "Eye has not seen, nor ear heard, nor have entered into the heart of man the things which God has prepared for those who love Him."[11] As I continue to walk with the God of miracles, I know that He has more wonders to show me. That promise will be wholly fulfilled when I have departed my earthly body and am united with my loving heavenly Father in the New Jerusalem.

67

THE MIRACLE COIN

URING THE DECADES that I have walked with God, He has communicated His will to me in several ways. To begin with, I have the peace of God as an umpire in my spirit. I have the clear guidance of the Word of God, where the Bible clearly states, "Your word I have hidden in my heart, that I might not sin against You."[1] I have had available the advice of godly friends in keeping with the biblical injunction, "In a multitude of counselors *there is* safety."[2] I have been privileged to be led in prayer to certain verses of Scripture that have served as clear answers to questions that I may have. And, particularly, I have been guided by the precise word of the Lord to me saying, "This is the way. Walk ye in it."[3]

There is one means of guidance, however, that I have been reluctant to use. We are told in the Book of Judges that an Israeli farmer named Gideon was suffering under the oppression of a group known as the Midianites.[4] Gideon was told by an angel that he was chosen by God to lead the force that would liberate Israel from the crushing yoke of the Midianites. Gideon had seen the angel up close and had heard a clear direction.

The instruction given to him, however, was far outside what we would call his comfort zone. After the angel had left him, Gideon asked the Lord for a sign. Gideon put a sheepskin on the ground outside his house and asked the Lord to keep the fleece dry in the early morning, although dew would cause the ground around it to be wet.

Sure enough, Gideon got up the next morning and found that the fleece was dry. Still not certain that his calling was valid, though, he asked the Lord to let the fleece be wet and the surrounding ground around remain dry the following day. The next morning, the fleece was soaking wet, and the surrounding ground was completely dry. Now he was sure of the sign from God.

In contemporary evangelical terminology, asking for a sign became known as "putting out a fleece." Someone seeking to know God's direction would ask that a specific thing happen or not happen to indicate God's guidance on a particular course of action.

You remember the story of our television station in Lebanon. When George Otis offered to give CBN that station, Dede and I had already received clear guidance from Scripture that we should take over the station. But I also realized what an incredibly risky move it would be to take over a television station in the middle of a war zone. I delayed action on receiving the Lebanese station until I could put out my version of Gideon's fleece.

I prayed to the Lord and said, "Lord, if it's Your will that we go forward to build and operate the station in Lebanon, please send me something of gold as a sign that this is of You."

On the way to work that day I told my secretary, Barbara Johnson, to notify our mail room to be on the lookout for something of gold. I waited one day and no gold, then another day, and no gold. And then on the third day, a miracle happened.

At the time, I was still living on the Frederick College campus outside an area known as Churchland. Dede and I maintained a box at the Churchland Post Office that we used for our personal bills and some of our communications so that our personal mail was kept separate from the much larger mail volume that flowed in and out of CBN.

That evening I drove from my office in Virginia Beach and met Dede at a nearby restaurant. She had picked up our personal mail at the post office and brought it with her to the restaurant. As she put the few pieces of mail down on our table, I picked up one postmarked from California from a man that I had known from the Full Gospel Business Men's Fellowship International. His name was Frank Foglio. He said that the Lord had instructed him to contact me because he had come into possession of a rare 24-karat gold medallion struck by the famed artist Pablo Picasso. Inside the letter was a picture of this medallion. God had not just sent me a common garden-variety Krugerrand. He had sent me—as the sign I was looking for—an artistic rarity, of which only eight existed in the world.

The added part of this miracle is that only a few people knew the existence of my personal post office box, and certainly Frank Foglio was not one of them. How did he get the post office box number? How did he know to send it? And how did he know to send along a picture of this artistic rarity?

I knew that I had heard from the Lord. What more sign could I ask for? God wanted us to go forward to operate a station in Lebanon, and this was all the confirmation I needed.

I contacted Frank Foglio and thanked him. Later, he graciously gave one of the coins to CBN. Its origin was certified by Picasso's daughter, Paloma, and was appraised some years ago by Sotheby's at $35,000.

68

"I WILL BLESS THOSE WHO BLESS YOU"

I N 1971 AN officer in the Ugandan army led a revolt against the civilian leaders of that country and established himself as president of Uganda. That officer was Idi Amin, who can only be described as a cruel monster. He mercilessly tortured his enemies, and in private he practiced cannibalism with human flesh that he stored in refrigerators. Despite his malevolent nature he was protected by Saudi Arabia and was also given access to the podium of the United Nations.[1]

As I understand it, his dispute with Israel arose when it withdrew certain technological assistance it had been providing to Idi Amin. In 1976, to show his power, Idi Amin was involved in the highjacking of a French airliner full of passengers.[2] He held the plane's passengers captive at the airport in Entebbe.[3]

When negotiations broke down and it appeared that Idi Amin was contemplating the execution of some of the innocent civilians, Israel performed a daring maneuver. Its military flew a couple of troop transports directly into the airport at Entebbe, neutralized the guards, and took control of the airfield. They then stormed the hangar where the prisoners were being held and shouted in Hebrew to the passengers to lie down. They shot and killed most of the Ugandan guards who had been holding the prisoners captive and who, not understanding Hebrew, had remained standing.

The Israeli officer who commanded this daring raid was named Yoni Netanyahu, an Israeli Defense Forces officer who commanded an elite commando unit. In the firefight that ensued, this brave Israeli was killed but became a national hero.[4]

His younger brother was Benjamin "Bibi" Netanyahu, who was studying at the Massachusetts Institute of Technology (MIT) at the time and later returned to Israel, where he rose in prominence to become prime minister. Before Bibi Netanyahu became prime minister, we became fast friends. As a matter of fact, he clearly said that he knew that evangelical Christians were the strongest supporters of the nation of Israel aside from the Jewish people themselves. Bibi and I shared some very precious moments when President Bill Clinton had attempted to wear him down in order to extract concessions that Clinton thought would be helpful to the United States. But Bibi was not my only bridge of fellowship to the Jewish people.

Years ago I learned of a wonderful organization called the Holyland Fellowship of Christians and Jews headed by Rabbi Yechiel Eckstein. We were privileged at CBN to give this splendid organization its first major contribution, and over the years, Yechiel and I became fast friends.

Each year in Israel there is a prestigious conference featuring addresses by Israeli politicians and people of note. Yechiel arranged for me to address the Herzliya Conference at the Lauder School of Government, Diplomacy, and Strategy in Herzliya, Israel, at the end of 2003.

I took the opportunity to assure the assembled audience that evangelical Christians throughout the world were the friends of Israel, and they could rely on us because of our shared biblical roots. It was an excellent opportunity to pour out my heart to the leaders of the nation of Israel. When I finished, I was given a standing ovation, and one of the attendees said to me, "This is an address worthy of a president."

I've chosen to include this speech, "Why Evangelical Christians Support Israel,"[5] on these pages because my talk lays out with great specificity the relationship that CBN has enjoyed over the years in support of God's chosen people. I am convinced that one clear reason for God's favor toward us has been our unyielding support for His chosen people.

Please keep in mind that I delivered this speech on December 17, 2003, when Yasser Arafat, the leader of the PLO, was still alive. He would die about a year after my talk, on November 11, 2004.

One day in the late nineteenth century, Queen Victoria of England reportedly asked her prime minister, Benjamin Disraeli, this question: "Mr. Prime Minister, what evidence can you give me of the existence of God?"

Disraeli thought for a moment and then replied, "The Jew, your majesty."

Think of it: according to Disraeli, the primary evidence that God exists is the existence of the Jewish people...a people who in 586 BC were deported to Babylon, yet returned after seventy years to rebuild a nation. Who were again brutally massacred and dispersed by the Romans in AD 70, yet after countless centuries of diaspora, expulsions, pogroms, ghettos, and attempts at genocidal extermination, have clung to their faith, their customs—and now after some 2,500 years of wandering have returned to the land promised by God to their ancestors.

A new nation began in that land in 1948 named after their ancestor Jacob, whose divinely appointed name in Israel means "Prince with God." And to fulfill another ancient prophecy, God moved on the heart of Eliezer Ben-Yehuda, whose son Ehud told me that, while his father was living in Eastern Europe, he heard a voice and saw a light directing him to bring forth for the Jewish people a pure language—Hebrew—the language of the Torah and of the ancient prophets.

Yes, the survival of the Jewish people is a miracle of God. The return of the Jewish people to the land promised to Abraham, Isaac, and Jacob is a miracle of God. The remarkable victories of Jewish armies against overwhelming odds in successive battles in 1948 and 1967 and 1973 are clearly miracles of God. The technological marvels of Israeli industry, the military prowess, the bounty of Israeli agriculture, the fruits and flowers and abundance of the land, are a testimony to God's watchful care over this new nation and the genius of this people.

Yet what has happened was clearly foretold by the ancient prophet Ezekiel, who, writing at the time of the Babylonian captivity, declared this message for the Jewish people concerning latter days:

"For I will take you out of the nations; I will gather you from all the countries and bring you back to your own land...I will give you a new heart and put a new spirit in you...to follow my decrees and be careful to keep my laws. You will live in the land I gave your fore-fathers; you will be my people and I will be your God. I will save you from all your uncleanness.

"I will call for the grain and make it plentiful...I will increase the fruit of the trees and the crops of the field, so that you will no longer suffer disgrace among the nations because of famine...

"This is what the Sovereign Jehovah says, 'On the day I cleanse you from all your sins, I will resettle your towns, and the ruins will be rebuilt. The desolate land will be cultivated instead of lying deso-late in the sight of all who pass through it. They will say, "This land that was laid waste has become like the garden of Eden; the cities that were lying in ruins, desolate and destroyed, are now fortified and inhabited."'

"Then the nations around you that remain will know that I, Jehovah, have rebuilt what was destroyed and have replanted what was desolate. I, Jehovah, have spoken, and I will do it." Ladies and gentlemen, evangelical Christians support Israel because we believe that the words of Moses and the ancient prophets of Israel were inspired by God. We believe that the emergence of a Jewish state in the land promised by God to Abraham, Isaac, and Jacob was ordained by God.

We believe that God has a plan for this nation, which He intends to be a blessing to all the nations of the earth.

Of course, we, like all right-thinking people, support Israel because Israel is an island of democracy, an island of individual freedom, an island of the rule of law, and an island of modernity in the midst of a sea of dictatorial regimes, the suppression of indi-vidual liberty, and a fanatical religion intent on returning to the feu-dalism of eighth-century Arabia.

These facts about modern-day Israel are all true. But mere polit-ical rhetoric does not account for the profound devotion to Israel that exists in the hearts of tens of millions of evangelical Christians.

You must realize that the God who spoke to Moses on Mount Sinai is our God. Abraham, Isaac, and Jacob are our spiritual patri-archs. Jeremiah, Ezekiel, and Daniel are our prophets. King David, a man after God's own heart, is our hero. The Holy City of Jerusalem is our spiritual capital. And the continuation of Jewish sovereignty over the Holy Land is a further bulwark to us that the God of the Bible exists and that His Word is true.

And we should clearly take note that evangelical Christians serve a Jew that we believe was the divine Messiah of Israel, spoken of by the ancient prophets, to whom He entrusted the worldwide dissemination of His message to twelve Jewish apostles.

It should be noted that today Christianity, with well over two billion adherents, is by far the fastest-growing religion in the world. Within twenty years that number will swell to three billion. Of these, at least six hundred million are Bible-believing Evangelicals and Charismatics who are ardent supporters of the nation of Israel. In twenty years that number will reach one billion. Israel has millions of Christian friends in China, in India, in Indonesia, and throughout Africa and South America, as well as North America.

To our Jewish friends, we say: We are with you in your struggle. We are with you as a wave of anti-Semitism is engulfing the earth. We are with you despite the pressure of the Quartet [the United States, the European Union, the United Nations, and Russia] and the incredibly hostile resolutions of the United Nations. We are with you despite the threats and ravings of Wahhabi jihadists, Hezbollah thugs, and Hamas assassins.

We are with you despite oil embargos, loss of allies, and terrorist attacks on our cities.

We evangelical Christians merely say to our Israeli friends, "Let us serve our God together by opposing the virulent poison of anti-Semitism and anti-Zionism that is rapidly engulfing the world."

Having affirmed our support, I would humbly make two requests of our Israeli friends:

First, please don't commit national suicide. It is very hard for your friends to support you if you make a conscious decision to destroy yourselves.

I hardly find it necessary to remind this audience of the stated objectives of Yasser Arafat, the PLO, Hamas, Hezbollah, and Islamic Jihad. Their goal is not peace but the final destruction of the State of Israel. At no time do they, or their allies in the Muslim world, acknowledge the sovereignty of Israel over even one square inch of territory in the Middle East.

If a Palestinian state is created in the heart of Israel with sovereign power to deploy troops, import modern weapons—even weapons of mass destruction—and operate with full secrecy and diplomatic immunity, the ability of the State of Israel to defend itself will be fatally compromised.

The slogan "land for peace" is a cruel chimera. The Sinai was given up. Did that bring lasting peace?

No.

Southern Lebanon was given up. Did that bring lasting peace?

No.

Instead, Hezbollah rode tanks to the border of Israel, shouting, "On to Jerusalem!" Now as many as ten thousand rockets aimed at Metula, Qiryat Shemona, and all of Northern Israel have been put in place throughout southern Lebanon.

Arafat was brought up at the knees of the man who yearned to finish the work of Adolf Hitler. How can any realist truly believe that this killer and his associates can become trusted partners for peace?

I am aware of the deep feelings of many Israelis who yearn for peace. Who long to be free from the terror of the suicide bombers of the intifada. I would draw their attention to the fact that during the Cold War, the American people yearned to be free from the constant threat of a nuclear holocaust.

Then, at Reykjavik, Iceland, on the occasion of a summit between President Ronald Reagan of the United States and Premier Mikhail Gorbachev of the Soviet Union, what seemed like an incredible opportunity for peace was presented to President Reagan by Mr. Gorbachev. An offer was made for hitherto undreamed of reductions in nuclear weapons. Gorbachev's offer included everything the US arms negotiators had wanted, except one thing. The condition for the Russian offer was to be the agreement by the United States to abandon the so-called "Star Wars" Strategic Defense Initiative.

Mr. Reagan carefully considered the offer—then reluctantly said no. Without the Strategic Defense Initiative, there would be no deal. Gorbachev was stunned. Then both leaders, with sadness in their hearts, adjourned the meeting and departed Reykjavik.

Once again, the world was hovering on the brink of nuclear annihilation. The American liberal press was apoplectic at Reagan's decision. But he held firm.

Now we all know that he was right. The Russians could not compete with the United States in a nuclear arms race, and Gorbachev knew it. The bluster was over—the threats were over—Reagan had won by standing firm. Soon freedom broke out in Poland...in Hungary...in East Germany. The Berlin Wall came down. The barbed wire fences came down. And Soviet Communism came down.

The world is safe from superpower nuclear terror. This terror is no more because one strong leader stood against public opinion—against the advice of many of his own counselors—and said *no*! May the leaders of Israel in 2004 have the courage to look the nations of the world in the eye, and when your national interests demand it—say *no*!

Second, the world's Christians ask that you do not give away the treasured symbols of your spiritual patrimony.

I read recently in the *Wall Street Journal* an article written by an American Jewish commentator who remarked that the Temple Mount and what is termed the "Wailing Wall" are "sacred stones and sites," but hardly worth bloodshed.

Just think—the place where the patriarch Abraham took Isaac to offer him to God. The place bought by King David from Araunah where the Angel of the Lord stood with drawn sword. The place of Solomon's temple. The place of the Holy of Holies. The place where Jesus Christ walked and taught. The very spiritual center of the Jewish worship of the one true God—nothing but a pile of sacred stones—unworthy of sacrifice? What an incredible assertion!

Ladies and gentlemen, make no mistake—the entire world is being convulsed by a religious struggle. The fight is not about money or territory; it is not about poverty versus wealth; it is not about ancient customs versus modernity. No—the struggle is whether Hubal, the Moon God of Mecca, known as Allah, is supreme, or whether the Judeo-Christian Jehovah God of the Bible is supreme.

If God's chosen people turn over to Allah control of their most sacred sites—if they surrender to Muslim vandals the tombs of Rachel, of Joseph, of the patriarchs, of the ancient prophets—if they believe their claim to the Holy Land comes only from Lord Balfour of England and the ever-fickle United Nations rather than the promises of almighty God—then in that event Islam will have won the battle. Throughout the Muslim world the message will go forth—"Allah is greater than Jehovah. The promises of Jehovah to the Jews are meaningless. We can now, in the name of Allah, move to crush the Jews and drive them out of the land that belongs to Allah."

In short, those political initiatives that some have asserted will

guarantee peace, will in truth guarantee unending struggle and ultimate failure. Those political leaders who only understand the secular dimension of Israel's existence and who cavalierly dismiss the
spiritual dimension will find that they receive the mess of pottage of
Esau rather than the inheritance of Jacob.

On Christmas Day in 1974, I had the privilege of interviewing
Prime Minister Yitzhak Rabin for my television program, *The 700
Club*. Rabin lamented the fact that after Israeli military victories,
the nation had been stopped from achieving a peace treaty.

That was thirty years ago. Israel seemed as isolated and alone
then as it does today. As I concluded my interview, I asked Prime
Minister Rabin a final question. "What would you want the United
States to do now for Israel?"

He replied without hesitation. "Be strong! Be strong!"

That evening I joined, for dinner, a group of several hundred
people who had accompanied me from the United States. We were
meeting in the large dining room of the InterContinental Hotel on
the Mount of Olives in Jerusalem, whose floor-to-ceiling windows
gave a stunning view of the illuminated Temple Mount. As I related
to the group the substance of my meeting, I began to recall the
feeling of sadness which had come from the Prime Minister—the
sense of the isolation of his nation. That evening, I made a solemn
vow to God that, despite whatever might happen in the future, I and
the organizations I headed would stand in support of Israel and the
Jewish people. Ladies and gentlemen, I am proud to say that I have
kept that vow each year since 1974.

In closing, I would deliver to Israel in 2004 the message Yitzhak
Rabin delivered to the United States on Christmas Day in 1974. For
you are the living witnesses that the promises of the Sovereign Lord
are true. "Be strong! Be strong!"

He will be with you, and so will your evangelical friends. Thank
you, and God bless you!

69

DROUGHT, CBN'S DRAMATIC
FORESTATION PLAN

IN MARCH 1985 then vice president George Bush invited me to join him and his wife, Barbara, on a trip to Sudan. The purpose was to meet with Sudanese President Gaafar Nimeiry. Bush's team, of which I was a part, was warmly received by President Nimeiry, and we were entertained at a lavish outdoor banquet in the capital city of Khartoum.

After a couple of days of official meetings and ceremonies, a few of us were flown in a twin-engine military aircraft to the northern part of the country, where we visited a major refugee camp for the survivors of the conflict between Somalia and Ethiopia, in a region known as Tigre-Eritrea.

I had been able to rent a 747 cargo plane that we filled with $250,000 worth of donated medicine. I presented this medicine to the vice president, who in turn made it available to the Sudanese government to alleviate the suffering of the refugees. We flew to an airfield in North Sudan and then were taken by convoy down roads with billowing dust all the way to the refugee area.

When we arrived at the camp, I was introduced to amazingly beautiful people who, despite their suffering, were dancing with joy just to be alive. A closer look revealed signs of remarkable privation, however. Then we went to the medical center at the heart of the encampment, where an unappetizing-looking gruel made up of cornmeal and native vegetables was cooking in a black cast-iron kettle.

The next thing we noticed was how the doctors weighed each of the little children to determine the level of their privation. As each child was weighed, his or her weight was recorded in kilograms, prompting Vice President Bush to turn to me for a quick calculation into pounds and ounces. One little boy was at least three or four years old, but malnourishment had dropped his weight to two and a half kilos, or five and a half pounds.

I remember talking to one woman who had walked for eight weeks across the desert to reach this place of safety. We asked her why she had made this dangerous trek on foot. She replied, "The soldiers stole all our food. We had nothing left to eat. We had to come here, or we would die."

It was on this trip that I saw the true heart of Barbara Bush. Not only did she bravely taste the food being served from this huge pot but she also took little children into her arms and hugged them. Her legs were covered with the dust and grime of that place, but with Barbara there was no show and no airs. She was a wonderful, caring mother deeply concerned about the plight of suffering children.

We returned to Khartoum, where George Bush received word that the Russian General Secretary of the Central Committee of the Communist Party, Konstantin Chernenko, had died. This meant Bush was slated to attend the funeral as a representative of the United States.

I wasn't invited to join the trip to Moscow, so I arranged to fly from Sudan up to Israel, and from Israel to Geneva, where I later rejoined the Bush party. As I flew in the small plane over North Africa, though, I saw something remarkable.

In the air there were little puffs of clouds that seemed to be rising from a few trees in the Sahara Desert, a vast, sandy waste. The Sahara Desert, I was told, was slowly creeping south, and the area of creep was known as the Sahel.[1] It was so clear that trees would be the answer to this spreading desert. I felt the prompting of the Lord to have three million trees planted along a fifteen-mile stretch that could serve as a source of moisture for this encroaching desert, which was leaving so many of the African people in desperate poverty.

When I think of the huge amounts of money spent on military weapons and the enormous overhead of the United Nations, I marvel why our government and the United Nations don't spend a small amount of money to set up a significant forest barrier to alleviate the blistering climate found in North Africa.

There is a major pilot project south of Sudan that was established by Dr. Chris Reij, a sustainable land management specialist with decades of experience in the restoration of degraded land in semiarid regions.[2] Dr. Reij had carved out room for a small lake, drilled the appropriate water wells, and planted a small forest around the area.

Through careful maintenance he had established a virtual paradise where the birds came back, the jungle animals returned, and plant life flourished. What this brilliant man had established was clear. Unproductive areas throughout our planet can be returned to their original state if we, as God's representatives, merely take the effort to restore the original ecosystem.

That's all part of being a good steward, just like when God took Adam and "put him in the Garden of Eden to work it and take care of it," as His Word says in Genesis 2:15 (NIV).

70

RETIREMENT PLANS CANCELED!

W HEN I WAS sitting in the Grand Hotel across from Disneyland in 1975, as I described earlier, God spoke to me to "buy all the land and build a school for His glory." In a subsequent revelation the Lord showed me that what was then known as CBN University was to have within itself distinct schools that could challenge the bastions of secular society.

Our first school was a Graduate School of Communications. We then added a School of Education and a School of Divinity. We added schools and students until our student body was close to five hundred, and our faculty was growing.

At that time I was privileged to meet the head of a small school in Michigan that encompassed a number of the disciplines that I was trying to build at CBN University. Dr. Dick Gottier agreed to leave his prestigious position at that university and become president of CBN University. With his dedication to the Lord and his academic experience, he seemed to be an ideal choice to move our fledgling school into the future. Along the way some problems developed, and in a meeting with our board of trustees, they agreed to part ways.

About this time I heard about the "curse of the trustees." It seemed that illness, family problems, and financial problems fell upon those who were willing volunteers for the leadership of CBN University. To the few who stood up to the challenge, there seemed to be a desire to break the university free from the principles of its founding. Although the CBN headquarters was just a stone's throw away from the classroom buildings of CBN University, some students began to call the CBN building "the forbidden city."

There is a principle in God's kingdom that demands that religious institutions submit to duly anointed leadership. When such leadership is absent, what results is disorder and chaos.

CBN University had its own board of trustees appointed by the board of directors of CBN. The university board chair was the wife of a Republican congressman. Her name was Dee Jepson.

In one of our university board meetings it became apparent that we needed an identifying name. CBN University was not adequate. Dee Jepson suggested renaming the school Regent University, explaining that a regent was one who held office in the absence of the sovereign. The "sovereign" for us, of course, was Jesus Christ.

We all liked the name and the concept. Our lawyers found no conflict in the United States with any educational institution bearing the same name. So we voted with no disrespect or hostility in any way to our founding parent, and we renamed CBN University, Regent University.

Although our fledgling university grew under various forms of leadership, a crisis forced us to make a dramatic change. It had to do with how major universities across the nation began offering single, specialized courses to a wide variety of students through recorded courses taught by distinguished specialists in their respective fields.

At Regent University I embraced the concept and attempted to develop a curriculum based on recorded lectures by gifted faculty. We took the Latin words *lux vera*, which means light and truth, and trademarked it to describe this body of courses. The concept of this expanded university seemed splendid on paper, but in reality it lacked financial underpinning because all of the courses were taught for free.

When I reached my eightieth birthday, I felt I had spent many years in the trenches and had fought the good fight. I decided it was time to leave the battle to younger people, so I notified the CBN Board of Directors that I was planning to go off the air, and I notified the Regent University Board of Trustees that I was stepping down as chancellor.

The God I serve, however, refused to accept my resignation because He had something more for me. Members of the board at CBN urged me to reconsider because they still needed me as the host of our flagship television show, and the board at Regent pointed out that since we were without a president at that time, according to our bylaws, the chancellor was required to assume the job of president.

As soon as I stepped into the role of president at Regent University, a bolt of God's power coursed through me. I no longer felt my age. I no longer felt fatigued, and I no longer felt like walking away. The God whom I served had more for me to do, and He then made available to me the strength necessary to fulfill these tasks with joy.

To let the staff know that I had their best interests at heart, I immediately instituted a 3 percent boost in everyone's salary, and then I reorganized the structure into several divisions under executive vice presidents who would report to me instead of reporting to a provost. The Lord gave me the ability to spot talent, and there was plenty of it waiting to be recognized. Some people were clearly out of place and were phased out. We began a massive program of continual hiring, training, and replacement. Our staff grew to about eighteen hundred, and along with that growth was a significant increase in the intellectual quality of our students and the skill level of our employees.

We emphasized over and over again the word that the Lord had spoken at the Tower of Babel: "If as one people speaking the same language they have begun to do this, then nothing they plan to do will be impossible for them."[1] Together we had one goal, and that was to serve the Lord. We reminded ourselves over and over again that the school belonged to the Lord, not to us. We set lofty goals, but under no circumstance were we to be under the bondage of trying to attain these goals in our own strength. We would rely on Him and work together and love each other and expect miracles.

I had spent decades in enterprises that depended on advertising. I felt it was clearly necessary that our university advertise so that we could attract more students and more revenue. Regent's vice president over marketing determined that the appropriate amount needed to begin such a campaign was ten million dollars. But all of our advertising money would be wasted unless we had in place the resources to handle the inquiries that would come from the advertising.

I learned that across the country, a few universities had adopted a fast-growth model. Remembering the words of Scripture that said, "For by wise counsel you will wage your own war, and in a multitude of counselors *there is* safety,"[2] I invited a group of learned and experienced counselors to join with key leaders of our university for a weekend high in the mountains surrounding Hot Springs, Virginia.

There was the man who had helped shape the course of one of the fastest-growing universities in America. There was a former president of the University of Phoenix. There was another expert in university growth. There were a couple of vice presidents from Regent, including our vice president of Academic Affairs.

Hour after hour we listened to proposals and then voted on the spot whether these proposals should be adopted or rejected.

The recent news is filled with headlines about Hollywood stars who were bribing officials in order to get their children accepted at prestigious universities such as the University of Southern California. My theory was the exact opposite. Universities should be set up to accommodate students and to make it easy for them to enroll. It used to be considered a mark of distinction for a parent to say proudly that their child was accepted at Harvard, or their child was accepted at Yale, or their child was accepted at Princeton. My theory was that universities needed to be welcoming and make quality education available to the broadest number of students possible consistent with higher educational excellence.

As we sat around a big table high in the Virginia mountains, several principles stood out. We were building a store, but imagine a store opening and only having beans for sale. That meant that we had to have a varied course offering or our advertising would be wasted.

In the same vein, if there was no one in the store to wait on the customers, they would soon turn around and walk out. The last thing we wanted was to have salespeople who felt their job was to insult the customers rather than welcome them manning the counters. In short we needed a complete overhaul.

Around the table the opportunity to speak was available to all of the participants. Concepts were put forward and recorded by the secretary, who was taking notes. Here are some of the things we came up with:

+ We had been operating on the semester system, so if a student wanted to enroll, he or she had to do so either in September or in February. Beyond that, there was no opportunity. We voted to discontinue the two-semester rule and open our enrollment a total of six times a year rather than two. This was a bit tough on the faculty, but it certainly made it easy to attract students.

+ We learned that one particular school had hide-bound, old-school thinkers handling requests for admission. They not only ignored prospective students but in some cases they actually insulted them. We determined that the university needed to establish a centralized admissions program with access to appropriate databases and student aid opportunities so that prospective students could have intelligent enrollment opportunities available on demand.

    Out of that came a decision to make an office building available across from our campus where several hundred fully trained enrollment counselors would be working under the inspired leadership of a lady named Heidi Cece. In subsequent years, Heidi's team achieved such professionalism that it took them exactly seven seconds to respond to an inquiry from a prospective student. When a legitimate applicant was on the line, he or she would find all of the necessary paperwork done immediately, and the enrollment was accomplished in record time.

+ We noted one particular annoyance, and that was the requirement that each applicant submit three letters of recommendation. We agreed this was an absurd requirement. Consider how it would play out: Young Johnny would go to his next-door neighbor and say, "Mr. Smith, I wish to enroll in Regent University. Would you please write me a letter of recommendation?"

Mr. Smith would then write something along these lines: "Young Johnny is a hardworking, eager young man who used to deliver my newspapers, and I know that he would fit in perfectly at Regent University." In truth, what Mr. Smith should have written was something more like this: "Young Johnny is a spaced-out drug user who actually shot my cat with a BB gun. He would better be considered at a reform school than Regent University." Of course, the truthful letter never got sent. But no admissions officer in his right mind would accept these so-called letters of recommendation at face value, so we eliminated this particular annoying requirement to ease the application process.

+ We determined that monies spent on retention were vastly more effective than those spent on the acquisition of students, so I established a Center for Student Happiness at Regent. We enlisted the support of faculty and deans to make at least four "touches" on behalf of each student—for academic well-being, for physical well-being, for spiritual well-being, and for financial well-being. Every student at our university learned that we were there to ensure his or her success. We were not their adversaries, but we were their friends, meant to see them succeed.

+ At our meeting we wrestled with the appropriate formula to determine the cost of acquiring a student and the cost of operating the university on a per-student basis. The discussion became so intense that one of our vice presidents resigned at the end of one of the meetings. Since that time, Sherri Stocks Miller has brilliantly led that phase of our endeavor to undreamed-of heights. Sherri

not only has determined the costs of acquisition and the
cost of retention but she also knows which ZIP codes
are most likely to bring us students and which courses
have the greatest appeal.

It was evident to me that the cost of health care was taking a dispro-
portionate share of our nation's gross national product, so we began a
College of Healthcare Sciences that would teach hospital administration, the principle of health insurance, and nursing.

Soon after, we learned of a nationwide shift in nursing accreditation.
Traditionally nurses were certified with a registered nurse (RN) qual-
ification. Sophisticated positions being offered by hospitals around
America, however, demanded nursing with broader-based education.
The hospitals were seeking employees with a Bachelor of Science in
nursing in addition to the RN.

I was wonderfully helped in all of this by my wife, Dede, who has
a master's degree in nursing from the Yale School of Nursing and who
had taught nursing at Tidewater Community College as an assistant
professor.

We filed a proposal with the state of Virginia, with the Southern
Association of Colleges and Schools, and with the accrediting body
for nursing education to grant a Bachelor of Science in nursing and,
along with it, a Master of Science in nursing and a doctor of nursing
practice. After a couple of years our university had received all of the
appropriate certifications for all these highly desirable degrees.

Then we learned that nurses with advanced training were called
nurse practitioners, and in rural areas these gifted people began
to assume the function of medical doctors when such doctors were
unavailable. Instead of the minimum wages that had once been paid
to nurses, these nurse practitioners were drawing salaries that ranged
from $100,000 to $200,000. Nurses with our Bachelor of Science in
nursing are eagerly sought with very substantial wages.

While our health sciences college was being established, a friend
named Rick Michaels visited me and asked if I had heard of something

called a cyber range. So I inquired of Rick Michaels what a cyber range entailed and what it cost.

A cyber range is a device that can identify hackers attempting to break into sophisticated databases. Rick said that Raytheon would charge about fifty million dollars for such a device. I was told of a consortium in Florida that was attempting to share one, but there was no university in the United States that had such a facility. I learned that the giant Israeli conglomerate called Elbit had a subsidiary called Cyberbit that was marketing cyber ranges in the United States.

I didn't wish to use any intermediate agent for a cyber transaction, so I had our university staff make contact with Cyberbit. Their American president graciously agreed to meet with me at the Homestead Resort in Hot Springs, Virginia. After dinner I asked the price of his cyber range. He told me it was a tiny fraction of what Raytheon charged. I then asked if he could finance it, and he replied in the affirmative. I then asked if he could get it operating by the end of summer, and he confirmed that he could. I asked if he could give me an exclusive for the geographic region and for university use, and he agreed that he could. With that in mind, I signed an agreement to acquire the most sophisticated cyber range that would be in the possession of any university in the United States.

I was not fully aware of what was being opened up to me by my heavenly Father. He had put Regent University in the middle of two of the most desirable college courses in America. When the cyber range went into action, it was an absolutely amazing experience. We signed up an array of clients, including the US Navy Cyber Command, the Tactical Air Command, Homeland Security, and the FBI. One international company brought its worldwide executive force to our campus to receive training. The vast National Security Agency and the Department of Homeland Security designated Regent University as a National Center for Academic Excellence in Cyber Defense Education for the BS in Cybersecurity. Our work was written about in *Wired* magazine and by a company in the United Kingdom that reported on advances in cyber education.

I marvel that the God who controls the whole universe would instruct His servant to prepare His university for a leading role in what is the most important technology in our modern world.

At our brainstorming meeting in the mountains, we talked about filling the store with something other than cans of beans. Since then Regent University has put in place 135 graduate and undergraduate areas of study on campus and online. The student body has experienced dramatic growth; in the fall of 2019 we totaled 10,425 students.[3] But the goal the Lord has given to me is establishing a major international university with at least three hundred thousand students who come from nations all around the world.

The motto of Regent University is "Christian Leadership to Change the World." The Lord spoke to me to build a school for His glory, and it is my firm conviction that our Lord is fulfilling the exact word that He spoke.

71

GOD STILL SPEAKS

IN WHAT IS called the "Parable of the Sower," which I refer to as the "Parable of the Soils," Jesus spoke of various grounds into which the seed of the gospel fell.[1] In one the plant came up luxuriantly, but it was choked out by weeds and ultimately died. In that Jesus was warning us about being encumbered with the cares of this life and the deceitfulness of riches and other things entering in, and the Word of God becomes choked and unfruitful.

It is so easy when a person like me is faced with the cares of so many hundreds of employees, contract negotiations, audience reviews, building projects, budget restraints, and regulatory issues to become totally absorbed in the cares of this life. For this reason I have from time to time set apart several days that I could spend in earnest prayer and Bible study so the gospel would find a warm place in my heart.

Some people like to make resolutions at the beginning of a new year. In my case, I like to take off some days between Christmas and New Year's that I can spend in earnest prayer and seeking God. I pray and read the Bible and then wait on the Spirit for His inspiration. I have with me a yellow pad so that I can write down whatever is being said. God in His goodness gives me advice, correction, and key points for our respective organizations for the new year. Along the way, He gives me in rather broad strokes what the world can expect in the year to come.

I have established on New Year's Day a combined staff meeting of the CBN, Operation Blessing, Regent University, and other related organizations. We have a time of prayer and praise and then share with one another what God has shown us. Out of this has come what we call media blitzes in various countries and whole regions of the world that God wants us to target with our ministry. With the direction that we receive, all of us are energized to move forward with unity to take on ever-increasing challenges and to believe God for His miraculous provision.

My word from the Lord in 2019 was profound. The Holy Spirit urged me with the words of Jesus: "Until now you have asked nothing in My name. Ask, and you will receive, that your joy may be full."[2] Our chapel was packed at the prayer meeting, and as we prayed I urged every single person to ask God what they wanted from Him. In my case, the answers were already coming in a dramatic fashion because the Lord says, "Therefore I tell you, whatever you ask for in prayer, believe that you have received it, and it will be yours."[3]

My three lifelong prayer requests are said over and over again: I want wisdom, I want anointing, and I want favor. Recently I asked God for a special glimpse of His power because the world was entering into a state of confusion. We need to know the reality of the Rock that holds it all together. I have been astounded at the beginning of the new year that world events are unfolding in exactly the way the Lord spoke to me in my annual prayer retreat. Whatever others may say about me, I say to anyone who is reading this book: The promises of God are for His people, and He is saying, "Until now you have asked nothing in My name. Ask, and you will receive, that your joy may be full!"

Epilogue

W HEN I LOOK back over the years, I see some works that the Lord has led me to establish that I hope will survive any times of trouble that may come on the face of the earth.

I carry with me the marvelous realization that I have been married to a beautiful lady for sixty-five years. I have not only four wonderfully talented children but fourteen healthy, intelligent, and spiritually alive grandchildren, one of whom—my granddaughter Cally—gave birth to my fifteenth great-grandchild. And now I learn that two more of my granddaughters are expecting children, which would give me my sixteenth and seventeenth great-grandchildren.

What more of a blessing can any human being ask for than what has been bestowed upon me by a gracious God as I have walked with Him for ninety years.

The apostle Paul wrote, "I know whom I have believed and am persuaded that He is able to keep what I have committed to Him until that Day."[1]

As I conclude *I Have Walked With the Living God*, I can say with great certainty that He who causes everything to be has never failed me once. He has never disappointed me. He has always been there when I needed Him. He is my closest friend and the anchor of my soul. What He has done for me He will do for you. He is waiting for His creatures to acknowledge that "He is, and that He is a rewarder of those who diligently seek Him."[2]

We read that the patriarch Abraham "believed in the LORD; and he counted it to him for righteousness."[3] The Bible tells us that "the eyes of the Lord run to and fro throughout the whole earth, to show Himself strong on behalf of those whose heart is loyal to Him."[4]

I have asked God for wisdom, and He has given it to me. I have asked God for His anointing, and He has given it to me. I have asked God for favor, and He has given it to me. The Bible says, "No good thing will He withhold from those who walk uprightly."[5]

There are many, many more instances when our Lord has spoken to me, when His Spirit has led me, and when His hand has reached out to hold mine. The Bible tells us that "Jesus Christ is the same yesterday, today, and forever."[6]

I have walked with the living God. I urge you to begin the adventure of a lifetime and begin your walk with the living God today.

Notes

Preface

1. Philip Reynolds, "Regent University Enrolls 11,000th Student," Regent University, October 17, 2017, https://www.regent.edu/news-events/regent-university-enrolls-11000th-student/.
2. "About the American Center for Law and Justice," ACLJ, accessed February 17, 2020, https://aclj.org/our-mission/about-aclj.
3. "Disney Buys Fox Family Channel," CBS News, July 23, 2001, https://www.cbsnews.com/news/disney-buys-fox-family-channel/.
4. Sallie Hofmeister, "Walt Disney to Acquire Fox Family," *Los Angeles Times*, July 21, 2001, https://www.latimes.com/archives/la-xpm-2001-jul-21-fi-24859-story.html.
5. "1988 Republican Party Presidential Primaries," Wikipedia, accessed February 17, 2020, https://en.wikipedia.org/wiki/1988_Republican_Party_presidential_primaries.
6. Isaiah 30:21, KJV.

Chapter 1

1. Isaiah 30:21, NIV.
2. "Ted Turner and CNN," Pop History Dig, updated August 23, 2019, pophistorydig.com/topics/tag/ted-turner-cable-tv.

Chapter 2

1. United States Federal Communications Commission, *Federal Communications Commission Reports: Decisions and Reports of the Federal Communications Commission of the United States, July 10, 1959, to January 8, 1960, vol. 27* (Washington, DC: United States Government Printing Office, 1961), 142–43, https://tinyurl.com/ungztga.

Chapter 3

1. "YHWH," Dr. Michael S. Heiser, accessed February 20, 2020, https://drmsh.com/the-naked-bible/yhwh/.
2. "Milestones: Westinghouse Radio Station KDKA, 1920," Engineering and Technology History Wiki, updated December 18, 2019, https://ethw.org/Milestones:Westinghouse_Radio_Station_KDKA,_1920.
3. "The Fireside Chats," History, updated June 7, 2019, https://www.history.com/topics/great-depression/fireside-chats.
4. "History: Radio," PBS, December 2, 2008, https://www.pbs.org/wnet/makeemlaugh/comedys-evolution/history-radio/35/.
5. Jeff Suess, "Our History: P&G Put the 'Soap' in 'Soap Opera,'" *Cincinnati Enquirer*, October 4, 2017, https://www.cincinnati.com/story/news/2017/10/04/our-history-p-g-put-soap-soap-opera/732149001/.
6. Mrs. Arthur Bell, *Lives and Legends of the Great Hermits and Fathers of the Church, With Other Contemporary Saints* (London: George Bell & Sons, 1902), 107, https://books.google.com/books?id=ZhEAAAAAYAAJ&pg.
7. Pat Robertson with Jamie Buckingham, *Shout It From the Housetops* (Alachua, FL: Bridge-Logos, 1972), 230–31, https://books.google.com/books?id=gGZsPV6tk74C&pg.
8. Zechariah 6:15.
9. Robertson with Buckingham, *Shout It From the Housetops*, 210.

10. "Ephemera of the Christian Broadcasting Network (CBN)—Collection 240," Billy Graham Center, updated May 2, 2001, https://www2.wheaton.edu/bgc/archives/guides/240.htm.
11. Zechariah 4:10, NLT.

CHAPTER 4

1. "Robertson, Absalom Willis (1887–1971)," Biographical Directory of the United States Congress, accessed February 22, 2020, https://bioguideretro.congress.gov/Home/MemberDetails?memIndex=r000317.
2. "Harry F. Byrd (1887–1966)," Encyclopedia Virginia, accessed February 22, 2020, https://www.encyclopediavirginia.org/byrd_harry_flood_sr_1887-1966.
3. Brent Tarter, "Byrd Organization," accessed February 22, 2020, https://www.encyclopediavirginia.org/byrd_organization.
4. Tarter, "Byrd Organization."
5. "A. Willis Robertson (1887–1971)," Encyclopedia Virginia, accessed February 22, 2020, https://www.encyclopediavirginia.org/Robertson_A_Willis_1887-1971.
6. "A. Willis Robertson (1887–1971)," Encyclopedia Virginia.
7. "A Pay Cut for Representatives During the Great Depression," History, Art & Archives—US House of Representatives, March 16, 1933, https://history.house.gov/Historical-Highlights/1901-1950/A-pay-cut-for-Representatives-during-the-Great-Depression/.

CHAPTER 5

1. "Genealogy Report: Descendants of John Garnett," Genealogy.com, accessed February 22, 2020, https://www.genealogy.com/ftm/w/a/g/Rick--Waggener/GENE3-0017.html.
2. "Ruby Bridges," Biography, updated January 16, 2020, https://www.biography.com/activist/ruby-bridges.
3. "The Birmingham Campaign," PBS, accessed February 22, 2020, http://www.pbs.org/black-culture/explore/civil-rights-movement-birmingham-campaign/.
4. "I Have a Dream…," The Nobel Price, accessed February 22, 2020, https://www.nobelprize.org/prizes/peace/1964/king/lecture/.

CHAPTER 6

1. "Patton Family at VMI," Virginia Military Institute, accessed February 22, 2020, https://www.vmi.edu/archives/genealogy-biography-alumni/featured-historical-biographies/patton-family-at-vmi/.
2. "Shorter Catechism of the Assembly of Divines: The 1647 Westminster Confession and Subordinate Documents," A Puritan's Mind, accessed February 22, 2020, https://www.apuritansmind.com/westminster-standards/shorter-catechism/.

CHAPTER 7

1. "Washington and Lee University," *Encyclopaedia Britannica*, accessed February 22, 2020, https://www.britannica.com/topic/Washington-and-Lee-University.
2. "Washington and Lee University," *Encyclopaedia Britannica*.
3. "Washington and Lee University," Unigo, accessed February 22, 2020, https://www.unigo.com/colleges/washington-and-lee-university/q-and-a/describe-the-students-at-your-school-6/3.
4. Merriam-Webster, s.v. "magna cum laude," accessed February 22, 2020, https://www.merriam-webster.com/dictionary/magna%20cum%20laude.

5. Joe Sommerlad, "North Korea at 70: How the Personality Cult of Kim Il-Sung Shaped a Nation," *Independent*, September 7, 2018, https://www.independent.co.uk/news/world/asia/north-korea-70th-anniversary-kim-il-sung-personality-cult-history-a8527696.html.

6. "This Day in History—June 30, 1950: President Truman Orders U.S. Forces to Korea," History, accessed February 23, 2020, https://www.history.com/this-day-in-history/truman-orders-u-s-forces-to-korea.

7. Volker Janssen, "History Stories: The Most Harrowing Battle of the Korean War," History, updated January 31, 2019, https://www.history.com/news/korean-war-chosin-reservoir-veterans-stories.

8. Floyd W. Henderson, "Lessons From Korea," *Military*, accessed February 23, 2020, http://milmag.com/2015/03/lessons-from-korea/.

Chapter 8

1. "Town, Gown, and the Great Depression: Yale and New Haven During the Construction of Yale's Original Residential Colleges," Yale Historical Review, accessed February 23, 2020, https://historicalreview.yale.edu/sites/default/files/files/YHR_YaleIssueMcCullough2.pdf.

2. Randall Herbert Balmer, *Encyclopedia of Evangelicalism* (Louisville, KY: Westminster John Knox Press, 2002), 515, https://books.google.com/books?id=syUupeVJOz4C&pg.

3. "Whiffenpoofs: America's Oldest Collegiate A Cappella Group," The Whiffenpoofs, accessed February 23, 2020, https://www.whiffenpoofs.com.

4. Tod Galloway et al., "The Whiffenpoof Song," Lyrics, accessed February 23, 2020, https://www.lyrics.com/lyric/2303861/The+Whiffenpoof+Song.

5. "Marbury v. Madison Establishes Judicial Review," History, accessed February 23, 2020, https://www.history.com/this-day-in-history/marbury-v-madison-establishes-judicial-review.

6. Albert Jenner, "Reviewed Work: *Moore's Federal Practice* by James W. Moore," *Yale Law Journal* 72, no. 8 (July 1963): 1662–65, https://www.jstor.org/stable/794528?seq=1.

Chapter 9

1. "Papers of Medical Philanthropist and NIH Benefactor Mary Lasker Added to the National Library of Medicine's Profiles in Science Web Site," National Institutes of Health, June 21, 2007, https://www.nih.gov/news-events/news-releases/papers-medical-philanthropist-nih-benefactor-mary-lasker-added-national-library-medicines-profiles-science-web-site.

Chapter 10

1. Acts 7:22.
2. Galatians 2:20, kjv.

Chapter 12

1. "Augustine of Hippo, Quotes," Goodreads, accessed February 26, 2020, https://www.goodreads.com/quotes/42572-thou-hast-made-us-for-thyself-o-lord-and-our.
2. Romans 10:9.
3. 2 Corinthians 5:17.

Chapter 13

1. Romans 8:14.
2. Colossians 3:15.

3. John Wesley, *The Works of John Wesley: Thoughts, Addresses, Prayers, Letters*, vol. xi (Grand Rapids, MI: Zondervan Publishing House), 444, https://books.google.com/books?id=w1pHAQAAMAAJ&pg.

Chapter 14

1. "Men's Track and Field: Patrick Robertson," Washington and Lee University, Generals Athletics, accessed February 23, 2020, https://generalssports.com/sports/mens-track-and-field/roster/patrick-robertson/3421.

Chapter 15

1. Marble Collegiate Church, "Dr. Norman Vincent Peale," accessed February 23, 2020, http://www.marblechurch.org/connect/library/vincent-peale.
2. "Marble Collegiate Church," Wikipedia, accessed February 23, 2020, https://en.wikipedia.org/wiki/Marble_Collegiate_Church.

Chapter 17

1. Jeremiah 12:5.
2. Psalm 37:4.

Chapter 20

1. "Six-Day War," History, updated August 21, 2018, https://www.history.com/topics/middle-east/six-day-war.
2. Luke 21:24.

Chapter 22

1. Katherine Blocksdorf, "Comparing Horse to Human Age," The Spruce Pets, updated September 11, 2019, https://www.thesprucepets.com/comparing-horse-to-human-age-1887320.
2. Bob Brown, "Seabiscuit Is Still the Stuff of Dreams," ABC News, January 6, 2006, https://abcnews.go.com/2020/story?id=123683&page=1.
3. "The Legend of Seabiscuit and the Santa Anita Handicap," US Racing, accessed February 24, 2020, https://www.usracing.com/news/analysis/legend-seabiscuit-santa-anita-handicap.
4. Jeanne Grunert, "Movements for Each Level of Dressage," Mom.com, accessed February 24, 2020, https://animals.mom.me/movements-level-dressage-3977.html.
5. "Ufano," SpanishDict, accessed February 28, 2020, https://www.spanishdict.com/translate/ufano.
6. Numbers 12:3.
7. Revelation 19:11, 14, niv.

Chapter 24

1. Ephesians 6:12, kjv.
2. Ezekiel 28:14 says, "You were the anointed cherub who covers; I established you; You were on the holy mountain of God; You walked back and forth in the midst of fiery stones." Ezekiel 14 and Isaiah 28 state that these angels were on top of the mercy seat.
3. Bible Study Tools, s.v. "Satan," accessed February 24, 2020, https://www.biblestudytools.com/dictionary/satan/.
4. Matthew 17:21, kjv.
5. Matthew 28:18–19, niv.

Chapter 25

1. Ted Turner, *Call Me Ted: My Life, My Way* (New York: Grand Central Publishing, 2008), https://books.google.com/books/about/Call_Me_Ted.html?id=O8bQBgj2znwC.
2. "Heritage USA," Wikipedia, accessed March 2, 2020, https://en.wikipedia.org/wiki/Heritage_USA.
3. Reynolds Holding, "Why Libby's Defense Failed," Time, March 6, 2007, http://content.time.com/time/nation/article/0,8599,1596626,00.html.
4. "United States v. Libby," Wikipedia, updated November 22, 2019, https://en.wikipedia.org/wiki/United_States_v._Libby.
5. "Bakker Guilt Is Affirmed, but Sentence Overturned," *Baltimore Sun*, February 13, 1991, https://www.baltimoresun.com/news/bs-xpm-1991-02-13-1991044074-story.html.
6. "Tammy Faye Messner Dies at Age 65," ABC News, July 21, 2007, https://abcnews.go.com/Entertainment/story?id=3400151&page=1.

Chapter 28

1. Psalm 46:10.
2. Mark 1:35.
3. "Count Your Blessings," Timeless Truths, accessed March 2, 2020, https://library.timelesstruths.org/music/Count_Your_Blessings/.
4. Philippians 4:6–7.
5. Psalm 119:165, kjv.
6. John 16:24, kjv.
7. Luke 10:40.
8. Luke 10:40.
9. Luke 10:42.

Chapter 29

1. John 14:12.

Chapter 30

1. Luke 6:38, niv.

Chapter 31

1. Becky Little, "Martin Luther Might Not Have Nailed His 95 Theses to the Church Door," History, updated August 31, 2018, https://www.history.com/news/martin-luther-might-not-have-nailed-his-95-theses-to-the-church-door.
2. Genesis 12:3.

Chapter 32

1. Romans 4:19–21.
2. Zechariah 4:6, kjv.

Chapter 34

1. "Cape Henry," *Encyclopaedia Britannica*, accessed February 24, 2020, https://www.britannica.com/place/Cape-Henry.
2. Matthew L. Becker, *The Self-Giving God and Salvation History: The Trinitarian Theology of Johannes von Hofmann* (New York: T&T Clark International, 2004), 12.

CHAPTER 35

1. "Fiscal Year 2019 Budget, Summary and Background Information," US Department of Education, accessed February 24, 2020, https://www2.ed.gov/about/overview/budget/budget19/summary/19summary.pdf.

CHAPTER 38

1. Isaiah 58:5, NIV.
2. Jim Collins, *Good to Great: Why Some Companies Make the Leap…and Others Don't* (New York: HarperBusiness, 2001).
3. "President Clinton Urges Full Funding for International Debt Relief for Poor Countries," White House Archives, October 3, 2000, https://clintonwhitehouse4.archives.gov/textonly/WH/new/html/Tue_Oct_3_100040_2000.html.
4. Christopher Wilson, "U.S. House Approves Third World Debt Relief," CNN, October 25, 2000, https://edition.cnn.com/2000/ALLPOLITICS/stories/10/25/congress.aid.reut/index.html.
5. "Debt Relief Under the Heavily Indepted Poor Countries (HIPC) Initiative," International Monetary Fund, March 19, 2019, https://www.imf.org/en/About/Factsheets/Sheets/2016/08/01/16/11/Debt-Relief-Under-the-Heavily-Indebted-Poor-Countries-Initiative.
6. Andrew Glass, "Clinton Signs 'Welfare to Work' Bill, Aug. 22, 1996," *Politico*, August 22, 2018, https://www.politico.com/story/2018/08/22/clinton-signs-welfare-to-work-bill-aug-22-1996-790321.

CHAPTER 39

1. Romans 15:20.
2. 1 Corinthians 3:12–15.
3. Proverbs 24:6.
4. James 4:6.
5. Proverbs 13:20.
6. 2 Chronicles 10:7, NIV.
7. 2 Chronicles 10:10–11, NIV.
8. 2 Chronicles 10:16, NIV.
9. John 13:14.

CHAPTER 40

1. "November 22, 1963: Death of the President," John F. Kennedy Presidential Library and Museum, accessed February 13, 2020, https://www.jfklibrary.org/learn/about-jfk/jfk-in-history/november-22-1963-death-of-the-president.
2. "Connecting Two Lions – Martin Luther King and Robert Francis Kennedy," Independence Hall Association, July 4, 1995, https://www.ushistory.org/people/twolions.htm.
3. "Results of the 1968 Election," *Encyclopaedia Britannica*, accessed February 13, 2020, https://www.britannica.com/event/United-States-presidential-election-of-1968/General-election-campaign#ref285853.
4. Nate Rawlings, "Richard Nixon's Plumbers," *Time*, May 17, 2011, http://content.time.com/time/specials/packages/article/0,28804,2071839_2071844_2071846,00.html.
5. "40 Years On, Woodward and Bernstein Recall Reporting on Watergate," NPR, June 13, 2014, https://www.npr.org/2014/06/13/321316118/40-years-on-woodward-and-bernstein-recall-reporting-on-watergate.

6. John O'Connor, "I'm the Guy They Called Deep Throat," *Vanity Fair*, October 17, 2006, https://www.vanityfair.com/news/politics/2005/07/deepthroat200507.

7. "Representative and President Gerald R. Ford of Michigan," History, Art & Archives, United States House of Representatives, accessed February 13, 2020, https://history. house.gov/Historical-Highlights/1901-1950/Representative-and-President-Gerald-R--Ford-of-Michigan/.

8. Robert Strong, "Jimmy Carter: Life Before the Presidency," Miller Center, University of Virginia, accessed February 13, 2020, https://millercenter.org/president/carter/life-before-the-presidency.

9. "Jimmy Carter Returns to Teaching Sunday School," *Politico*, November 3, 2019, https://www.politico.com/news/2019/11/03/jimmy-carter-sunday-school-065149.

10. White House press release, October 17, 1975, Box 17, Gerald R. Ford Presidential Library, accessed February 13, 2020, https://www.fordlibrarymuseum.gov/library/document/0248/whpr19751017-006.pdf.

11. Tom Infield, "The Last Time a Pa. Primary Mattered," The Philadelphia Inquirer, March 24, 2008, https://www.inquirer.com/philly/news/politics/elections/The_last_time_a_Pa_primary_mattered.html.

12. Christopher Lydon, "Jimmy Carter Revealed: Rockefeller Republican," *The Atlantic*, July 1977, https://www.theatlantic.com/magazine/archive/1977/07/jimmy-carter-revealed-rockefeller-republican/404908/.

13. Tom Hayden, "Jimmy Carter: The Unchanging of the Guard," *Rolling Stone*, March 10, 1977, https://www.rollingstone.com/politics/politics-news/jimmy-carter-the-unchanging-of-the-guard-189354/.

14. "The Iranian Hostage Crisis," Office of the Historian, accessed February 12, 2020, https://history.state.gov/departmenthistory/short-history/iraniancrises.

15. Elaine Kamarck, "The Iranian Hostage Crisis and Its Effect on American Politics," Brookings, November 4, 2019, https://www.brookings.edu/blog/order-from-chaos/2019/11/04/the-iranian-hostage-crisis-and-its-effect-on-american-politics/.

16. Mark Bowden, "The Desert One Debacle," *The Atlantic*, May 2006, https://www.theatlantic.com/magazine/archive/2006/05/the-desert-one-debacle/304803/.

17. Nancy Mitchell, "How the U.S. Aided Robert Mugabe's Rise," *Washington Post*, November 26, 2017, https://www.washingtonpost.com/news/made-by-history/wp/2017/11/26/how-the-u-s-aided-robert-mugabes-rise/.

18. "Robert Mugabe, Zimbabwe's Strongman Ex-President, Dies Aged 95," BBC News, September 6, 2019, https://www.bbc.com/news/world-africa-49604152.

19. Michael Lind, *Vietnam: The Necessary War* (New York: Touchstone, 2002), 26.

20. "1980 Electoral College Results," National Archives, The Office of the Federal Register, reviewed on December 16, 2019, https://www.archives.gov/electoral-college/1980.

21. "Iran Hostage Crisis Ends," History, A&E Networks, updated January 16, 2020, https://www.history.com/this-day-in-history/iran-hostage-crisis-ends.

Chapter 41

1. Dave Schwensen, "The Beatles at Shea Stadium," The Beatles at Shea Stadium, accessed February 14, 2020, http://www.beatlessheastadium.com/contributors.htm.

2. Shannon Woodland and Andrew Knox, "Nedra Ross: 'The Right Ronette,'" CBN, accessed February 14, 2020, https://www.cbn.com/cbnmusic/interviews/700club_nedraross031507.aspx?mobile=false&u=1.

3. Woodland and Knox, "Nedra Ross: 'The Right Ronette.'"

4. "1964: The Ronettes Tour With Opening Act the Rolling Stones," *Rolling Stone*, accessed February 14, 2020, https://www.rollingstone.com/culture/culture-lists/

women-who-rock-greatest-breakthrough-moments-160844/1964-the-ronettes-tour-with-opening-act-the-rolling-stones-223959/.

5. Natalie Weiner, "What Is It About The Ronettes' 'Be My Baby'? Some of the Countless Artists to Lift the Iconic Drum Beat Weigh In," *Billboard*, July 14, 2017, https://www.billboard.com/articles/columns/pop/7866041/the-ronettes-be-my-baby-drum-intro-artists-sample-interview.

6. "The Ronettes," Rock & Roll Hall of Fame, accessed February 14, 2020, https://www.rockhall.com/inductees/ronettes.

CHAPTER 42

1. "Cultural Revolution," History, A&E Networks, updated June 6, 2019, https://www.history.com/topics/china/cultural-revolution.

2. Kui Shin Voo and Larry Hovee, "The Lamb of God Hidden in the Ancient Chinese Characters," *CEN Technical Journal* 13, no. 1 (1999): 81, https://www.ocf.berkeley.edu/~wwu/chinese/lamb_chineseChars.pdf.

3. "Li," *Encyclopaedia Britannica*, accessed February 17, 2020, https://www.britannica.com/topic/li-Chinese-philosophy.

4. Eleanor Albert, "Christianity in China," Council on Foreign Relations, updated October 11, 2018, https://www.cfr.org/backgrounder/christianity-china.

CHAPTER 43

1. 1 John 2:2, KJV.

2. Proverbs 11:27, NIV.

CHAPTER 44

1. "Crisis of Confidence," PBS, accessed February 12, 2020, https://www.pbs.org/wgbh/americanexperience/features/carter-crisis/.

2. Phil Shenk, "Washington for Jesus," *Sojourners*, June 1980, https://sojo.net/magazine/june-1980/washington-jesus.

3. "History Timeline," Historic Jamestowne, Howell Creative Group, accessed February 12, 2020, https://historicjamestowne.org/history/history-timeline/.

CHAPTER 45

1. Psalm 37:23.

2. "Reaching Children With God's Love," Trinity Broadcasting Network UK, July 25, 2019, https://tbnuknewsletter.org/2019/07/25/reaching-children-with-gods-love/.

3. Gene Zubovich, "Russia's Journey From Orthodoxy to Atheism, and Back Again," Religion & Politics, October 16, 2018, https://religionandpolitics.org/2018/10/16/russias-journey-from-orthodoxy-to-atheism-and-back-again/.

4. William J. Brown and Kevin R. Crawford. "Provoking Biblical Conversations through Popular Media: Lessons Learned from *The Shack* and *Superbook*," *Global Conversations* 1, no. 1 (Fall 2013): 16, https://pdfs.semanticscholar.org/1112/a2fc38f5aa6dc4b4475e3cd129820f026aee.pdf.

CHAPTER 46

1. Julie Zeveloff, "See Why Beirut Was Once Known as 'The Paris of the Middle East,'" Business Insider, December 26, 2014, https://www.businessinsider.com/photos-of-beirut-lebanon-1965-2014-12.

2. Christina Abellan Matamoros, "How Does Lebanon's Government Work?," Euro News, updated January 4, 2020, https://www.euronews.com/2019/10/21/how-does-lebanon-s-government-work-euronews-answers.

3. "PLO," History, A&E Networks, updated August 21, 2018, https://www.history.com/topics/middle-east/plo.

4. "The Lebanon War: Operation Peace for Galilee (1982)," Israel Ministry of Foreign Affairs, accessed February 13, 2020, https://mfa.gov.il/MFA/AboutIsrael/History/Pages/Operation%20Peace%20for%20Galilee%20-%201982.aspx.

5. "U.N. Resolution on Golan," *New York Times*, January 21, 1982, https://www.nytimes.com/1982/01/21/world/un-resolution-on-golan.html.

6. "Camille Chamoun," *Encyclopaedia Britannica*, accessed February 13, 2020, https://www.britannica.com/biography/Camille-Chamoun.

7. Kirsten E. Schulze, *Israel's Covert Diplomacy in Lebanon* (New York: Macmillan, 1998), 89.

8. John Yemma, "Report From South Lebanon: Major Haddad and His Men," The Christian Science Monitor, March 30, 1981, https://www.csmonitor.com/1981/0330/033077.html.

9. "George K. Otis," Ohio History Central, accessed February 13, 2020, https://ohiohistorycentral.org/w/George_K._Otis.

Chapter 47

1. Scott Span, "The Rule of 72 and Retirement Planning," The Balance, updated February 6, 2020, https://www.thebalance.com/whats-the-rule-of-72-4040505.

Chapter 48

1. Genesis 11:6, niv.

Chapter 49

1. "Don't Ask Me, Ask God," Internet Movie Database, Amazon, accessed on February 13, 2020, https://www.imdb.com/title/tt1252282/plotsummary.

Chapter 51

1. "ACLU," History, updated August 21, 2018, https://www.history.com/topics/gay-rights/aclu.

2. "Engel *v.* Vitale," Oyez, accessed February 13, 2020, https://www.oyez.org/cases/1961/468.

3. "School District of Abington Township, Pennsylvania *v.* Schempp," Oyez, accessed February 13, 2020, https://www.oyez.org/cases/1962/142.

4. "1936 Constitution of the USSR," Bucknell University, accessed February 13, 2020, https://www.departments.bucknell.edu/russian/const/36cons04.html.

5. Rory Carroll, "America's Dark and Not-Very-Distant History of Hating Catholics," *Guardian*, September 12, 2015, https://www.theguardian.com/world/2015/sep/12/america-history-of-hating-catholics.

6. "Jefferson's Letter to the Danbury Baptists," Library of Congress, accessed February 13, 2020, https://www.loc.gov/loc/lcib/9806/danpre.html.

7. John S. Baker Jr., "Wall of Separation," *The First Amendment Encyclopedia*, accessed February 13, 2020, https://www.mtsu.edu/first-amendment/article/886/wall-of-separation.

8. "Richmond, State of Virginia. In Convention, Wednesday, the 25th of June, 1788," Library of Congress, accessed February 13, 2020, https://www.loc.gov/resource/bdsdcc. c1201/?st=text.

9. "Board of Education of Westside Community Schools *v.* Mergens By and Through Mergens," Oyez, accessed February 13, 2020, https://www.oyez.org/cases/1989/88-1597.

10. John 3:27; Matthew 15:13, NIV.

11. "About Jay Sekulow," American Center for Law and Justice, accessed February 13, 2020, https://aclj.org/jay-sekulow.

CHAPTER 52

1. Hal Brands, "The Vision Thing," Miller Center, University of Virginia, accessed February 13, 2020, https://millercenter.org/issues-policy/foreign-policy/the-vision-thing.

2. "Robertson Claims Michigan Victory," *Sun-Sentinel*, May 29, 1986, https://www.sun-sentinel.com/news/fl-xpm-1986-05-29-8602010306-story.html.

3. Brian McVicar, "Grand Rapids Businessman Peter Secchia Attending George H.W. Bush Funeral," Michigan Live, updated January 29, 2019, https://www.mlive.com/news/grand-rapids/2018/12/grand_rapids_businessman_phila_1.html.

4. "Iowa Caucus History: George Bush Beats Expectations Against Ronald Regan in 1980," Iowa PBS, accessed February 13, 2020, http://www.iowapbs.org/iowapathways/artifact/iowa-caucus-history-george-bush-beats-expectations-against-ronald-reagan-1980.

5. "Caucus Results," Iowa Publications Online, accessed February 13, 2020, http://publications.iowa.gov/135/1/elections/10-5.pdf.

6. David Yepsen, "Presidential Caucuses in Iowa," Iowa Publications Online, accessed February 13, 2020, http://publications.iowa.gov/135/1/elections/10-5.html.

CHAPTER 53

1. Steve Koczela, "How N.H. Went From Deep Red to Swing State Over the Course of a Few Elections," New Hampshire Public Radio, June 7, 2016, https://www.nhpr.org/post/how-nh-went-deep-red-swing-state-over-course-few-elections#stream/0.

2. "Presidential Primaries and Caucuses Republicans 1988," PrimaryCaucus, accessed February 14, 2020, https://sites.google.com/site/primarycaucus/home/republicans1900.

3. "Christian Coalition," Law Library, accessed February 14, 2020, https://law.jrank.org/pages/5212/Christian-Coalition.html.

4. "'These Are the Boys of Pointe Du Hoc'; Remembering Ronald Reagan's Words and Legacy on the 75th Anniversary of D-Day," Reagan Foundation, May 28, 2019, https://www.reaganfoundation.org/media/354665/75th-anniversary-of-d-day-press-advisory.pdf.

5. "Explosion of the Space Shuttle Challenger Address to the Nation, January 28, 1986," NASA History Office, NASA, accessed February 14, 2020, https://history.nasa.gov/reagan12886.html.

6. "Read My Lips: No New Taxes," History, A&E Networks, accessed February 14, 2020, https://www.history.com/speeches/read-my-lips-no-new-taxes.

7. Brian Domitrovic, "Bush's 1990 Tax Increase Was Comprehensively Destructive," *Forbes*, December 9, 2018, https://www.forbes.com/sites/briandomitrovic/2018/12/09/bushs-1990-tax-increase-was-comprehensively-destructive/#15130a7b5a10.

Chapter 54

1. Jim Anderson, "Baker-Aziz Talks Fail," United Press International, January 9, 1991, https://www.upi.com/Archives/1991/01/09/Baker-Aziz-talks-fail/4770663397200/.
2. R. J. Reinhart, "George H. W. Bush Retrospective," Gallup, December 1, 2018, https://news.gallup.com/opinion/gallup/234971/george-bush-retrospective.aspx.
3. "Bush Orders Operation Desert Shield," History, A&E Networks, accessed February 14, 2020, https://www.history.com/this-day-in-history/bush-orders-operation-desert-shield.
4. Jason M. Breslow, "Colin Powell: U. N. Speech 'Was a Great Intelligence Failure,'" PBS, May 17, 2016, https://www.pbs.org/wgbh/frontline/article/colin-powell-u-n-speech-was-a-great-intelligence-failure/.
5. "The Iraq War," Council on Foreign Relations, accessed February 14, 2020, https://www.cfr.org/timeline/iraq-war.
6. Mark Thompson, "How Disbanding the Iraqi Army Fueled ISIS," Time, May 29, 2015, https://time.com/3900753/isis-iraq-syria-army-united-states-military/.
7. Zack Beauchamp, "The Conflict Between Iraqi Sunnis and Shias Sustains ISIS," Vox, November 17, 2015, https://www.vox.com/2018/11/20/17995846/the-conflict-between-iraqi-sunnis-and-shias-sustains-isis.

Chapter 55

1. Matthew Continetti, "A Decade of Reed," Washington Examiner, June 27, 2005, https://www.washingtonexaminer.com/weekly-standard/a-decade-of-reed.

Chapter 56

1. Adrienne S. Gaines, "Charles Blair, Pioneering Charismatic Pastor, Dies at 88," Charisma, accessed February 14, 2020, http://www.charismamag.com/site-archives/570-news/featured-news/6510-charles-blair-pioneering-charismatic-pastor-dies-at-88.
2. Paul Moore, "Investment Squabble Goes On and On," Denver Business Journal, updated July 9, 2000, https://www.bizjournals.com/denver/stories/2000/07/10/story8.html.
3. Moore, "Investment Squabble Goes On and On."

Chapter 57

1. Robert M. and Maxine K. Reed, The Encyclopedia of Television, Cable, and Video (New York: Van Nostrand Reinhold, 1992), 197.
2. Maria Einstein, Media Diversity: Economics, Ownership, and the FCC (Mahwah, NJ: Lawrence Erlbaum Associates, 2004), 144.
3. Geraldine Fabrikant, "Murdoch Set to Buy Family Cable Concern," New York Times, June 12, 1997, https://www.nytimes.com/1997/06/12/business/murdoch-set-to-buy-family-cable-concern.html.
4. "News Corp. and Haim Saban Reach Agreement to Sell Fox Family Worldwide to Disney for $5.3 Billion," Saban Capital Group, July 23, 2001, https://www.saban.com/News-Corp-and-Haim-Saban-Reach-Agreement-to-Sell-Fox-Family-Worldwide-to-Disney-for-5-3-Billion/.
5. Robert Browning, "Andrea del Sarto," Poetry Foundation, accessed February 14, 2020, https://www.poetryfoundation.org/poems/43745/andrea-del-sarto.
6. "Number of Internet Users in China from 2017 to 2023," Statista, accessed February 14, 2020, https://www.statista.com/statistics/278417/number-of-internet-users-in-china/.

7. "Court Oks PetroKazakhstan Sale to CNPC," China Daily, October 10, 2005, http://www.chinadaily.com.cn/english/doc/2005-10/26/content_488017.htm.

CHAPTER 58

1. "Warfarin (Coumadin®)," US Department of Health and Human Services, accessed February 14, 2020, https://dphhs.mt.gov/Portals/85/dsd/documents/DDP/MedicalDirector/Warfarin.pdf.
2. Jeffrey L. Saver, "Time Is Brain—Quantified," *Stroke* 37, no. 1 (2006), https://doi.org/10.1161/01.STR.0000196957.55928.ab.

CHAPTER 59

1. 1 Corinthians 2:4.
2. "Power and Authority," Acton Institute, accessed February 14, 2020, https://acton.org/research/lord-acton-quote-archive.
3. C. Clifton Black, "The 'Good News' of the New Testament," Bible Odyssey, accessed February 14, 2020, https://www.bibleodyssey.org/en/tools/ask-a-scholar/good-news-of-the-nt.
4. 1 Timothy 2:5.
5. Abigail J. Estes, "Martin Luther and the Priesthood of All Believers: The Foundation of Reform and Spark of Revolution," Hanover College, accessed February 14, 2020, https://history.hanover.edu/hhr/18/HHR2018-estes.pdf.
6. 1 Peter 2:9.
7. Wayne Jackson, "The True Meaning of Grace," *Christian Courier*, accessed February 14, 2020, https://www.christiancourier.com/articles/1279-true-meaning-of-grace-the.
8. John 20:22, NIV.
9. Acts 1:8.
10. "Christian Movements and Denominations," Pew Research Center, December 19, 2011, https://www.pewforum.org/2011/12/19/global-christianity-movements-anddenominations/.
11. Katie Reilly, "Read Hillary Clinton's 'Basket of Deplorables' Remarks About Donald Trump Supporters," *Time*, updated September 10, 2016, https://time.com/4486502/hillary-clinton-basket-of-deplorables-transcript/.
12. Psalm 2:1, 4.

CHAPTER 60

1. Rustam Qobil, "Soviet-Era Nuclear Testing Is Still Making People Sick in Kazakhstan," Public Radio International, March 13, 2017, https://www.pri.org/stories/2017-03-13/soviet-era-nuclear-testing-still-making-people-sick-kazakhstan.

CHAPTER 61

1. Luke 4:18, NIV.

CHAPTER 62

1. "Cobalt Reserves Worldwide as of 2019, by Country," Statista, accessed February 14, 2020, https://www.statista.com/statistics/264930/global-cobalt-reserves/.
2. "Leopold II," *Encyclopaedia Britannica*, accessed February 14, 2020, https://www.britannica.com/biography/Leopold-II-king-of-Belgium.
3. "Leopold II," *Encyclopaedia Britannica*.

4. John-Thor Dahlburg, "Nation Suffered as Dictator Drained Riches," *Los Angeles Times*, May 17, 1997, https://www.latimes.com/archives/la-xpm-1997-05-17-mn-59626-story.html.

5. "Mobutu Dies in Exile in Morocco," CNN, September 7, 1997, http://www.cnn.com/WORLD/9709/07/mobutu.wrap/.

6. "Laurent Kabila," *Encyclopaedia Britannica*, accessed February 17, 2020, https://www.britannica.com/biography/Laurent-Kabila.

7. "Debunked: The Polio Vaccine and HIV Link," The History of Vaccines, accessed February 28, 2020, https://www.historyofvaccines.org/content/articles/debunked-polio-vaccine-and-hiv-link.

Chapter 63

1. "Mohammad Zahir Shah," *Encyclopaedia Britannica*, accessed February 17, 2020, https://www.britannica.com/biography/Mohammad-Zahir-Shah.

2. "Soviet Invasion of Afghanistan," *Encyclopaedia Britannica*, accessed February 17, 2020, https://www.britannica.com/event/Soviet-invasion-of-Afghanistan.

3. Dorothy C. An, "Afghan Soldier Speaks of Soviet Atrocities," The Harvard Crimson, February 26, 1986, https://www.thecrimson.com/article/1986/2/26/afghan-soldier-speaks-of-soviet-atrocities/.

4. "Afghanistan Opium Survey 2018," United Nations Office on Drugs and Crime, accessed February 17, 2020, https://www.unodc.org/documents/crop-monitoring/Afghanistan/Afghanistan_opium_survey_2018_socioeconomic_report.pdf.

Chapter 64

1. Revelation 12:4.

2. Revelation 12:9.

3. "Dr. D. G. S. Dhinakaran," Jesus Calls, accessed February 17, 2020, https://www.jesuscalls.com/about-founders-profile-dr-d-g-s-dhinakaran.

4. Julie McCarthy, "The Caste Formerly Known as 'Untouchables' Demands a New Role in India," NPR, August 13, 2016, https://www.npr.org/sections/goatsandsoda/2016/08/13/489883492/the-caste-formerly-known-as-untouchables-demands-a-new-role-in-india.

5. McCarthy, "The Caste Formerly Known as 'Untouchables' Demands a New Role in India."

6. "Dalit Girl Beaten Up as Her Shadow Falls on High Caste Muscleman," *Times of India*, June 16, 2015, https://timesofindia.indiatimes.com/india/Dalit-girl-beaten-up-as-her-shadow-falls-on-high-caste-muscleman/articleshow/47691186.cms.

7. See Daniel 10.

8. Matthew 12:29.

9. See Acts 19:11–20, NIV.

10. Acts 19:13, NIV.

11. Acts 19:15, NIV.

12. See Luke 8:26–39.

13. Matthew 28:18, NIV.

14. "What Is the Meaning of *Exousia* in the Bible?," Got Questions, accessed February 17, 2020, https://www.gotquestions.org/exousia-meaning.html.

15. "What Is the Meaning of the Greek Word *Dunamis* in the Bible?," Got Questions, accessed February 17, 2020, https://www.gotquestions.org/dunamis-meaning.html.

16. Acts 1:8, NIV.

17. 1 Peter 5:8.

18. "A Mighty Fortress," Hymnary, 1529, https://hymnary.org/text/a_mighty_fortress_is_our_god_a_bulwark.

CHAPTER 65

1. Isaiah 14:12.
2. Ezekiel 28:14.
3. Ezekiel 28:14.
4. Ezekiel 28:15.
5. Ezekiel 28:2.
6. 1 Peter 5:6.
7. 1 Peter 5:5.
8. Proverbs 9:10.
9. Isaiah 42:8.
10. Luke 17:10.
11. Daniel 4:30, NIV.
12. Daniel 4:32, NIV.
13. Philippians 2:6, NIV.
14. John 13:14.
15. Luke 22:27.
16. 2 Corinthians 12:7–9.
17. 2 Corinthians 12:10.
18. Galatians 4:14.
19. 2 Corinthians 12:7–9.
20. Jakon Hays and Maureen Watts, "Frank Batten Sr. Timeline," *Virginian-Pilot*, September 10, 2009, https://www.pilotonline.com/news/obituaries/article_bd3a13c3-6e56-5b0f-84f7-22b47e5f1c99.html.
21. Hebrews 12:11.
22. "Red Hat: How They Developed a Big Idea That Shook Up a Huge Market," Growth Hackers, accessed February 17, 2020, https://growthhackers.com/growth-studies/red-hat-how-they-developed-a-big-idea-that-shook-up-a-huge-market.

CHAPTER 66

1. Exodus 3:14, KJV.
2. Psalm 91:14.
3. Psalm 91:14, NIV.
4. Psalm 91:14, NIV.
5. Psalm 91:15.
6. Psalm 91:15.
7. Psalm 91:15.
8. Psalm 91:15.
9. Psalm 91:16.
10. Psalm 91:16.
11. 1 Corinthians 2:9.

CHAPTER 67

1. Psalm 119:11.
2. Proverbs 24:6.
3. Isaiah 30:21, KJV.
4. See Judges 6, NIV.

Chapter 68

1. "Idi Amin," Biography, updated April 17, 2019, https://www.biography.com/political-figure/idi-amin; Paul Hofmann, "Amin, at U.N., Appeals to Americans to Rid Their Society of Zionists," *New York Times*, October 2, 1975, https://www.nytimes.com/1975/10/02/archives/amin-at-un-appeals-to-americans-to-rid-their-society-of-zonists.html; "Idi Amin: 'Butcher of Uganda,'" CNN, August 16, 2003, https://www.cnn.com/2003/WORLD/africa/08/16/amin.obituary/index.html; "Idi Amin," *Guardian*, accessed February 20, 2020, https://www.theguardian.com/news/2003/aug/18/guardianobituaries.
2. "Idi Amin," Biography.
3. "Yonaton 'Yoni' Netanyahu," Jewish Virtual Library, accessed February 20, 2020, https://www.jewishvirtuallibrary.org/yonaton-quot-yoni-quot-netanyahu.
4. "Yonaton 'Yoni' Netanyahu," Jewish Virtual Library.
5. Pat Robertson, "Why Evangelical Christians Support Israel," accessed February 20, 2020, http://www.patrobertson.com/Speeches/IsraelLauder.asp.

Chapter 69

1. Fred Carver, "As the Sahel Becomes Sahara," United Nations Association – UK, September 18, 2017, https://www.climate2020.org.uk/sahel-becomes-sahara/.
2. "Chris Reij," World Resources Institute, accessed February 17, 2020, https://www.wri.org/profile/chris-reij.

Chapter 70

1. Genesis 11:6, NIV.
2. Proverbs 24:6.
3. "Regent Facts," Regent University, accessed February 17, 2020, https://www.regent.edu/about-regent/regent-facts/.

Chapter 71

1. See Matthew 13.
2. John 16:24.
3. Mark 11:24, NIV.

Epilogue

1. 2 Timothy 1:12.
2. Hebrews 11:6.
3. Genesis 15:6, KJV.
4. 2 Chronicles 16:9.
5. Psalm 84:11.
6. Hebrews 13:8.

My **FREE GIFT** to You

Dear Reader,

I'm so happy you read my book. I hope my story inspires you to step out in faith and experience the reality of God.

As a thank-you…

I am offering you a gift:

E-book: *Ten Laws for Success*

To get this **FREE GIFT**, please go to:

PatRobertsonBooks.com/gift

Thanks again and God bless you,

Pat Robertson

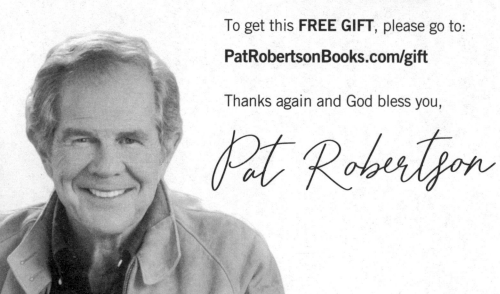